Watergate's Forgotten Hero

Watergate's Forgotten Hero
Frank Wills, Night Watchman

Adam Henig

Foreword by JaQwan J. Kelly

McFarland & Company, Inc., Publishers
Jefferson, North Carolina

LIBRARY OF CONGRESS CATALOGUING-IN-PUBLICATION DATA

Names: Henig, Adam, author. | Kelly, JaQwan J., writer of foreword.
Title: Watergate's forgotten hero : Frank Wills, night watchman / Adam
Henig ; foreword by JaQwan J. Kelly.
Other titles: Frank Wills, night watchman
Description: Jefferson, North Carolina : McFarland & Company, Inc.,
Publishers, 202 | Includes bibliographical references and index.
Identifiers: LCCN 2021022105 | ISBN 9781476684802 (paperback : acid free paper) ∞
ISBN 9781476643151 (ebook)
Subjects: LCSH: Watergate Affair, 1972–1974. | Wills, Frank, 1948–2000. |
United States—Politics and government—1969–1974. |
Watchmen—Washington (D.C.)—Biography. | North Augusta
(S.C.)—Biography. | BISAC: HISTORY / United States / 20th Century
Classification: LCC E860 .H46 2021 | DDC 973.924092 [B]—dc23
LC record available at https://lccn.loc.gov/2021022105

BRITISH LIBRARY CATALOGUING DATA ARE AVAILABLE

ISBN (print) 978-1-4766-8480-2
ISBN (ebook) 978-1-4766-4315-1

© 2021 Adam Henig. All rights reserved

*No part of this book may be reproduced or transmitted in any form
or by any means, electronic or mechanical, including photocopying
or recording, or by any information storage and retrieval system,
without permission in writing from the publisher.*

Front cover image: Frank Wills in front of the Watergate Complex
for a *JET* magazine cover article to commemorate the one year
anniversary of the break-in. Photograph by Maurice Sorrell
(courtesy Carol McCabe Booker).

Printed in the United States of America

*McFarland & Company, Inc., Publishers
Box 611, Jefferson, North Carolina 28640
www.mcfarlandpub.com*

For my father,
Gerald S. Henig,
and
in memory of my mother,
Lori Henig

Table of Contents

Acknowledgments	ix
Foreword by JaQwan J. Kelly	1
Preface	3
1. "Impenetrable" Security	7
2. The Break-In	10
3. Savannah	19
4. North Augusta	33
5. Job Corps	42
6. Watergate	50
7. Metro Police	59
8. The Caper	67
9. Opportunity Knocks	80
10. Delusions of Grandeur	90
11. From Bad to Worse	109
12. Downward Spiral	128
13. "I've Done My Work"	144
Epilogue	159
Chapter Notes	165
Bibliography	183
Index	195

"No one could have conceived that the call would lead to infamy for many, nor could any have deemed, least of all he, that for him it would lead to oblivion.... And so it might be said that his life did end with that phone-call."[1]
—John B. Sanford (1989), Hollywood screenwriter blacklisted during the Red Scare of the 1950s

Acknowledgments

Most biographers will tell you they spend more time researching than writing. Even with the advancements in technology and Internet search engines, we are still dependent on others to provide us with information.

The material in my book would not be as rich in detail without the help of the following individuals and institutions: Carol Waggoner-Angleton (Augusta University); Carolyn Chun (California State University, East Bay); FBI archives; Lauren Acker (Department of History and Geography, Georgia College); Lisa L. Denmark (Department of History, Georgia Southern University); Rick Watson and Diana S. Leite (Harry Ransom Center, The University of Texas at Austin); Independent Researcher Rebekah Dobrasko; Jennifer Roesch (John F. Kennedy Presidential Library); Lewis Wyman (Library of Congress); Corey Rogers (Lucy Craft Laney Museum of Augusta, Georgia); Mena-Keona S. Nokes-Drake, Tab Lewis, and Abigail Malangone (National Archives and Records Administration); Kristen Newby (Ohio History Center); Felicia Parker-Cox (Office of Representative Dwight Evans, PA-03); Alana Lewis (Paine College, Augusta, Georgia); Library staff (Department of Special Research Collections, University of California, Santa Barbara); Steve Batt and Betsy Pittman (Thomas J. Dodd Research Center, Archives & Special Collections, University of Connecticut Library); Stacey Wiens (Kenneth Spencer Research Library, University of Kansas Libraries); Georgia Historical Society; Kate Moore and Graham Duncan (Hollings Special Collections Library, University of South Carolina); Vanderbilt Television News Archive staff.

Acknowledgments

I am especially grateful to Honey Ryan, a Savannah-based researcher, who tracked down Frank Wills' home address in a 1948 city phone directory, accessed Wills' social security card application and death certificate, and provided critical information about his childhood. Also, thank you to City of Savannah Research Library & Municipal Archives Director Luciana Spracher, who put me in touch with Ms. Ryan.

For insight on Wills' early years in Savannah, I am indebted to Savannah-based author and historian Martha Keber, who connected me with Lindsay Resnick of Cuba Family Archives for Southern Jewish History, which eventually led to Lee Shonfield, whose family employed Wills' mother. A special thank you to Martha and Lindsay, and especially to Lee, who shared his memories of "Frankie" and his mother Margie, helping me to understand better Wills' formative years.

If personal papers and official records serve to fill the missing gaps in a biography, the personal interview helps bring the subject to life. Many of the interviews I conducted came about because of the willingness and effort of one person, Wayne O'Bryant. O'Bryant was invaluable providing access to Wills' family and friends. Aiken County Historical Museum Director Brenda Baratto graciously introduced me to O'Bryant, who lined up several interviews for my visit to North Augusta, Wills' hometown. Not only was O'Bryant my conduit into Frank's past, but his insight into Wills and the community he grew up in was invaluable. I am grateful to those who took time out of their day to sit down for an interview: Stephanie Coleman, Cathy and Reco Grant, Mallory Millender, Martez Mims, William Mims, Mary Newsome, Pamela Oliver, Austin Rhodes, Preston Sykes, Carrie Williams, Eugene Williams, and Eddie and Shirley Wills. JoAnn Hooper, Frank's girlfriend, neighbor, and mother of his daughter, was especially helpful in providing an honest portrayal of her best friend.

In addition, there were several people who shared their recollections of Wills by phone or through email: Paul Brock, Bruce Givner,

Acknowledgments

Professor Nathaniel Irvin, Jr., Professor Martha Keber, Don Rhodes, and Walter B. Simmons. I also want to thank Carol McCabe Booker, widow of journalist Simeon Booker. Although she never met Frank Wills, her late husband, Simeon, penned numerous articles about him for *JET* magazine. Carol generously provided me exclusive access to Simeon's papers as well as her editorial pen. A thank you to James West, who put me in touch with Ms. Booker.

For their encouraging comments and detection of either stylistic or factual blunders, I am indebted to Cathy Curtis, Don Rhodes, Herb Boyd, John A. Farrell, Joseph Rodota, Kathy Schienle (a thank you to Rosemarie Robotham for recommending Kathy), Nell Boeschenstein, and WiseInk Creative Publishing's Graham Warnken. And to the talented JaQwan Kelly, who would be an ideal candidate to portray Frank Wills in a full-length biopic, I am thankful for his enthusiastic support.

For being supportive and always curious about my literary progress, I am truly grateful to my family: My sisters, Jennifer and Rebecca, and their husbands, Russ and Matt, and my four nieces; my in-laws Frank and Evelyn Muro; my brothers-in-law and sisters-in-law and their families. Also, for their interest and encouragement, I would like to acknowledge my co-workers, lifelong friends, and neighbors. Lastly, and certainly not least, I am indebted beyond words to my wife, Jennifer, and our two boys, Jacob and Alex, future bibliophiles; they are my rock and reason for getting up every morning.

With great pleasure, I have dedicated this book to my parents. My father, Professor Emeritus Gerald S. Henig, has been at my side throughout this entire process, from conception to publication. I am thankful and fortunate to have him in my life. And in loving memory of my mother, Lori Henig, a teacher by profession, who always encouraged me to read and love books.

Foreword

by JaQwan J. Kelly

My introduction to Frank Wills began when I portrayed him in the final scene of the Steven Spielberg film *The Post* (2017). Like most people who did not live through the Watergate scandal, I was not familiar with the details of the break-in, let alone Wills' role in the affair. Ordinarily, for the acting role I was given, there was no need to conduct extensive research. I was only a "day player," which meant it didn't take longer than a day to shoot my scene. But I was determined to learn as much as I could about my character. I knew there was more to Frank than what had been included on his Wikipedia page, but since there was hardly any in-depth material available, I took a leap of faith. From New York City, I flew to Frank's hometown of North Augusta, South Carolina, and met his cousin Eddie Wills, who drove me around and showed me Frank's elementary school, his neighborhood, church, and gravesite.

After release of *The Post*, I wasn't ready to let go of Frank. I wanted to tell his story and the best way I knew how was through cinema. Partnering with Giant Island Films, I reprised my portrayal of Frank in a short film called *He, the People*. Prior to production, I met Adam Henig during a fundraising drive. We may have lived on opposite ends of the country and come from different backgrounds, but he was the only other person I knew who was as intrigued with Frank's life as much as I was.

Watergate's Forgotten Hero explains, for the first time from

Foreword by JaQwan J. Kelly

Frank's perspective, what happened on the night of the break-in and the misery that it caused him. As you'll see, Frank Wills was indeed a hero. His alertness in the face of danger revealed—unintentionally—what was *really* happening inside the Nixon White House—political corruption and abuse of power. He also shows us that even heroes are not immune to racial injustice and exploitation.

Adam Henig deserves immense credit for his tenacity and fervor, reminding us that Frank's story remains relevant and poignant and should not be forgotten because obstruction and deceit at the highest levels of government can recur, as we have recently witnessed. Hopefully, if our country reaches that threshold again, there will be another Frank Wills that can save our nation, but this time, not at his (or her) personal expense.

JaQwan J. Kelly is a New York City–based actor, writer, and producer. He has been featured in Hulu's WuTang: An American Saga, *CBS's* Blue Bloods, *HBO's* Mrs. Fletcher, *and Steven Spielberg's Academy Award–nominated film* The Post.

Preface

"You're writing a book about who?" was the usual response when I mentioned that I was working on a biography of Frank Wills. No one in my circle and beyond had ever heard of him including several who boasted a comprehensive knowledge of Watergate. Was it worth four years of my life juggling family and a full-time job to recreate the life of this little-known security guard?

In fact, the author who ignited my interest in Wills never pursued his initial inclination to write about him. That author, Alex Haley, who produced the best-sellers *Roots* and *The Autobiography of Malcolm X*, actually inspired my literary career. Haley was the subject of my first book, *Alex Haley's* Roots: *An Author's Odyssey*. A pioneering journalist in his day, Haley was one of the first African Americans to write for mainstream (i.e., white) magazines, such as *Playboy*, *Reader's Digest*, and *Cosmopolitan*. Haley's subjects varied, but he focused much of his work on popular figures in the Black community: Martin Luther King, Jr., Muhammad Ali, and Miles Davis, to name but a few. One of his lesser-known subjects was a St. Petersburg, Florida, civil rights activist, Dr. Ralph Wimbish, who, in 1961, led the efforts to integrate Major League Baseball's spring training. I thought Wimbish deserved a full-length study. Hence, my second book, *Baseball Under Siege: The Yankees, the Cardinals, and a Doctor's Battle to Integrate Spring Training*.

In 1983, Haley approached Frank Wills about collaborating on a memoir, similar to what he had done with Malcolm X. On several occasions, the author met with Wills and conducted a series of interviews. Wills thought he had finally hit the jackpot. Unfortunately for

Preface

him, Haley failed to follow through on the project. However, I held on to the 100-word news brief that detailed their literary plans. The more I read it, the more I was convinced that Haley had missed a golden opportunity: A $2-an-hour night watchman working at the Watergate Office Building in Washington, D.C., detected a burglary in progress, reported it, and, unknowingly, shaped the course of American history. In the wake of that unprecedented political upheaval, here, too, was an opportunity to explore the fate of Frank Wills, a Black man in 1970s America caught up in a power struggle dominated solely by white men.

Thankfully, Haley had recorded on cassette tapes and saved Wills' interviews. Currently housed in Ohio's National Afro-American Museum and Cultural Center, the interviews shed invaluable insight on Wills' formative years in Savannah. Indeed, they serve as a springboard of what it meant to be Black, poor, and fatherless in the United States during the second half of the twentieth century.

To gain further insight on the life and times of Frank Wills, I interviewed members of his family, his girlfriend, childhood friends, neighbors, a radio personality he had often contacted, and a Democratic National Committee volunteer he had encountered at the Watergate Office Building on the night of the break-in. In terms of archival material, I found most helpful the famed *Washington Post* reporters Bob Woodward and Carl Bernstein papers (which had a file exclusively on Wills), located at the Harry Ransom Center at the University of Texas at Austin. To recreate the night of the break-in, I relied heavily on federal court transcripts and declassified FBI files. How Wills fared after his moment in the limelight is chronicled by numerous journalists, the best accounts written by *JET* magazine reporter Simeon Booker.

What they reveal is that Frank Wills' actions in the early morning of June 17, 1972, were not a source of heroic pride, but in the end caused him bitterness and disappointment. This tragic outcome, however, should not blind us to the fact that Wills' discovery of the

Preface

burglary at the Watergate served as a catalyst for the exposure of one of the most corrupt administrations in the history of the presidency. Once his story is better known, perhaps fewer people will ask "Who?" when Frank Wills' name is referenced.

CHAPTER 1

"Impenetrable" Security

June 30, 1971
Washington, D.C.

"I want them just to break in and take it out. Do you understand?" the president asked. "Just go in and take it. Go in around eight or nine o'clock."[1]

President Richard Nixon was meeting with Chief of Staff H.R. Haldeman in the Oval Office. Haldeman had learned early in his tenure that when his boss gave an order, no matter how ridiculous (or illegal), it was to be implemented. A few months before, Daniel Ellsberg, a disgruntled defense analyst, had leaked the Pentagon Papers—thousands of pages that detailed military secrets and politically sensitive information concerning the ongoing, publicly unpopular Vietnam War—to the national press. Once the papers were published, it had led to further public outcry. More files were housed at the Brookings Institution, the Washington, D.C.–based liberal think tank, waiting to be leaked. Obsessed with his reelection a year and a half away, Nixon wanted those documents destroyed. The war had already doomed Lyndon B. Johnson's presidency. Nixon was determined not to let the same fate happen to him.

Within days of Nixon's order, two men from his reelection campaign, with briefcases in hand, entered the Brookings front lobby and asked to see Morton Halperin. He had served as the deputy assistant secretary of defense for international security affairs in the Johnson

Administration, where he oversaw the production of the Pentagon Papers. After Nixon took office, Halperin worked as an assistant to National Security Advisor Henry Kissinger, but resigned in disagreement with the administration's role in the Vietnam War. Once the papers were leaked to the news media, Halperin, a friend of Ellsberg, was put on the President's infamous "Enemies List." Halperin was now a senior fellow at Brookings.

At around 7:30 p.m., the two men were greeted in the Brookings lobby by Roderick Warrick, a tall, lean, Black security guard wearing a dark-blue uniform. He was unarmed. The men claimed they had an appointment with Halperin and needed to meet the former White House deputy in his fifth-floor office.

No, Warrick said. If they wanted to visit with Mr. Halperin, they needed to pick up the phone and have him come down to the lobby to escort them personally to his office. The men repeated that Halperin was expecting them and insisted on going up to the office unattended. New to the position but trained to challenge any visitor without proper identification, Warrick held his ground. He would not allow them upstairs unless Halperin was present. The men finally left the building, reporting to their superiors that Brookings had "impenetrable" security.[2]

Roderick Warrick would later be hailed a hero. Historians point to this altercation as the "first of the illegal activities" that ultimately led to Nixon's downfall.[3] The Trinidad native contended he was just doing his job.

Described as a "tough, by-the-book, no-nonsense employee who faithfully upheld his responsibility of guarding the staff and the building," Warrick spent the next three decades working in nighttime security at Brookings.[4] Whether it was denying access to an absent-minded academic who had left his office keys at home or refusing entry to the organization's new vice president without proper identification (Warrick hadn't been introduced to him yet), he epitomized the job he was hired to do. He may have had the "most complaints against him of any employee," his supervisor confided, but no

Chapter 1. *"Impenetrable" Security*

significant criminal activity occurred on his watch.[5] "Who are you here to see, please," was Warrick's standard greeting to an unknown visitor. Although he was highly praised by Brookings' management and recognized by scholars for his role, Warrick never allowed that event to affect the way he conducted his job or his life.

A year later and two miles away, another tall, slim, unarmed, Black night watchman wearing a blue uniform dealt with a more serious incident involving other Nixon henchmen.

CHAPTER 2

The Break-In

June 16, 1972
Washington, D.C.

It was a typical summer evening in DC—warm and sticky.

As most residents were coming home from a day's work, Frank Wills was getting ready to start his. Crawling out of bed, the twenty-four-year-old African American night watchman was scheduled for his usual graveyard shift, midnight to 8:00 a.m., at the Watergate Office Building.

For the past year the lanky South Carolinian lived on the third floor of a boarding house at 1315 Twenty-Second Street NW in DuPont Circle, the heart of the capital less than a mile away from the White House. Wills' one-room apartment—which he thought of as a bird cage because of its minuscule size—had a worn carpet, a bed barely long enough to sleep in, a small color television, and plastic daisies as the centerpiece on a table near the window. He shared a bathroom down the hallway with eight other tenants on the floor. His weekly rent was fourteen dollars.

Able to sleep for only five hours, he passed the remaining time before his next shift—as he usually did—playing with his cat, Tuffy, watching television, assembling model airplanes, and listening to a police scanner in the background on a short-wave radio. At the dinner hour, Wills rode the bus across town to the Southern Dining Room. Still far more comfortable in the backwoods of South Carolina

Chapter 2. The Break-In

Wills in his one-room apartment. Photograph by Maurice Sorrell (courtesy Carol McCabe Booker).

than in a big city, he ate by himself at this down-home restaurant, popular among Blacks who migrated from the South. Treating himself to the closest thing he had to a home-cooked meal, Wills had steak with rice and gravy, salad, and peach pie. The tab was $1.75. Afterward, he took the bus to Georgetown and wandered the streets window-shopping, something he did often while waiting for his shift to begin. Before he went home, he hiked to the Potomac River, found a quiet area, and meditated, thanks to the Beatles, who recently popularized the ancient Eastern exercise.

Notwithstanding an ongoing fling with a maid he had met at work, Wills was essentially a loner. He lived by himself, ate by himself, spent his leisure time by himself. Even his job involved minimal social interaction. Nor did he have any interest in what was happening in the world. Maybe it was for the best. Current events in recent weeks were anything but uplifting: the war in Vietnam saw no end in sight; anti-war protestors throughout the nation continued to rage on America's streets; commercial airlines were subjected to a rash of hijackings; and on May 15, presidential candidate and segregationist Alabama governor George Wallace suffered an assassination attempt.

When Wills returned to his room, it was time to get ready for work. He took a shower, the second of the day, a ritual he practiced regularly. He got dressed in his company-issued uniform: blue button-down shirt, blue slacks, and blue jacket, which included a pocket for his can of Mace.

Upon his arrival in Washington from Detroit more than a year earlier, Wills had been able to secure employment at General Security Services (GSS). Given his prior experience as a department store security guard in the Motor City, he was able to join the Security Force division. Yet, despite the steady employment and his promotion to the rank of corporal, Wills felt he "wasn't going anywhere" with his current job.[1] On his twenty-minute walk to work, the young watchman contemplated "getting a better job and making some money."[2] Little did he know that a once-in-a-lifetime opportunity would materialize that very evening.

For the previous six weeks, Wills had been assigned to protect the Watergate Office Building, an eleven-story office tower located at 2600 Virginia Avenue NW. Its central location enabled building management to lease space to government agencies (e.g., the Federal Reserve) and political organizations such as the Democratic National Committee (DNC), its headquarters for the past five years.

Wills' daily duties were to check every door, hallway, parking garage, and potential entry point of the office building to ensure they were locked and secured. If he observed any suspicious activities, he was required to contact his supervisor or, if needed, the police. Never armed with a gun, Wills had few ways to protect himself against an intruder.

Chapter 2. The Break-In

That evening, he arrived fifteen minutes early to his midnight shift. The guard he was relieving, Fletcher Pittman, told him he would be on his own. Leroy Brown, who was supposed to work alongside Wills, had left his shift earlier because he was not feeling well. Wills signed in on the employee log and called the GSS answering service to report that he was on duty.

Normally, activity at an office building like this one wound down by the dinner hour. Lately, though, the building had had a steady flow of young energetic workers who were arriving at and leaving from the sixth-floor DNC offices. With less than five months until Election Day, the DNC was in full swing, its staff not allowing a single minute to be wasted. "The phones constantly rang; typewriters banged and clacked; enthusiastic workers conversed—lots of hyperactivity everywhere," as one intern recalled, all in preparation for the Democratic National Convention in Miami that was scheduled to take place in three weeks.[3] Recently, guards had reported that "party workers often labored into the morning hours" making final preparations.[4] But on that night, the Watergate was eerily silent.

***

Twenty minutes into his shift, beginning in the building's basement, Wills set out for his first patrol. The basement was comprised of three levels, each serving as an access point to the underground parking garage. Taking the elevator to the second level, known as B-2, Wills saw that the first of three doors that led to the parking garage was locked. Check. He checked the second door. It was unlocked.

Caught by surprise, he saw that a piece of gray gaffer tape was affixed to the latch. He had encountered this before. To save time when going back and forth with heavy equipment, building janitors would occasionally cover a door latch to avoid having to stop and pull out a key when re-entering the building. Even office workers—including those from the DNC—would use this time-saving method. When Wills removed the tape, he noticed that the latch was full of cotton and paper. That wasn't normal. Unfazed, he pulled the material out of the latch and moved on to the final door on the second floor. It too was unlocked, taped, and stuffed with cotton and paper. He cleared the latch and secured the door. Now the second floor was clear.

He walked down a flight of stairs to check the basement's third floor (B-3). As was the case with the previous floor, the first door was secure, but the next two doors were not locked. One had tape and paper inside the latch, while the other simply had not been secured.

Wills headed to the first floor (B-1) and found all the doors were secured. At 12:20 a.m., back at his post in the main lobby, he wrote in the security log, "B-2 level stuff [*sic*] with paper. Both doors. Also, one Door on B-3 level was open, the other was stuff [*sic*] with paper."[5] Something was not right. If one door was taped, that would not have been alarming, but four doors were unsecured, three of which had their latch openings packed with cotton and paper—highly unusual!

Concerned about what he'd observed, Wills phoned his boss, Captain Bobby Jackson. Jackson, the "roving supervisor" that evening, was making his own rounds at a GSS-guarded facility ten miles away in Takoma Park, Maryland, and was not picking up.[6] Wills left a voicemail at the company's answering service. Rather than wait for Jackson to respond, the young night watchman called Jackson's superior, Major Ira O'Neal.

A recently retired veteran of the U.S. Air Force, O'Neal supervised fifty-one GSS security guards, including those who worked at the Watergate. When Wills called, O'Neal was off-duty, asleep at his home. Awakened by the call, he assumed the situation was not as dire as Wills presented it to be. O'Neal was aware, he said later, that office workers had "used this technique to avoid walking around the block to the main entrance of the building."[7] He instructed Wills to continue checking all the doors of the remaining eleven floors as he normally would and report back. It was likely a fluke.

As Wills continued his patrol, Bruce Givner, a twenty-one-year-old DNC intern, entered the main lobby from the stairwell.

Chapter 2. The Break-In

An incoming senior at UCLA, Givner—whose first day had been forty-eight hours earlier, on June 14—was excited about his summer job. In preparation for the upcoming Miami convention, he was one of many interns tasked with calling and coordinating the "political movers and shakers" throughout the country.[8] He was also a self-described "errand boy," cruising on his motorcycle to and from Capitol Hill, hand delivering confidential documents to high level party officials.[9] His college professor had told him it would be "an experience of a lifetime."[10] Of course, Givner had no clue how true those words would prove to be.

He was the last worker—or rather, volunteer, because he wasn't paid—to leave the DNC offices that evening. While his fellow interns and supervisor had called it quits at 9:00 p.m., Givner had remained to take advantage of the free long-distance phone service to call friends in his Ohio hometown, Lorain. An hour later, he needed to relieve himself. That was a problem. Since the office was closed, if he went to the men's room in the lobby, the office door would lock behind him, so that he couldn't return (apparently, he didn't consider taping the latch). Thinking that he might have to leave early, Givner had another idea.

"I remembered the small balcony outside and a flower-filled planter lodged against its front railing," he wrote in his memoir.[11] While he was zipping up, Givner looked at the plants he ruined and apologized (he actually said, "sorry"). Later, he described it as "the most noteworthy pee break in American political history," since it allowed him to remain at the DNC headquarters two more hours, forestalling entry of the burglars, who were in the garage, awaiting the signal to enter the building.[12]

Shortly after midnight, Givner had wrapped up his calls. He was famished. He turned off the lights in the office and headed for the stairwell, opting to walk down six flights instead of taking the building's elevator. When Wills saw Givner, he asked him to sign out in the visitors' log. "Nah, you don't need that. I've been here all day," Givner said. "Since I didn't sign in when I got here, I don't think I need to sign out."[13] Wills didn't press the matter, perhaps seeing no reason to pursue it.

After some small talk, Givner asked Wills if he'd care to join him across the street at the Howard Johnson's Motor Lodge & Restaurant, where he was going to place a take-out order. Known for its slogan, "Someone you know, wherever you go," the motel chain featured a quaint twenty-four-hour coffee shop.[14] Though Wills was only thirty minutes into his shift, his concern with the unlocked doors packed with paper and cotton conveniently fell to the wayside. The night watchman took his first break of the evening, turning off the lights in the building's main lobby, and walking across the street with Givner.

Although they were close in age, worked at the same facility, and were new to the Watergate (Wills was assigned to the building the previous month), these two young men had little in common. Givner, who was white, was on his way to a successful legal career in sunny Southern California, while Wills, who hadn't finished high school, was working blue collar jobs. Normally, their paths would never have crossed, but on June 17, they did.

Both men ordered the same meal: a cheeseburger, a milkshake, and french fries. Waiting for their orders, they engaged in small talk. Once the food was ready, Givner hopped on his motorcycle. "See you soon," he told Wills.[15] Givner took off to his cousin's house. Wills went back to the building. The two men would never see each other again.

While Wills had been away, Captain Jackson, his immediate supervisor, had called and left a message for him to complete his rounds and then return the call. Wills chose to sit down at the guard's desk and enjoy his meal, putting his rounds and the call to his boss on hold.

At approximately 1:30 a.m., nearly an hour after he stepped away to buy food, Wills resumed his duties. Instead of checking the upstairs offices as Jackson requested, Wills went to the basement. He took the elevator to B-2, where he'd originally begun his

Chapter 2. The Break-In

shift and once again checked the door. It was at that moment that Wills knew he was not alone in the building. The tape had been reapplied.

With a can of Mace and, if need be, his bare fists as his only protection, Wills was not adequately equipped (or trained) to confront an intruder. Was there more than one? Were they armed? What was their target?

With no clear idea how to proceed, Wills returned to the main lobby, where he encountered Walter Hellams, a Federal Reserve Board guard in charge of protecting the agency's eighth-floor office suite. Wills updated Hellams about the situation; the other guard instructed Wills to call the police. He was reluctant. Fearful of being punished or, worse, losing his job for not following up with his bosses sooner, he tried to circumvent the situation by contacting Fletcher Pittman, the guard he had replaced from the previous shift. Maybe there was a logical explanation. But Pittman said that no locks were

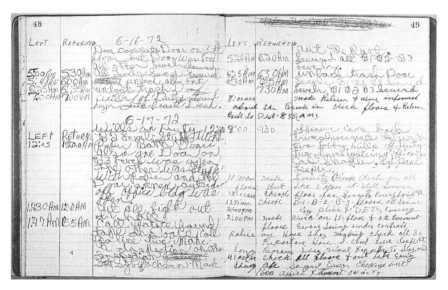

Security log Frank Wills used to record his activities on the night of the break-in, June 17, 1972 (PF-(usna)/Alamy Stock Photo).

taped during his watch. Now, Wills knew he was in trouble. Having no choice, he called his supervisor, Captain Jackson.

The B-2 level door had been retaped, Wills reported. Jackson ordered him to call the police. At approximately 1:47 a.m., Wills updated the security log: "Call police found tape on doore [*sic*]."[16] In that moment, Frank Wills' life changed forever. And so would the nation's.

CHAPTER 3

Savannah

December 24, 1997

More than a quarter-century after placing that historic phone call, igniting the greatest American political scandal of the century, Frank Wills, now forty-nine years old, was walking alone down a winding, rural road on Christmas Eve in North Augusta, South Carolina, where he had lived as a child.

Wills was no longer the famous night watchman. Middle-aged, he'd stayed slim, but his hairline had receded and there were noticeable wrinkles around his face. He was walking on the shoulder of Five Notch Road, near where he grew up. Carrying two paper bags, Wills did not have an umbrella or a hat to protect him from the pouring rain on that cold and windy December day. While most of his neighbors gathered to celebrate the holiday with their families, Wills was alone, heading to his modest four-room, 885-square-foot house. Once hailed by politicians, Black activists, and the media as an American hero, he was no longer in the public eye except every five years during the anniversary of the break-in.

Despite the inclement conditions, no one pulled over to offer him a ride. Even a childhood friend, who was on his way home to see his aging parents, noticed Wills but didn't offer him a lift. Longtime residents from the neighborhood knew Wills and remembered his adoring mother, Marjorie, who had passed away five years earlier. She was his lone confidante. Wills wasn't doing well before she died. He was in worse shape now.

Watergate's Forgotten Hero

To understand how Frank Wills managed to go from indistinguishable night watchman to celebrated folk hero to national embarrassment to, finally, a heartbreaking and cautionary celebrity tale, one need look no further than his roots.

***

On February 4, 1948, a warmish and partly humid day in Savannah, Georgia, Frank Wills was born. While the weather was mild, the news of the day was not.

Addressing the devastation of World War II, U.S. Secretary of State George C. Marshall requested "another billion" from Congress for Europe's restructuring efforts.[1] While Europe and Japan wrestled with reconstruction, the global community was in mourning over the January 30 assassination of Indian civil rights leader Mahatma Gandhi. Although a lone gunman was responsible, Indian authorities believed he had not acted alone; a manhunt was under way. Back home, the nation was in the midst of an economic boom, as millions of young men who had fought overseas increased the ranks of the workforce and the student bodies of the universities. The Republican-controlled Congress was making it difficult for Democratic President Harry S. Truman, now seeking election in his own right, having been elevated to the office three years earlier upon the death of Franklin D. Roosevelt.

In Georgia, residents were gearing up for a fiery gubernatorial showdown between the challenger, staunch segregationist Eugene Talmadge, and the current governor, Melvin E. Thompson, who was more moderate on race issues (at least in comparison to his opponent). It wasn't just another governor's race. The election's outcome would determine the state's response to growing racial unrest.

Throughout the South, many African Americans had returned from the war unwilling to accept the decades-long, racially restrictive Jim Crow laws. Political and cultural changes were sweeping through the South, especially in Atlanta. Sensing white backlash, Talmadge courted the state's white, rural citizens by making the

Chapter 3. Savannah

election about race. A vote for his opponent was a vote to cede power to Blacks.

Victorious, Talmadge rewarded his supporters by fostering a culture of "fear, intimidation, [and] threats of violence" toward African Americans in the state, "all with impunity, all in the interests of 'true white Southerners.'"[2] In the thriving metropolis of Atlanta, however, residents of color had fewer restrictions imposed on them than their rural neighbors. The Black citizens of Georgia's second-largest city, Savannah, experienced a similar situation.

Savannah, with a population of 150,000, had a reputation of being more welcoming toward African Americans than any other city in the state save Atlanta. Located on Georgia's eastern seaboard, Savannah utilized its geography to serve as a major economic trade portal in the Southeast region. Not only a bustling commercial center, the port city also enabled foreigners to come and go, creating a more tolerant culture than most other Southern towns. Still, some visitors had not arrived of their own volition. Dating back to 1755, Savannah was a destination for African slaves. Compelled to abolish slavery in 1865 by ratification of the Thirteenth Amendment, Georgians, like most white Southerners, devised ways to maintain a form of quasi-slavery. As was the case with nearly every city and town in the South, Savannah adopted Jim Crow laws, ensuring "a viselike grip over virtually every aspect of life in the city" to the detriment of people of color.[3] Compared to whites, African Americans earned two-thirds less, and their unemployment rate was twice as high. Even the most benign situations fell prey to segregation. When the traveling display of the original Constitution and Declaration of Independence came through town in 1948, Blacks and whites had separate viewing lines. It took nearly a century after the Civil War for the walls of segregation in Savannah to begin crumbling.

When Frank Wills was born, the civil rights movement was gaining a foothold in Black Savannah. Led by clergy and the local branch of the National Association for the Advancement of Colored People (NAACP), African American residents organized and forced the city to drop its segregated employment practices. Black civic leaders, notably, Dr. Ralph Mark Gilbert—who had helped reestablish the local NAACP chapter after the national office revoked its membership for failing to pay its dues—demanded that the city provide people of color with job opportunities beyond the departments of sanitation and maintenance. The city's Black-owned businesses, which had been vibrant since the beginning of the century, were entering their most profitable era. In fact, the local economy was so robust that because of the shortage of workers, white-owned downtown businesses reluctantly hired Black men and women— unheard of a few years earlier—to work as salesclerks in retail stores.

Despite the gains, racism was far from eradicated in Savannah. The Ku Klux Klan (KKK) was active, with many in power at the local and state level either openly involved or covertly sympathetic to its cause. For Black residents, obtaining basic medical care, labor protections, banking and mortgage opportunities, and adequate education remained challenging. Even using public or business bathrooms required strategic planning. If an African American family were shopping in downtown Savannah, no one, including a child, was allowed to use a store's restroom reserved for white customers, forcing parents to plan ahead.

When African Americans made political gains, they often had unintended consequences. Angry white rural voters, displeased by the growing economic and political power of urban Blacks, supported a statewide poll tax, designed to hinder voter turnout. The Klan did its part, ramping up its visibility on the streets of Black neighborhoods when an election neared. Even the city phone directory was divided along racial lines. If you were a person of color, there was a "C" next to your name, indicating you were "colored."[4] Entries were alphabetized by last name; the head of the household (almost always a male) was listed first, followed by address, occupation, and employer. In the 1948 Savannah city directory, among the tens of thousands of households listed, one of the few not headed by

Chapter 3. Savannah

a male was Marjorie Wills.' She had a "C" next to her name. She and her son Frank lived at 746 East Gwinnett Street in Apartment F.

***

Born in 1908, Marjorie Anna Wills, known as Margie to family and friends, was the daughter of Cornelius Wills (1882–1947) and Ida Boeler (1890–1931) of North Augusta, South Carolina. Located about 125 miles northwest of Savannah, North Augusta lies directly on the border of Georgia and is a bridge and river away from Augusta, a much larger metropolis.

Marjorie was one of seven children. No one knows why as an adult she left North Augusta for Savannah. Four of her siblings— Hampton, Nellie, Gladys, and Catherine—remained in North Augusta, while two moved out of state: Francis went south to Florida, and George traveled in the opposite direction to Indiana. It's likely Marjorie left for a love interest.

Frank did not know his father, Oliver (whether it is his given name or surname is unknown). With no male listed beside Marjorie's name in the city directory and no marriage or divorce records, it's likely that Oliver was a boyfriend. This was not unusual.

"Lot of boys didn't know their fathers," ninety-three-year-old lifelong Savannah resident Walter B. Simmons recalled well over a half-century later.[5] Fatherless homes were a fact of life in Savannah's Black neighborhoods. Because of chronic unemployment within the African American community, most of these men were unable to financially provide for their household. They became a liability to their family. If they couldn't find work but continued living at home, the family would not qualify for welfare. With no adult male living in the home, the single mother was eligible to receive a government subsidy. Thus, unless the father had a steady paycheck, there was little financial incentive for him to stay.

There were two other members of the Wills household that little is known about. A year after the break-in, in an interview with *Washington Post* reporters Bob Woodward and Carl Bernstein, Wills

Watergate's Forgotten Hero

confided that he had two younger brothers who died from infections that might have been avoided by uncontaminated bathing water. Wills was a child living in Savannah when those tragedies occurred. Neither the names of the boys nor their ages at death are known. Considering Marjorie's limited resources and the circumstances under which she was raising her sons, the loss of a child to preventable disease was not unusual at that time. Even with significant medical breakthroughs during the first half of the twentieth century, the health disparity between whites and Blacks remained vast, particularly for African Americans living in the South. Simply put, Black Southerners—especially youth—died in disproportionately greater numbers than their white counterparts. In 1950, the infant mortality rate for whites was 26.5 deaths per 1,000 births. For African Americans, it was almost double: 44.5 deaths. Only 25 percent of African American births in the South occurred in a hospital (as opposed to 68 percent for whites)—a direct result of segregated medical facilities that lacked an adequate number of physicians. Due to causes ranging from inadequate access to clean drinking water and the lack of indoor plumbing—an indicator of housing quality—to overcrowded housing conditions and poor air quality, Blacks in the South were more susceptible to illness and disease. This might help to explain why Marjorie's sons died prematurely. The impact this tragedy had on her and Frank is not known, but it is reasonable to assume the trauma remained with them forever.

Marjorie and Frank lived in an East Savannah apartment, a block away from a major thoroughfare, East Broad Street. They resided in a predominately African American working class community. Although some residents in the neighborhood were better off than others, Frank described his childhood as a "life in poverty and deprivation ... each day was a struggle for survival."[6] Even in the 1940s, it was not uncommon to find residents without access to electricity and running water. Marjorie probably obtained water from an outside pump, lit her apartment using kerosene lamps, and cooked on a wood burning stove.

Chapter 3. Savannah

Fortunately for her and her son, they lived within walking distance of shops and grocery stores, the majority of which were owned and operated by African Americans. If something was not available in East Savannah, Marjorie and Frank could take the bus to West Broad Street, which was *the* Black business district of the city. The west side of West Broad Street (the east side was for whites) included almost every professional and commercial establishment an African American family would need that was inaccessible elsewhere: banks, a movie theater, a pharmacy, a dry goods store, grocery stores, an ice cream parlor, medical offices, and funeral establishments. But there were times when a Black family would have to venture downtown, and that posed a dilemma.

Downtown Savannah was one of the few neighborhoods where whites and Blacks interacted. Because storeowners were white, there was an established, but unspoken understanding of what African Americans could and could not do inside their businesses. If Marjorie was shopping for a pair of shoes for her son, for instance, Frank would have to wait outside while she looked inside the store for him, because only one member of a Black family at a time was permitted to enter the premises. The shopkeeper no doubt kept a close eye on her, and offered minimal assistance. When she found what she was looking for, she'd have to hope the shoes were the right size, because her son would not be allowed to try them on before they were purchased. If they didn't fit her son, she had no recourse, a costly reminder of their second-class status.

***

To add to their struggles, Black people in Savannah had difficulty obtaining a fair living wage. The Black middle class, relatively small in number, included business owners and the college-educated, such as teachers, lawyers, or physicians. The vast majority of African Americans, however, had little if any hope of entering the middle class. Because most white unions barred people of color from joining, they were forced to organize their own unions or accept

25

Watergate's Forgotten Hero

low-paying jobs that offered no opportunity for career advancement or labor protections. At best, an uneducated Black male might be fortunate to secure a job at a shipyard or a shrimp factory, or as a porter on a Pullman train. But most people of color worked as maids and butlers for wealthy whites or as day laborers fixing streets, maintaining the city's sewers, or sharecropping under the blistering sun.

Marjorie was fortunate in this regard. She had two jobs that were highly desirable within the Black community: working for a sugar refinery and as a maid for a Jewish family. She worked for the Savannah Sugar Refinery in Port Wentworth, about ten miles northwest of the city. Without access to an automobile, Marjorie traveled to and from the refinery by bus, which probably required a transfer, ensuring an even lengthier workday. Despite this inconvenience, what made working at the refinery desirable were the added benefits such as access to a company store and affordable medical care (a rarity for Southern Blacks). At the Savannah Sugar Refinery, for "ten cents a week," workers could receive medical care from an on-site physician.[7] Typically at a refinery, most of the nonwhite workforce was male and worked on the dock, spending every day hauling 300-plus-pound bags of sugar. Women worked in nonfactory positions, such as office secretary or in the employee cafeteria. Although the refinery was considered a preferred place of employment for Blacks in Savannah, it remained a product of its times. If there was company housing, it was segregated, as was schooling offered for the employees' children. Like any other employer (including the state government), the refineries paid Black workers less than their white equivalents for doing the same jobs. It would be safe to assume that an African American rarely if ever was promoted to a managerial position.

In later years, Wills told an interviewer that his mother also had been employed as a domestic in a Jewish household. Whether she served in that capacity initially as a side job while working at the sugar refinery is not clear, though such a position—part-time or not—had to be advantageous in light of what we know about Jews in the South. Whatever the reason, perhaps because of their shared

Chapter 3. Savannah

historical experience as outcasts and victims of indescribable cruelty, Blacks and Jews in the South, by the middle of the twentieth century, had developed a unique relationship.

Jewish small business owners, for example, "earned a reputation among African Americans for being more willing than other white businessmen to offer both credit and basic courtesy to Black customers."[8] This open mindedness also extended to employment. Like their Gentile counterparts, Jews relied on Blacks to serve as caretakers of their homes, grounds, cars, and children. But a domestic working in the kitchen of a Jewish family had to possess (or develop) skills that satisfied the culinary tastes and dietary laws of their employer. If you could prepare matzo ball soup and kugel, you were in demand. "Learning to cook Jewish food," Eli Evans noted in his memoir, *The Provincials: A Personal History of Jews in the South*, "was a skill that led directly to secure permanent employment." If an employer moved, there was always another Jewish family "eager to hire a cook who knew what a gefilte fish was and that Friday night was chicken soup night."[9]

Marjorie may not have prepared gefilte fish, but Henry and Sadye Shonfield found her to be reliable when it came to the household's daily cooking and cleaning needs and, most importantly, able-bodied when it came to looking after their inquisitive six-year-old son, Lee. Because of the couple's work schedule, they were dependent on a maid to keep their home tidy and supervise their only child.

While Sadye was born and raised in Savannah, Henry emigrated from Poland at the age of ten with his divorced mother. His strong work ethic, necessitated by poverty at an early age, eventually paid off when he secured a loan to open his own shoe store from a sympathetic banker who did not discriminate against lending to a Jew. Years later, according to Lee, his father helped organize a credit union dedicated to loaning money to Jewish merchants.

Understanding the dark side of anti–Semitism, Henry and his Jewish business partner (whose last name was Schwartz), most likely opted not to name their downtown store after their ethnic sounding surnames and settled on a non-ethnic one, "Stewart's." Theirs was one of the few stores downtown that did not place restrictions on African Americans patronizing the premises; in later years, they hired a Black saleswoman, an unthinkable decision in that era. After his partner left the business, Henry had managed the day-to-day store operations, while Sadye worked as the bookkeeper and part-time saleswoman. Eventually, the shoe store prospered, and the family upgraded its residence from a cramped upstairs apartment to a single-family home in a more desirable, middle-class neighborhood.

Lee Shonfield's earliest memory of hired help was Lena, a Black maid he adored. She was his "surrogate mother" even though she only stayed with the family until he was six years old.[10] After Lena left, Marjorie was hired. With Lee in school, Margie, as she was known to the family, had fewer childrearing responsibilities. Still, Lee's memories of Margie—in contrast to Lena—were not warm and fuzzy. "She was very angry and bitter," he recalled, and he was intimidated by her unyielding presence.[11]

Every morning, Margie took the bus to her employer's home, walked from the bus stop to the Shonfields, and worked until late afternoon. On occasion, Henry was able to give her a lift to her residence. When Lee accompanied his dad on one of those rides, he was surprised to see where Margie and her son Frank lived. The apartment complex, located in the center of Savannah, was rundown and surrounded by derelict open lots—a contrast to his family's oak and palmetto tree–lined neighborhood. Like most Black help, Margie would take home leftover food; on occasion, she received hand-me-downs for Frank. Although many families would invite their maid to family functions and, in some cases, almost treat her like a member of the family, such generosity was not to be misinterpreted. The racial divide was ever present, and African Americans were fully aware never to cross it.

When Margie began working for the Shonfields, "Frankie"—as

Chapter 3. Savannah

Frank, age five, in Savannah, Georgia, at the home of his mother's employer, the Shonfields (courtesy Lee Shonfield).

he was then known—was about a year old, five years younger than Lee.[12] The age difference didn't matter to Lee (an only child) once Frankie was old enough to walk and talk. The boys interacted mostly on the weekends and during the summer when the Shonfields relocated to their two-story bungalow on Tybee Island, a small town off the Savannah coast known for its picturesque beaches. To escape the oppressive heat—there was no air conditioning during those days— many people left the city for the coastal town. During the week, Margie and Frankie would stay at the two-story house, living on the

Henry and Sadye Shonfield with their son, Lee, in 1952 (courtesy Lee Shonfield).

first floor in the single room maid quarters while the Shonfields were upstairs. Even though it was about twenty miles from Savannah, Henry still commuted to work every day.

It was during these summers that Lee witnessed how "unreasonably strict" Margie was with her son. If Frankie did something wrong, "she would make him sit in a chair [for long periods of time]

Chapter 3. Savannah

and he could not move. She scolded him a lot."[13] And since he suffered from asthma, when Margie punished him, he would often get an attack, finding it difficult to breathe. It was sad for nine-year-old Lee to watch.

No doubt, Margie was under a lot of personal strain, not to mention the institutional racism inflicted upon her. As on the mainland, segregation in the beach community was rigorously enforced. The only African Americans allowed on the island were those who worked. Once their shift ended, there was little if any opportunity to enjoy the amenities. Not allowed to use the beach, some Blacks circumvented the Jim Crow laws at night when there were fewer people present and they were less likely to be seen.

Radio was Margie's salvation. She listened to gospel music and soap operas, but one of her favorite programs was "Queen for a Day," Lee recalled.[14] Started in 1945, the format was simple: a group of women, preselected, each had to explain a financial or emotional hardship they had recently experienced. The host would follow up, asking them why they should be queen for a day. Using an applause meter, the studio audience would decide who deserved to win based on the most compelling response. Winners walked away with what they actually needed—from medical care to a washing machine—along with many other prizes such as household appliances or even a romantic vacation for the woman and her husband. Like most avid listeners, Margie's hopes to improve her lot—realistic or not—were no doubt raised.

***

Poor, Black, and a single mother, Marjorie had few reasons to stay in Savannah. She knew she could receive much-needed support if she moved to North Augusta, South Carolina, where her family was based. Sometime around 1954, after working for the Shonfields for a half-decade, Margie decided to quit her job. Her younger brother Hampton drove to Savannah and brought his sister and nephew, who was about six years old, back to her hometown. The timing and specific reason for their departure remain a mystery; no doubt Marjorie hoped that she and Frank could make a fresh start.

Lee and Frankie's paths, interestingly, would intersect again, but never face to face.[15] Lee went off to college, attended medical school at Medical College of Georgia, served in the Army Medical Corps, and completed his residency at the University of Cincinnati. He settled in Cincinnati, practiced psychiatry, and, with his wife, a native of Savannah, raised their family. Frank Wills' outlook would not be as promising.

CHAPTER 4

North Augusta

When Marjorie and her son Frank arrived in North Augusta, the region had gone through a major economic transformation. With an economy that was once based on farming, textile mills, and boutique tourism, North Augusta (located in Aiken County) had benefited from the nation's post–World War II boom, especially with the construction of the U.S. Atomic Energy Commission's (AEC) Savannah River Site. A nuclear power facility that spanned more than three counties and covered over 450 square miles, the River Site would be the AEC's biggest public works program to date. Requiring forty thousand workers to complete its construction, no project, as one scholarly study has pointed out, "had a greater impact on post–World War II South Carolina."[1]

The Wills family's new community looked more like the "New South," a region that was finally shedding its agrarian image and establishing itself as an industrial center.[2]

The city of North Augusta was founded in 1906 by James Urquhart Jackson, a savvy financier and visionary railroad tycoon who realized the benefits of the city's mild weather and accessible transportation routes by rail and steamboat. With the help of his brother Walter, the Jacksons modernized North Augusta by building rail, road, and water infrastructure while turning the town into a vacation destination for the wealthy (business tycoons John D. Rockefeller and Harvey Firestone), famous (baseball great Ty Cobb), and powerful (U.S. Presidents William Howard Taft and Warren G. Harding). The city had become synonymous with luxury, hoping to be known as the "winter resort of the South."[3] When word spread throughout the nation about this up-and-coming town, it reached the heads of the growing movie industry. Trying to determine where to relocate their studios from their current base in New York City, movie moguls were torn between North Augusta and Hollywood. Only a daylong trip by train from Gotham as opposed to the three-thousand-mile distance of Hollywood, North Augusta had the inside track. But James Jackson and his fellow residents resisted the offer, worried about losing the city's small-town appeal. In 1916, one of Jackson's resorts, Hampton Terrace, recently renovated, burned down due to faulty wiring. With limited funds—he failed to insure the resort—he tried rebuilding it but was unsuccessful. Falling on hard times, Jackson died in 1925.

North Augusta grew steadily and retained its quaint allure, especially for white residents, though it never regained its reputation for being a first-class resort town. Residents didn't have to worry about the big-city issues, such as crime or insufficient housing, that Augusta, its larger neighbor across the river, had to endure. But there were drawbacks. There was no hospital, for example, which forced residents to travel twenty minutes by automobile to the town of Aiken for medical care. Even so, North Augusta remained a picturesque, peaceful community to raise a family, that is, as long as you were white. In common with other Southern towns, North Augusta had a long history of Black oppression.

Before it was incorporated, North Augusta was first known as Savannah Town (est. 1670s), followed by Campbell Town (1770), and then Hamburg (1821). Hamburg was a major inland port until the railroad was extended across the river to Augusta, Georgia, in the 1850s. That rail extension was the catalyst for Hamburg's economic decline; the city was relegated to just another stop on the railway. After the devastation of the Civil War, white residents abandoned a number of smaller Southern towns. Hamburg had already been all but deserted; the war made it a "ghost town."[4] This situation created an opportunity for recently freed African Americans. Hoping to capitalize on Hamburg's riverfront location, Black farmers settled the

Chapter 4. North Augusta

land, with the goal of transforming it into a trading center. White resentment simmered, especially from ex-rebel soldiers who had not recovered emotionally or financially from the war. When these men witnessed firsthand the freedmen running their former town, it was too much to bear. Although Hamburg's Black residents were armed, they were no match for a state-supported militia made up largely of former Confederate servicemen. When an altercation erupted between the two sides on the Fourth of July in 1876, the outcome turned deadly. Outmanned and outgunned, the town's Black militia, which numbered thirty men, could not withstand three hundred white troops, who murdered five African Americans. It would be known as the Hamburg Massacre. The killers were never prosecuted, and the terror continued unabated as whites exerted complete control over the area, reinforcing it with "midnight rides," a tactic to intimidate the remaining residents of color.[5]

It wasn't until 1929, following a massive flood that forced residents to flee, that Hamburg was annexed to the city of North Augusta. Whites remained firmly in control while African Americans (who made up nearly 40 percent of the city's population) were regarded as second-class citizens. Politically oppressed and denied basic civil rights, people of color were afforded little if any economic opportunity in North Augusta, compelled to take jobs that whites were unwilling to fill. For every white male working on the train, there was a Black man laying down the railroad tracks. For every white female shopkeeper selling produce, there was a Black woman hauling those fruits and vegetables in a cart pulled by a farm animal. This prejudicial system had a direct impact on children of color. As a case in point, to combat the summer heat and humidity, thousands of white youth used the public swimming pools, while African American children resorted to swimming in an unsupervised and unsanitary lake. And this was only a small part of the problem.

"You didn't know what white people would do to you," Nathaniel (Nat) Irvin, Jr., a former resident and neighbor of Frank Wills, recalled. "Growing up here, people were afraid of the Klan getting you. Kids grew up hiding in the woods because when the Klan came through, it was time to disappear."[6]

For Marjorie Wills, returning to North Augusta was in some ways a step backward from the more progressive Savannah. As an African American woman with limited formal education, Marjorie had benefited from respectable jobs with reasonable accommodations in Savannah. In North Augusta, however, she wasn't able to obtain employment in a factory or mill, where there were too few positions and far too many applicants—a situation exacerbated by the nearby construction of the Atomic Energy Commission's nuclear power facility. It displaced eight thousand residents, "including an estimated three thousand African American sharecroppers who received no compensation at all."[7]

Marjorie worked as a servant for wealthy white families. With no means of transportation, she had to be driven by another worker or a sibling. Thin yet sturdy, Marjorie was a strong-willed, religious woman who rarely missed a prayer service at nearby Mount Transfiguration Baptist Church. On Sundays, her brother Hampton would drive her and Frank to church with his family.

Marjorie adored her son but never let him get away with any misdeed, big or small. "She was a no-nonsense person," a neighbor remembered.[8] When Frank joined the Mount Transfiguration Baptist Church's junior choir, his mom "insisted" he stick it out despite having a "terrible voice."[9] Although he may have strained reaching the higher notes in "What a Friend We Have in Jesus," he was a good sport about it, knowing how much it meant to his mother. She was "quite the disciplinarian," Frank's cousin Eddie Wills recalled.[10] When it came to Marjorie, her son did as she said.

Marjorie's first home in North Augusta was with her brother Hampton's family. It was ideal for Frank since his uncle's son, Eddie, was exact same age as his cousin—they were both born on February 4, 1948. After a brief stay, Marjorie and Frank moved near the center of town at 303 Euclid Avenue. Then, when Frank's great-aunt died, mother and son were invited to move in with their

Chapter 4. North Augusta

relatives. His second cousin, Martez Mims, looked back fondly when he lived with her family. She was a few years younger, and they had developed a sister-brother relationship. For a while things went smoothly, but as expected with long-term guests, tensions escalated.

Pamela Oliver, Martez's sister, recalled how her cousin Frank was in trouble frequently and could be quite "mischievous."[11] He had a habit of dropping his sneakers in the entryway where someone could trip on them. Losing her patience, Aunt Sadie, Marjorie's first cousin, exclaimed, "I'm sick of these sneakers! Y'all gonna have to leave!"[12]

No doubt, all this was difficult to process for a fatherless ten-year-old boy, who wanted to do what all kids his age did in the late 1950s rural South: ride bicycles, play baseball, shoot hoops, climb up to a tree house, and explore the wooded terrain. In those days, baseball was king. Virtually every young boy fantasized about hitting that game-winning home run in the bottom of the ninth inning or striking out the last batter in a World Series game. For Frank Wills and other African American youngsters coming of age during that era, top players like Jackie Robinson, Willie Mays, and Hank Aaron were viewed as heroes who defied the odds in racist America.

Whatever problems Marjorie and Frank encountered living with relatives, once they returned to their former residence at Euclid Avenue, a far more difficult issue had to be addressed. Could Frank receive an adequate education in a segregated and contentious school environment?

The quality of Black schools was in no respect equal to that of white ones. Teachers were paid less, facilities were older, books were more out of date, and spending per student was significantly lower. School officials failed to enforce the 1954 U.S. Supreme Court ruling in *Brown v. Board of Education*, which declared unanimously that racial segregation in public education was unconstitutional. On top of that, South Carolina was spending less per pupil, white or

Black, than any other state in the nation. Still, African American children suffered the most. Up until 1930, the state refused to issue high school diplomas to Blacks; even after it relented, progress was slow. In 1935, nearly eight thousand white students graduated high school in South Carolina compared to barely 300 African Americans. By 1940, those numbers had improved slightly: 10,717 vs. 1,009. To compound the problem, African American residents of the Palmetto State had to contend with the era's staunchest opponent of integration, Strom Thurmond.

The state's former governor and now a member of the U.S. Senate, Thurmond was determined to prevent implementation of the *Brown v. Board of Education* ruling. Turning a deaf ear to the Court's actual decision, Thurmond and his fellow South Carolinians devised a plan to increase educational funding for African Americans, hoping that equal separate facilities and resources would vitiate any need to overthrow segregated education in South Carolina. They even used public funds to bankroll the costs of out-of-state law school tuition for a Black student to prevent him from attending in state. The increased funding efforts for students of color fell short; white students still received a larger share of the pie. During the 1950s, the state spent an average of $159 for a white student versus $95 for an African American. In Aiken County, the difference was even more, $130 to $48.

Because allocated tax revenue to Black schools was considerably less, it meant that the length of the school year for African American students was eight months as opposed to nine months for their white counterparts. Furthermore, there were fewer books and supplies available, the teacher-to-student ratio was higher, and the average Black youngster spent more time traveling to school because of inadequate transportation. School officials overlooked no detail to keep the races separate. In Aiken County, the school administration installed a gasoline pump at a Black school for the "purpose of servicing the Negro school buses so that these buses would not have to drive to the [white] shop to be served."[13]

Chapter 4. North Augusta

Frank attended Triune, which was located in Belvedere, an unincorporated town inside the boundaries of North Augusta. Once Wills completed Triune, he was sent to the all–Black Jefferson High School. If Wills were white, he would have attended North Augusta High School, which was about two and a half miles from his house. Jefferson was twice the distance, although Wills' daily trip could have been even longer. Prior to 1955, he would have had to either cross state lines to attend Lucy Craft Laney High School in Augusta, Georgia, or go to the Bettis Academy in Edgefield County (fifteen miles from Wills' home) or Schofield High School in the city of Aiken (sixteen miles away).

Frank's yearbook photo at Jefferson High School, after which he dropped out.

Frank enjoyed English and science and participated in Future Farmers of America. His passion for reading made him excel in spelling; he won a classroom spelling bee, receiving a candy bar as a prize. But overall, he struggled academically. Those who knew him well remembered a teenager who was "smart in his own right," but was often unable to focus and his grades suffered.[14] Also, Wills found himself in trouble with Jefferson's administrators. On one occasion he was suspended from school for letting the air out of the principal's car tire. His cousin Pamela Oliver recalled how Marjorie was "very upset" over this prank, fearing her son was heading in the wrong direction.[15]

When Wills wasn't in school, he was at the Central Colored

School playground, a popular place for African American youth during after school hours. Disputes were settled there. Wills fought another boy, Nat Irvin, Jr., recalled. To those watching, it was obvious he had been victorious. Yet there was something troubling about his reaction. "I just remember looking at Frank, watching him continue to argue for no logical reason, and seeing a troubled soul," Irvin said. "It was not a normal reaction."[16]

While attending Jefferson, Wills was a loner. "I don't recall him having a lot of friends," noted Irvin. "He was an odd kind of person growing up."[17] Martez Mims remembered that he "didn't talk a whole lot."[18] One of Wills' few friends, Preston Sykes, confirmed that he was quiet and kept to himself. Although Marjorie was a supportive parent, protecting her only child, she had her limitations. Wills, an impressionable teenager, desperately needed an older male role model. Fortunately, one gentleman was willing to step up to the task.

***

The Rev. Nathaniel Irvin (father of Nat Jr.) was known never to "give up on anyone."[19] Born in 1929, Irvin was raised in an unincorporated area near North Augusta called Summer Hill. Like Wills, he was born to a single mother. But in contrast to Marjorie, Irvin's mother had no supportive network of relatives to help raise her six children in a home without electricity and indoor plumbing. Growing up, Irvin's life seemed bleak. He needed direction. His older brother, Leroy, advised: "get away ... [and go] to a place where nobody knew who you were."[20]

Irvin heeded his brother's counsel. He left Summer Hill, went to college, and became a history teacher and an ordained pastor. A popular educator, Irvin never forgot the names of his students. "And they never forgot him," according to his son.[21] Frank Wills was one of his students. As both a pastor and teacher, Irvin was well suited to serve as a "father figure for many young men."[22] Wills and Irvin developed a bond at Jefferson High School that would remain for the duration of Wills' life.

Chapter 4. North Augusta

Eventually, Marjorie and her son moved out of the Euclid Avenue residence into a home of their own a short distance to the east, at 204 West Five Notch Road. The six-thousand-square-foot vacant lot Marjorie purchased had been subdivided for a small home—and small it was. The 885-square-foot home was not constructed onsite but transported by a truck. A wood-frame, single-family residence, the four-room house—or "hut," as one of her neighbors would refer to it because of its tiny size—was located at the top of a sloped street.[23] It boasted a kitchen, a bathroom, and two bedrooms. The neighborhood was located in a more rural setting than their previous one, but it still offered easy access to the town. It was an ideal location for them because Marjorie's brother Hampton, and sister Gladys, lived around the corner. So did Preston Sykes.

Wills and Sykes immediately hit it off. Both only children, the two teens had a lot in common, including a passion for playing sports and exploring the woods, only steps away from their homes. When they weren't rummaging through the thickets, they freely ran around the neighborhood, often to the chagrin of Aunt Gladys, who was not averse to shouting at them and their parents from her porch. "Get these children out of the road!" she'd say, loud enough for everyone who lived nearby to hear.[24] It was the type of neighborhood where everyone knew each other.

But as his friends and cousins continued with their studies and made plans for college or jobs following graduation from Jefferson, Wills continued to struggle. There was a possibility he might be held back. On top of that, Wills had created another dilemma for himself. He had met a girl at a basketball game who attended the rival Augusta-based Lucy Craft Laney High School. They dated, and eventually she became pregnant. Frank planned to marry her, but got "chicken."[25] With a baby boy on the way compounding his subpar academic standing, the seventeen-year-old Wills, against his mother's wishes and the Reverend Irvin's counsel, dropped out of high school.

CHAPTER 5

Job Corps

Frank Wills, a poor Southern Black teenager with a child on the way and no high school diploma, had limited options. Fortunately, he had a knack for being in the right place at the right time.

In 1964, a year before Wills dropped out of Jefferson High School, President Lyndon B. Johnson had launched his "War on Poverty" initiative, an ambitious plan designed to address the economic and educational inequality between whites and people of color. It included federal job training for young men like Wills, to prevent them from falling into a cycle of poverty, chronic unemployment, and crime. The program was called Job Corps.

Under the leadership of the Office of Economic Opportunity director (and former head of the Peace Corps) Sargent Shriver, Job Corps was modeled after President Franklin D. Roosevelt's Civilian Conservation Corps (CCC), one of the many programs to put Americans back to work during the Great Depression. While the CCC was primarily focused on forestry (three billion trees were planted throughout its duration), the vision for Job Corps was broader in scope. Almost half the participants would be trained in conservation, but the remainder had the opportunity to acquire skills focused on "food service, auto and machine repair, construction trades, electrical appliance repair, service occupations, and industrial production"—the types of trades leading to a reliable and well-paid union job that could support a household in the 1960s.[1] Job Corps would take these young men (and women) out of their troubled environment and send them to out-of-state sites, where, in addition to occupational training, they

Chapter 5. Job Corps

would attend school (with a major emphasis on reading and math skills).

As a community leader, the Reverend Irvin was a vigorous advocate of the program. He had witnessed his former students enroll in Job Corps and return home more confident and employable. Irvin encouraged Wills to apply, but the odds were heavily against him: 300,000 applicants for 45,000 spots. Wills went to a local employment office and applied. Within two weeks, he was notified. By sheer luck, he had beaten the odds.

Once accepted, he was assigned to a men's center in Battle Creek, Michigan, nearly a thousand miles away, a bit scary for a young man who never traveled beyond Georgia and South Carolina. Determined to establish economic opportunities for himself, he left his home, mother, girlfriend, and baby son, Eugene.

Originally used as a World War I training facility for soldiers, the center was called Camp (later Fort) Custer, in honor of the famous General George Armstrong Custer. Wills and his fellow Job Corps cadets were housed, fed, and trained onsite. The typical enrollee was like Wills: Black, eighteen years old, and most likely a high school dropout. It was expected that participants, who could leave at any time, stay for up to twenty-four months.

Initially, Job Corps had bipartisan support, as *Washington Post* reporters John M. Berry and Art Pine pointed out: Democrats liked the program because it helped the urban poor; "Republicans embraced [it] as a respectable alternative to welfare."[2]

Like any innovative government program, however, it had its drawbacks and critics. Turnover was high. Almost half the enrollees quit within three months of signing up, usually due to "homesickness and [a] failure to adjust."[3] Those who did graduate were not automatically guaranteed a secure, well-paying job. When researchers tracked graduates of Job Corps, a third of the participants remained unemployed, and another third were hired for jobs that had little or nothing to do with their training.

Another problem was the cost. The logistics of recruitment,

Watergate's Forgotten Hero

housing, training, data collecting, and overall administration were significantly more expensive than running a local job training center, where enrollees did not need to be housed, fed, or schooled in academic subjects.

Many of the Job Corps sites were located in rural America, far away from the urban centers most of the enrollees were from. In addition, the white residents living near these centers were "resentful" that busloads of mostly African American and Hispanic young men had "invaded" their towns.[4] Battle Creek seemed to be the exception in view of its active community of color and rich heritage. The town boasted of a visit on the eve of the Civil War by the famous Black abolitionist leader Frederick Douglass. In the 1940s and 1950s, African Americans were heavily involved in the community's vibrant music scene. But racial justice was still a work in progress. It wasn't until 1963 that Battle Creek elected its first Black city commissioner. It was another four years before the school district appointed its first African American school principal.

While at Fort Custer, Wills "studied heavy machine operation" and learned to operate back loaders and graders.[5] He took classes toward a high school equivalency diploma, though he would not complete all the requirements. In the midst of Wills' tenure at Job Corps, the program's funding suffered a major curtailment. President Johnson moved from helping the poor to expanding America's involvement in Vietnam, diverting more and more revenue to the extraordinary costs of the war. Like many other social services under Johnson's presidency, Job Corps was a casualty of the conflict in Southeast Asia. When President Nixon entered the White House, the cuts to Job Corps continued. Even before he was elected president in 1968, on the campaign trail "he repeatedly held up the Job Corps as an example of an antipoverty program which should be eliminated."[6] Although he did not fulfill his promise, Nixon drastically reduced the program's budget by 30 percent. It's likely that Wills was not affected by the cut, and left of his own volition a year or so before.

Chapter 5. Job Corps

Out of the program and still without a high school diploma, nevertheless Wills landed on his feet. Using skills he acquired in Battle Creek, he found employment in nearby Detroit, the nation's automobile manufacturing capital.

Back home, however, Marjorie had a difficult time. Living alone, she missed having her only child present. This was painfully apparent when she attended a birthday party for her nephew, Eddie, who shared the same birthday as his first cousin Frank. At the gathering, Eddie later remembered, it seemed that Marjorie was actually celebrating her son's birthday in his absence.

Arriving in Detroit sometime in 1967 or 1968, Wills was hired to work at the Ford Motor Company assembly line in the city's suburb of Dearborn. At Ford, he was assigned to install the front and rear bumpers for the Mercury Cougar. As unfinished cars passed above Wills' head, forcing his neck to constantly stay at an uncomfortable forty-five-degree angle for eight hours a day, he was tasked with fitting bumpers on 75 to 100 vehicles. Although it may have seemed like a mundane task, it was stressful for Wills. He dreaded being the incompetent worker who was responsible for holding up the line of cars on the massive assembly line, which came to a halt when there was a delay.

With no family, few friends, and limited career options, all he looked forward to was Friday—payday. He did take pride seeing the Cougar on the road, pointing out to friends that he was the one who had installed the bumper. After being let go from Ford, he worked at Chrysler Motors. That job did not pan out either. Years later, when asked about his employment in Detroit, Wills said he left Ford because of his "asthma" and was not able to find steady work at Chrysler because he was "barred from union membership" (it's likely the rampant racism of the United Automobile Workers played a role).[7]

Unable to secure lasting employment at Ford and Chrysler, he went from "job to job," including a stint as a part-time security guard at a department store.[8] It was the first time he worked in an enforcement position. Hired as an "undercover store detective," Wills seemed to have a knack for identifying suspects before they left the store with the stolen merchandise.[9] On one occasion, he observed a gentleman putting clothing items in his pockets. It appeared to be a routine situation. Per store policy, Wills waited for the suspect to walk out the door before apprehending him.

But the perpetrator exited quickly and Wills had to confront him in the parking lot. At this point, Wills was alone and far enough from the store that he could not easily holler for assistance. He took his chances and asked the suspect to empty his pockets.

Instead, the suspect turned around and pointed a .38 caliber gun at Wills.

"Turn around. Walk back in that store and don't look back!" he demanded.[10]

Wills did as he was told.

When he went back inside, Wills told his manager, who called the police. The manager told him not to put himself in that situation again. Confront suspects immediately so you are within earshot of the store, he advised him.

Despite this incident, Wills had come to the realization that he enjoyed security work—the pay, status, and possibility of advancement. In April 1971, the twenty-three-year-old attended a party where he struck up a conversation with visitors from Washington, D.C. Wills was intrigued when he heard from the out-of-town guests that higher-paying jobs, especially for security guards, were plentiful in the nation's capital. Plus, it was geographically closer to North Augusta, making it easier for him to see his mother. The DC guests invited him for a visit. He took them up on the offer, boarding a Greyhound bus. He planned to stay only for one week but instead stayed for two. When he returned to Detroit, he packed his bags, and once again boarded a bus for DC, but this time he bought a one-way ticket.

When Wills arrived in Washington (the nation's first major city with a Black majority), it was still dealing with the aftermath of its

Chapter 5. Job Corps

own devastating riots following the 1968 assassination of Dr. Martin Luther King, Jr. The destruction had been cataclysmic. Even in the White House, President Lyndon Johnson could smell the smoke caused by the arsonists.

Older, wiser, and more confident, and perhaps thanks to Marjorie's influence, Wills avoided the pitfalls—drugs and violence—that engulfed many of DC's young Black men. Initially hired as a busboy and a hotel bellhop, soon Wills obtained a job as a security guard. Standing six feet tall and weighing 155 pounds, he was clean-cut and handsome, with closely cropped hair, a neatly trimmed mustache, and an engaging grin, which he usually suppressed. Retiring and soft-spoken, he had a drawl that clearly identified him as a Southerner. He never projected a threatening presence, but his height, quiet demeanor, and guard uniform conveyed a sense of importance.

***

Since 1960, the private security industry had rapidly expanded, generating $4 billion annually and employing nearly half a million guards nationwide. Whether it was protecting banks, corporations, hospitals, hotels, offices, private homes, special events, or government buildings, employers found it was cheaper to contract with a private agency than to hire off-duty police officers or maintain security personnel on their own payroll.

Most businesses sought night watchmen to patrol their property after hours. The watchmen's presence was to act as a deterrent, but if they did detect criminal activity, they were supposed to relay the information to their superior, or, if the situation warranted, to law enforcement directly. Rarely were these hourly paid private guards expected to apprehend criminals. They lacked the proper training and, as private citizens, had no legal authority. Training was minimal, usually one full day prior to the first assignment. In some cases, it would occur during the first day of work, with the new recruit shadowing a more experienced colleague. In fact, it was not "uncommon for a new guard to spend an hour or less with a supervisor and

Watergate's Forgotten Hero

then be assigned to work alone."[11] If a problem arose, the guard usually called the supervisor for support.

Private security companies were reluctant to invest in training their employees because of the high turnover rate, which explained the low pay. The average private security guard earned either minimum wage or slightly above it. In 1970, the federal minimum wage was $1.45. Most private security guards were paid between $1.60 and $2.50 an hour (equivalent to $9.85 and $15.50 in today's dollars).

In May 1973, Mary Margaret Hughes, affiliated with the industry magazine *Security World*, claimed "these are enormously underpaid men considering the nature of their work." She added, "Some agencies pay only minimum wage and force their guards to work overtime to make an adequate income. The wonder is that these men don't steal on the job, considering their wages."[12]

In the early 1970s, when Wills was entering the profession, a study of the private security industry was conducted. The typical guard was white, in his forties or fifties, lacked a high school diploma, had minimal security experience, and worked between sixteen and twenty-four hours a week, either as a patrolman (mobile) or night watchman (stationary). Often, security agents had another job to supplement their scant income. Most, when surveyed, had accepted the position because it was the "best job to be found."[13] Although Wills did not fit the profile, the study noted his demographic—nonwhite and under the age of twenty-four—as the fastest-growing in the field.

Within a month of his arrival in DC, Wills was hired by General Security Services (GSS) through an employment agency. He was paid slightly above minimum wage, which came to $80 a week (the equivalent of $500 today). Wills found a small, single-room apartment located in the northwest part of town on Twenty-Second Street, in a safe neighborhood (unlike the slums of the southwest quadrant).

Wills served as a watchman for various buildings in town during

Chapter 5. Job Corps

the day as well as after business hours. He was often assigned the "lonely midnight-dawn shift."[14] Working alone suited his introverted personality.

In May 1972, he was promoted and given notice to report to 2600 Virginia Avenue NW—the Watergate Office Building.

CHAPTER 6

Watergate

In the early 1960s, if certain members of the Washington, D.C., fine arts and planning commission had had their way, the proposed ten-acre, six-building complex would never have been built. It was too tall, too curvy, too bold, and too different from every other structure in the cityscape. The DC elite were desperate to save the nation's capital from this "architectural catastrophe."[1]

Aside from the complex's angular shape, the proposed height of the six buildings was cause alone to vote against it. If the plans went through, the skyline of the nation's capital would forever be altered, partially blocking the view of the Lincoln Memorial, the National Mall's most sacred structure. Even President John F. Kennedy was pulled into the debate. Privately, he sided with the commission— these buildings rising over 150 feet were too tall. The builders would have to compromise.

The project's critics wanted more than anything to maintain the city's architectural status quo of gothic, neoclassical. To them, the design was "blasphemous" and would "erode and destroy the qualities that give Washington its particular beauty."[2]

Nestled along the Potomac River, the proposed site was located at the former Washington Gas Light Company plant, in the historic Foggy Bottom neighborhood. Builders preferred this site because it was within walking distance of the U.S. State Department and the soon-to-be built National Cultural Center (renamed the Kennedy Center following the assassination) and only eight blocks from the White House.

Luigi Moretti, the Italian architect responsible for the uproar,

Chapter 6. Watergate

was not deterred. He may have relied on an interpreter during his stay, but the "bulky man with an expressive face" had vision, stubbornness, and access to the Vatican's deep pockets.[3] Often referred to by his admirers as the "Frank Lloyd Wright of Italy," Moretti, whose past projects included the 1960 Olympic Village in Rome, viewed DC as a poorly planned city filled with passé buildings that were an embarrassment for a global superpower.[4] Despite the country's claim to the biggest military and economy on the planet, the architectural façade of the U.S. capital could not hold a candle to its European counterparts—London, Paris, or Rome.

The proposed ten-acre, $50 million project was made up of curving concrete towers that would be built without a single straight line among them. Billed as a "city within a city," its selling point was that it was a high-end urban destination where all your needs were met—work, rest, and play.[5] In 1960, this was a new concept, not yet in vogue. The development would include three large apartment towers, a hotel, two office buildings, a post office, a grocery store, high-end retail boutiques, and a top-story restaurant, all bounded by lush, green open space. By June 1961, developers and the staff for the National Cultural Center agreed on a name, calling it the Watergate Towne Complex.

Not to be outflanked, project supporters enlisted the aid of local officeholders. Fearful that residents would follow the pattern of many American households, fleeing the urban center for quieter suburbs—in this case, northern Virginia or southern Maryland—DC government officials had to act fast. The project had the potential not only to slow the exodus but also to reshape and reenergize the region.

After much back-and-forth, a handful of concessions were made, notably the height requirement—it could not exceed the Lincoln Memorial. Once the green light was given, construction got underway. Built in a series of phases, the project took eleven years to complete, five years longer than originally planned.

***

Watergate's Forgotten Hero

Watergate East Apartments, the first of six towers, opened in 1965 and was hailed a success. "Georgetown's new rival for the title of Washington's best address" headed an advertisement for units.[6] It was only a matter of time before the Watergate name "would be synonymous with luxury like New York's Park Avenue and San Francisco's Nob Hill," declared local real estate agents.[7] Those able to afford any unit, let alone the most coveted, were likely empty nesters, mainly gray-haired lawyers, judges, diplomats, or politicians. After all, this was Washington, D.C.

To its critics' astonishment, the complex was a hit. Before Watergate East had opened its door, 80 percent of the apartments in the 110-foot-tall, "curving building [that was] shaped like a boomerang" were sold.[8] Perhaps Moretti expected a different type of resident to move into the Watergate. Built during the Kennedy and LBJ administrations, the builder might have imagined that his tenants—at least those working at the White House—would lean politically leftward. Because many of America's largest cities were Democratic strongholds, he and his colleagues probably assumed that progressives preferred a more urban lifestyle than their conservative counterparts, who were more comfortable in the quieter (and whiter) suburbs. By the time the second apartment tower was built in 1968, though, there was a new political party in power.

The lure of convenience and living in the "most expensive apartment house in town" attracted many of President Richard Nixon's staff.[9] The most prominent to take up residence was Attorney General John Mitchell. Although his wife Martha was bitter about leaving behind their twenty-room estate in Westchester County, New York, their multi-level, high-rise unit, which featured sweeping views of the Potomac and was one of the most expensive in the building, probably served to mollify her. Secretary of Commerce Maurice Stans and his wife Kathleen also purchased a lavish penthouse suite that was decorated in African décor, complete with tiger skins and elephant tusks (souvenirs from their recent safari). Rose Mary Woods, Nixon's secretary, moved in too, as did Transportation Secretary John

Chapter 6. Watergate

An aerial view of the Watergate Complex, Washington, D.C. Photograph taken by Carol M. Highsmith (Alpha Stock/Alamy Stock Photo).

Volpe, speechwriter Victor Lasky, Protocol Chief Emil "Bus" Mosbacher, and other members of the White House staff. "Why, we could have a Cabinet meeting here," a local real estate agent quipped.[10]

Watergate, though, was not just home to the Grand Old Party (GOP). Democratic Senators Alan Cranston of California and Wayne Morse, the Oregonian maverick, also lived at the complex. Nevertheless, the Watergate remained associated with the GOP, giving it the nickname "Republican Bastille."[11]

Its status as a palace of power, however, had its drawbacks.

In February 1970, hundreds of demonstrators, protesting the conspiracy trial of the Chicago Seven (a group of protestors who were charged for inciting a riot at the 1968 Democratic National Convention) attempted to "storm" the "Bastille" in demonstration against the dubious charges.[12] Scores of police officers successfully created a massive blockade around the complex, preventing any of the activists from harming the facility, its grounds, or the residents.

Watergate's Forgotten Hero

Aside from outside agitators, the buildings and their contents posed problems.

In March 1972, residents organized and filed a $1.5 million damage suit in United States District Court against the developers for a number of defective household appliances and structural deficiencies. More than "forty-five percent of the kitchen appliances furnished by the developers were defective," the air-conditioning units were not working in nearly three-quarters of the apartments, and there was significant "water damage" in nearly half the apartments from rainwater leakage caused by insufficiently sealed windows and cracks in the ceiling and walls.[13] And to top it off, Watergate residents complained about airplanes whizzing overhead during their "summer roof-garden cocktail parties."[14]

No matter the complaints, the complex did not lose its appeal. Besides its avant-garde style, what made Watergate stand out was its ability to incorporate the live-and-work synergy that is commonplace today but was an unfamiliar philosophy fifty years ago. In theory, a resident could leave from his or her apartment; work in one of the two office buildings; stop by an onsite retail store or salon, or relax at a restaurant; and then go home, all without having left the complex. Now, if it only had a tennis court and a movie theater, a resident remarked, then there really would be no reason to leave.

Of the six towers, two were used for offices—Watergate 600 and the Watergate Office Building, the larger of the two.

Located at 2600 Virginia Avenue Northwest, the Watergate Office Building was connected via T-shape to the 213-room Watergate Hotel. Although the two buildings had separate entrances and different addresses, they were jointly connected both above and below ground through an underground parking garage. More than 200,000 square feet of office space were available to lease.

In June 1967, the first tenant to move into the Watergate Office Building was the Democratic National Committee (DNC). DNC

Chapter 6. Watergate

chairman John M. Bailey was excited about the party's new location. In addition to its aerial view of the Potomac River, it offered more than five thousand square feet for less cost than its previous site. Because the DNC was lured to the building before construction was completed, the builders enticed its officials by adding something that no other floor featured—an outdoor terrace.

Bailey would not enjoy his party's new home for long. Following defeat in the 1968 presidential election, he resigned as DNC chairman, replaced by Lawrence O'Brien.

A Massachusetts native and lifelong Democrat, O'Brien's career in politics began when he worked for the dashing, thirty-five-year-old Congressman John F. Kennedy. With Kennedy planning a U.S. Senate run in 1952, O'Brien signed on, confirming his place on the Kennedy team. JFK was victorious, and after he was elected president in 1960, O'Brien served as one of his key advisors until that day in Dallas, November 22, 1963.

Recognized for his political acumen, O'Brien stayed on at the request of Lyndon Johnson. Appointed as postmaster general in 1965, O'Brien left three years later to be an advisor on the presidential campaign of Senator Robert F. Kennedy. Following Kennedy's assassination, O'Brien helped Johnson's Vice President, Hubert Humphrey, in his presidential bid, but to no avail. Nixon was elected.

At a time when the nation had fractured over the war in Vietnam and civil rights, Democratic leaders, shaken up by their party's defeat, considered O'Brien one of the leading candidates to head the DNC and beat Nixon in four years. And when Ohio-based shipbuilding magnate (and future New York Yankees baseball club owner) George Steinbrenner refused the invitation to lead the party, the DNC offered it to O'Brien, who accepted. His first test would be the 1970 midterm elections.

O'Brien's chief objective was to hold his party's majority in the House and Senate, and perhaps add a few seats in both chambers.

Watergate's Forgotten Hero

Politicos placed their bets on Nixon and the GOP, writing off O'Brien and the Democrats as "politically dead."[15]

To Nixon's irritation, the new DNC chairman, who coordinated campaigns in twenty-two states, proved he was a formidable political force. While he lost three seats in the Senate, he still managed to retain the majority and added an additional twelve seats in the House. The defeat stung Nixon, channeling his anger toward the DNC and its upstart leader.

Following the midterm elections, Nixon reached his "lowest point" since taking office.[16] Dealing with high unemployment and a war without end in Vietnam, Nixon's approval rating was lower than all of his recent predecessors. One had to go back to Truman to find a comparable rating at this period in a presidency. Polls indicated that if the 1972 election were held a year earlier, Nixon would lose.

Feeling vulnerable about his reelection chances, the paranoid president laid out his "secret agenda."[17] Continuing the pattern of unethical political tactics that had earned him the nickname "Tricky Dick," Nixon ordered members of his administration to bug, spy on, and investigate anyone he deemed an enemy (not surprisingly, O'Brien was at the top of the list). When Nixon tried recruiting the FBI to conduct secret surveillance of his political opponents, the agency's top official, J. Edgar Hoover, said he would not be a part of it. With no other options, Nixon and his inner circle of former FBI and CIA agents would do it themselves.

***

It began in early 1971.

Someone broke into O'Brien's DC apartment at the Sheraton Park Hotel, seizing documents pertaining to his law practice. Not long after, there was another break-in, at O'Brien's apartment in New York City. In the meantime, business associates had informed O'Brien they were being spied upon. When he went out to a restaurant, his waiter informed him that an unknown patron had asked

Chapter 6. Watergate

with whom O'Brien had dined in a previous visit. The harassment soon went beyond break-ins and spies; Nixon loyalists launched an all-out economic attack. First the companies and firms O'Brien conducted business with had their federal contracts terminated, and then the IRS placed O'Brien himself under investigation.

Among GOP operatives, the word was out: "Get O'Brien."[18]

The first known break-in by Nixon's men at the DNC offices in the Watergate was on May 5, 1972. Upon initial investigation, it looked like a standard robbery—a safe had been broken into, and $200 in cash and checks had been stolen. The DNC deputy treasurer filed a police report, and the office resumed its activities. Ten days later, the Democrats selected their presidential nominee, South Dakota Senator George McGovern.

Popular with the college-aged and left-wing ideologues, McGovern's team quickly took over the DNC operation and its offices. McGovern's staff was viewed by O'Brien and his colleagues—many of whom were former members of the Kennedy and/or Johnson administrations—as inexperienced and ill-equipped to run a presidential campaign. Whether it was their naiveté when it came to political strategy, their shaggy appearance, or their lack of funds (they had already fallen behind on their rent), the DNC offices reflected the campaign's informal and youth-infused culture. Office visitors rarely, if ever, needed an appointment. Once you entered the sixth-floor DNC headquarters office, you were likely greeted and scrutinized by an unpaid intern. The only formal security was the building's first-floor doorman.

During Memorial Day weekend, the office was burglarized again. This time the lock was picked, files were in disarray, and, unbeknownst to DNC officials, listening devices were installed on O'Brien's phone and that of another top party official. Luckily for the Democrats, the listening devices malfunctioned and the documents that were photographed proved "meaningless."[19] Upon viewing the material, Nixon's Attorney General John Mitchell, who was now serving as chairman of the Committee to Re-Elect the President

(CREEP), said: "This stuff isn't worth the paper it's printed on."[20] The burglars would need to return.

The DNC filed another police report. Detectives were on scene. Prints were lifted. The office locks were changed. There was still no suspect (or suspects).

A memo was sent to DNC staff: "Be more alert."[21]

CHAPTER 7

Metro Police

It was 1:52 a.m. when Officer Dennis P. Stephenson pulled his police cruiser into the parking lot of the Washington, D.C., Second District Police Headquarters at Twenty-Third and L Street NW. A call from the dispatcher came in: there was a burglary in progress at the Watergate Office Building. Low on gas and behind on his paperwork, Stephenson decided not to take the call. Ninety percent of these calls never materialized, he reasoned.

Heading toward the upscale Georgetown neighborhood, cruiser 727 was next in line to receive the dispatcher's notification. The police car was unmarked. So were the plainclothes driver and his two passengers.

Sergeant Paul Leeper and Officers John Barrett and Carl Shoffler were referred to as the department's "bum squad," a law enforcement unit that worked incognito.[1] The purpose of their disguise was to give the police an advantage during the course of any criminal activity, such as a mugging or a burglary.

"When someone's about to commit a crime," Leeper later explained to the *Washington Post*, "he usually looks around at the last minute. With us [the bum squad] he doesn't see anyone he's afraid of."[2]

Leeper, 33, was the driver. An eleven-year veteran, Leeper was in charge of the precinct's plainclothes division. It was his wife's birthday that day, and he was hoping to get off soon so he could go home, get some sleep, and take her out that evening. Sporting a tough man's goatee, he wore a bucket hat, construction boots, and a windbreaker with *George Washington University* emblazoned on it. Barrett and

Watergate's Forgotten Hero

Shoffler were just as mismatched in their attire as their boss. Barrett described his appearance as a "Junior Charlie Manson."[3]

As usual, the crew had been working beyond their normal shift, which had begun at 4:00 p.m. They were scheduled to be off at midnight, but due to a string of recent robberies, they were working overtime, hoping for a break in the case.

When the call came in, Car 727 was at Thirtieth and K Street NW. They made a U-turn and headed toward the Kennedy Center. Within ninety seconds, they had arrived at their destination, 2600 Virginia Avenue NW—the Watergate Office Building.

With plenty years of experience, Leeper and his unit knew there was no need to "jump out of the car and go running up there."[4] That would defeat their cover. The team was aware from a daily crime report they read before each shift that there had been a couple recent burglaries at this building, which was known to have been a "favorite [target] of Washington's burglars and sneak thieves for several years."[5]

Between 1:55 and 1:57 a.m., Car 727 pulled up to its destination, purposely parked about fifty feet from the main entry to avoid detection. Leeper and his men walked toward the building's entrance and marched up the steps to the main lobby door.

Barrett hit his badge against the window, hoping to get someone's attention.

"Police," he yelled to the nervous security guard walking toward him on the other side of the glass.

Frank Wills unlocked the door and allowed the three undercover officers inside the lobby. Wills attempted to explain the situation; however, Officer Shoffler had trouble following along. Wills was saying something about "there was somebody inside possibly."[6] Something about seeing "tape on a door."[7] Then, when he returned, he "saw the tape was back."[8] There was something about a "garage door at the B-2 level."[9] "[It was] very hard to judge his demeanor," Shoffler later testified in court. "We asked him to show us."[10] And Wills took the three police officers to the basement.

60

Chapter 7. Metro Police

In Wills' defense, he was a poorly trained, inexperienced security guard, and at the moment he had a potential burglary in progress in the building he was hired to secure. To exacerbate the problem, the police who had arrived could pass as members of Charlie Manson's clan. This was not a trainable situation for any low-level night watchman.

Wills led the officers to the second level of the basement. Unlike the first instance, when he had discovered the tape attached to the latch and removed it, Wills had left the reapplied tape intact.

Federal Reserve guard Walter Hellams joined the group and explained to the officers that the Reserve Board's eighth floor offices had been burglarized recently too.

Convinced something was amiss but skeptical on the details, Leeper was not taking any chances and ordered Wills to shut down the elevator. It would prevent anyone from the floors above from escaping without detection. The stairwell was now the only access point to exit the building. Leeper also told Wills to remain in the lobby—if he saw anyone trying to leave the building whom he didn't recognize, he was to call the police. The three police officers, each equipped with a .38 caliber revolver, took the stairwell and headed toward the eighth floor. Hellams joined them. Their first stop was the Federal Reserve office.

When they walked up the eight flights of stairs and entered the floor lobby, the officers asked Hellams to open the office door. He was having difficulty doing so. After assessing the area, the three officers observed there was no evidence of forced entry. Hellams was sent to assist Wills in securing the lobby.

The three officers split up. Barrett went up to the ninth floor. Leeper and Shoffler walked down to the seventh floor. Both floors were clear. They were beginning to wonder if it was a false alarm. They proceeded to the sixth floor.

Once they reached the entry door from the stairwell, Leeper and Shoffler immediately noticed the tape on the latch, the same type that was used in the basement.

Watergate's Forgotten Hero

"I started to think we did have a break-in [in progress]," Leeper recalled. "[My] adrenaline started pumping."[11]

Leeper ran up a flight of stairs and yelled for Barrett to come down. He quickly did, and the three men quietly entered the twenty-nine-room office suite of the Democratic National Committee.

It was obvious the lock on the front door had been tampered with. Inside the DNC suite, the three officers entered a massive office, large enough to accommodate nearly 100 workers.

A few of the lights were turned on, but it was dark enough to avoid visibility. Leeper, Barrett, and Shoffler split up and checked each office. Once an office was cleared, they moved on to the next one. Between the large amounts of paper thrown on the floor and the file drawers pulled out and left open, they were certain a burglary had taken place (little did they realize that the offices normally looked this disheveled). The question in the back of their minds, hands gripping their guns, was whether or not the burglars were still in the building.

Shoffler made his way to what looked like a conference room and noticed a chair had been used to prop open a door that led to an outdoor terrace. He signaled Leeper to join him. With his gun drawn, Shoffler "crawled" along the terrace.[12] He spotted a man on the opposite side of the street, standing on a hotel room balcony at the Howard Johnson's.

The man was holding a walkie-talkie and observing Shoffler's movement. Unsure who he was, Shoffler crawled back inside.

"What if he calls the police?" Shoffler asked his boss.

"Hell, Carl, we are the police!"[13]

Convinced they were not alone, the three officers pulled out chairs from each desk and checked underneath to see if a burglar was hiding. Working their way across the office suite, it appeared they had reached the end. One of the last rooms that had not been cleared was Larry O'Brien's office.

There were three cubicles that separated O'Brien's office from

Chapter 7. Metro Police

the rest of the suite. To create a level of privacy, each of the cubicles had a three-foot-high metal partition attached to the desk. On top of each partition was a three-foot-high, cloudy glass window.

The officers searched the first cubicle.

Nothing.

They searched the second cubicle.

Nothing.

Realizing there were fewer and fewer places left to hide, Officer Barrett had an overwhelming sense that "I better not go into the third cubicle."[14]

His partners were only a few paces away, but to Barrett, for all intents and purposes, they could have been a mile away. With the room pitch-dark, Barrett had no visible way of indicating to them his gut feeling without blowing their cover.

Outside that third cubicle, Barrett squatted what seemed an inch below the three-foot-high metal partition. If anyone was on the other side, he hoped they wouldn't see him. Barrett looked up. Along the cloudy glass partition, he saw what looked like an arm inches from his face. His face accidentally brushed against the glass. The arm quickly slid back down. Barrett drew his revolver and made his move.

"Hold it, come out!" he yelled, pointing his revolver at the assailant.[15]

Without a moment of hesitation, Leeper joined his partner, jumping on the desk of that third cubicle, pulling out his revolver, and pointing it at the ground.

Expecting one person's hands to be raised in the air, the officers received the shock of their lives.

Five sets of hands were raised high, covered in blue latex surgical gloves. The men they were attached to were dressed in sport coats and ties.

Concerned there might be more, perhaps behind him, Leeper, his gun in hand, scanned the vicinity. There was no one else.

Watergate's Forgotten Hero

"Are you the police?" one of the men asked a couple of times.[16] The officers responded in the affirmative. Not anticipating five burglars, they had only two pairs of handcuffs among the three of them. They'd have to wait for backup.

"Raise your arms and spread your feet," Leeper yelled at the suspects.[17]

Officer Barrett noticed one of the offenders was not raising his hands. He was clutching a black bag with a trench coat over his arm. Barrett demanded he drop the items and raise his hands. The man didn't move. Barrett "pointed his pistol directly at the man's chest."[18] Another suspect mumbled something possibly in Spanish, loud enough that the man put his hands up and the confrontation was averted.

Once the lights were turned on, it was apparent that the thieves had left the DNC office in shambles. In their possession, the well-dressed burglars were found with a walkie-talkie, two 35-millimeter cameras, forty rolls of unexposed film, lock picks, pen-size tear gas dispensers, and $2,293 in cash. The police determined that the cash had been intended, if necessary, to bribe a guard or two. Considering that amount was the equivalent of half Wills' annual salary, this was not an unreasonable assumption.

This was no ordinary robbery.

The culprits—James M. McCord, Bernard L. Barker, Virgilio R. Gonzalez, Eugenio R. Martinez, and Frank Sturgis—were brought downstairs and marched through the main lobby. Four of the five arrestees (Barker, Gonzalez, Martinez, and Sturgis) were Cubans and later determined that they had direct ties to the botched 1961 Bay of Pigs invasion. The fifth perpetrator (McCord) was an American. The tallest amongst them, McCord's "hard-edged features" suggested an occupation with the military or law enforcement.[19] Frank Wills watched them as they left the building. Within three hours of the arrests, Wills returned to his nightly routine—checking the door locks and securing each floor.

Chapter 7. Metro Police

A DC Metro officer at the crime scene contacted DNC Deputy Chairman Stanley L. Greigg. Greigg, awakened at his home, was in charge while O'Brien was in Miami finalizing details for the convention. Greigg was informed of the break-in and told to come to the Watergate. Under the misimpression that the culprits were run-of-the-mill hoodlums interested in stealing the staff's $150 typewriters, Greigg was taken aback when the officer explained, "these men we arrested were in business suits."[20] Within thirty minutes, Greigg arrived to find the office "littered with film and wires and electronic equipment."[21] Several police officers were scattered throughout the office, looking for clues and dusting for fingerprints.

Meanwhile, Sergeant Leeper was at the police station, completing the initial report. The five burglars he'd arrested were now in a holding cell. A fellow officer came by to chat.

"Do you know who that one guy is you've got locked up in there?" the officer asked.[22]

"Which one?" said Leeper.

The officer pointed. This was the man "of striking appearance" who'd asked Leeper if they were the police.[23]

"He said his name is Ed Carter."

"No," the officer shot back. "His name is James McCord. He's the director of security for the Committee to Re-elect the President of the United States."[24]

Paul Leeper, who'd voted for Nixon in 1968 because of the "President's professed belief in law and order," had not grasped fully that the arrests—which he deemed was "five of the easiest lock-ups"—would clearly be his most memorable and important.[25] As events unfolded, he and his partners would carry on their careers with the DC Metropolitan Police Department with a bit more recognition and perhaps a little extra swagger among their fellow officers.

Frank Wills' involvement in the apprehension of the burglars would not be neatly contained. The twenty-four-year-old high school dropout had not realized—nor had anyone else that morning at the crime scene—that his phone call to the DC police had triggered what would become the first chapter in the uncovering of the biggest political scandal in American history.

CHAPTER 8

The Caper

It was about 8:00 a.m., six hours following the arrests, when FBI Special Agent Angelo J. Lano received a call at his home. It was from FBI headquarters, ordering him to report to the Second District police station, where the evidence and suspects from the Watergate break-in were held.

Initially, Lano believed (for no apparent reason) that the criminals were professional jewel thieves. Upon arrival, he was handed a bag full of wires and other assorted electronic equipment. The DC police officers thought the equipment was bomb-making material. It wasn't, Lano immediately informed them. The electronics were designed for telephone bugging, tools FBI agents regularly used. At that moment, the burglary at the Watergate was no longer a jurisdictional matter for the Metropolitan Police Department. Because the scene of the crime was the headquarters of a national political party, the Feds got involved.

When intern Bruce Givner returned to the DNC offices later that afternoon, he encountered several "clean-cut men in gray suits with bulges" milling about the office.[1] At first, he didn't think there was anything unusual going on; after all, this was the office of a presidential campaign and "occasionally there were important people passing through."[2] But when he checked further, he was shocked to learn that there had been a break-in. When he confided to his supervisor that he had been the last to leave the office the day before, he was directed to speak with the authorities.

In just a few hours, the entire nation would learn what had happened at the Watergate earlier that morning.

Watergate's Forgotten Hero

"Five men wearing white gloves and carrying cameras were caught early today in the headquarters of the Democratic National Committee in Washington," *NBC News*' weekend anchor Garrick Utley reported. "They were caught by a night watchman and they did not resist arrest when the police came. They apparently were unarmed and nobody knows yet why they were there.... But I don't think that's the last we're going to hear of this story."[3]

It was the morning newspapers that would actually identify the Watergate security guard. On June 18, in the *Washington Post*'s front-page article "5 Held in Plot to Bug Democrats' Office Here," written by senior police reporter Alfred Lewis, Wills' name first appeared, about halfway through the article.

> The early morning arrests occurred about 40 minutes after a security guard at the Watergate noticed that a door connecting a stairwell with the hotel's basement garage had been taped so it would not lock. The guard, 24-year-old Frank Wills, removed the tape, but when he passed by about 10 minutes later a new piece had been put on. Wills then called police.[4]

Lewis' lengthy piece (which had multiple contributors, including metro beat reporters Bob Woodward and Carl Bernstein) mentioned "clandestine" operations, Fidel Castro, and CIA connections, suggesting the break-in may have had bigger implications.[5]

For reporter Simeon Booker and photographer Maurice Sorrell of *JET*, a nationally distributed weekly African American magazine, the story was too big to pass up. But what was the "Black angle"?[6]

JET magazine reporter Simeon Booker (courtesy Carol McCabe Booker).

Chapter 8. The Caper

With their DC Bureau office located on Pennsylvania Avenue a block west of the White House and a few more blocks east of the Watergate, the two men scanned reports about the burglary breaking over TV, radio, and the office's clicking UPI teletype. As soon as it became apparent that a key figure in the story was a young African American, Booker and Sorrell contacted Frank Wills and arranged to meet him there when his shift ended the following morning.

Born in Baltimore in 1918 but raised in Youngstown, Ohio, Simeon Saunders Booker, Jr., had always dreamed of becoming a professional writer. In 1942, after graduating from Virginia Union University (in Richmond), Booker followed through with his childhood aspiration when he went to work for the *Baltimore Afro-American.* Entering the profession on the cusp of the Civil Rights Movement in 1951 following a journalism fellowship at Harvard University, the up-and-coming Black reporter sought employment at a major newspaper. He sent out dozens of resumes to the leading papers of the day. Only one responded: the *Washington Post.* While he was honored to be working in the nation's capital as the first full-time African American journalist for a national news organization, Booker's tenure, to his disappointment, was brief.

When he introduced himself as a reporter for the *Post,* people were dubious. A Black reporter employed by a white-owned newspaper was unheard of. Nor had he escaped the blatant discrimination of DC, which seeped into the *Post* offices. "It was recommended to me that I use only the bathroom on the fourth floor."[7] Although he wasn't barred from using the company's cafeteria, he always ate alone. Hoping to better utilize his talents and serve his ambitions to reach a wider audience, Booker left the *Post* and accepted a job with *JET,* where he covered the Civil Rights movement from the front lines. His partner, Maurice Sorrell, also a trailblazer, was the first African American to become a member of the White House Photographers Association.

First thing in the morning on June 18, the two men from *JET* walked over to the Watergate Office Building, as Wills was about to

Watergate's Forgotten Hero

go off duty. After running through the events of the previous day, Wills took them to the sixth-floor stairwell and showed them the entryway where the tape had been applied. The door had already been removed, "seized as evidence."[8] Sorrell took photos while Booker asked Wills questions.

Noticing the door hinges on the floor, Wills picked them up.

"You might as well take these," he said to Booker, handing them to him. "They're just going to get thrown away."[9]

Still under the impression that it had been office equipment the burglars were after, Wills had no clue about the significance of the robbery

At around 8:00 a.m., after the interview and his shift was over, Wills jogged to his apartment, hoping the exercise would calm his nerves. When he arrived home, he was still jittery. He put drops in his eyes to alleviate the redness from his lack of sleep. The back-to-back graveyard shifts took their toll, and the drama of the burglary had drained him physically and emotionally.

Once settled, to his chagrin, there was a knock on the door. Because he was relatively new to the area and kept to himself, Wills had no idea who it could be. Holding his cat, he opened the door to find a petite white woman standing there. It was *Washington Post* reporter Karlyn Barker.

First *JET*, now the *Post*.

In only her second year on the job (coincidentally, she had been hired on the same day as fellow reporter Bob Woodward), Barker was dispatched by senior reporter Alfred Lewis to gather more information about the incident at the Watergate.

"Are you Frank Wills?"[10] Barker asked.

"Yes, I am."

"Mr. Wills, have you seen an article in the newspaper?"

Wills hadn't seen it.

"Did you know that the people that were arrested last night were carrying around items connected to Nixon's reelection campaign?"

Chapter 8. The Caper

"What?"[11] Wills wasn't aware. Curious about what she had to say, he let her in.

The journalist wanted to know everything about the night watchman and his role in the break-in: Who apprehended the burglars? How much did he make? Who did he work for? And what was his role in the arrest?

Taken aback by the questions, Wills (perhaps he enjoyed the sudden attention) warmed up to Barker, who found him "very nice" to talk to, even if he hadn't yet realized the magnitude of the situation.[12] It was obvious to any outsider this was "not the apartment of a hero."[13] The carpet was threadbare, and the only bright colors were those hideous plastic daisies on a table near the window. But Barker wasn't there to be impressed. She was there to write a story.

Intentionally misinforming her, Wills included himself in the apprehension of the burglars. "When we went inside," he told Barker, "all the office lights were on and we saw five men with foreign accents moving around and crawling on the floor. I think they were getting ready to leave because they had gathered up a lot of papers in three boxes."[14]

"One part of the office was really messed up. File drawers had been pulled out and paper was all over the floor.... [We] looked through the material the men were getting ready to carry out. One was something about national defense, and another was on a business firm."[15]

After the interview, Barker checked her notes with Lewis, the senior crime reporter, and she noticed that Wills' story "was somewhat different from official police reports of the first encounter with the intruders."[16] Over the years, there would be several discrepancies in Wills' account of what happened in the early morning of June 17, partly to protect himself from discipline by his employer for leaving his post while on duty and partly out of a desire to enhance his role in the capture of the burglars. Wills would later claim that he "assisted the police in collecting the various gear, equipment and disguises" from the scene of the crime and brought them down to the main lobby, where they would be taken in as evidence.[17] This scenario he described is highly unlikely to have occurred since there were several police officers on the scene within minutes of the apprehension and they, not Wills, undoubtedly would have been the ones to handle the evidence.

Barker's article, "Intruders Foiled by Security Guard," was published the day after Lewis' article and featured a biographical profile and photograph of Wills.

***

Inside the Beltway, politicos were "abuzz with rumors."[18] But outside DC, the news hardly made a blip. Aside from the *Post* articles and the ten seconds that had aired on NBC the night before, the break-in received surprisingly scant media coverage. The *New York Times* buried its article, "5 Charged with Burglary at Democratic Quarters," on page 30.[19] So did the *Boston Globe* (page 50). It failed to make the front page of the *Chicago Tribune* as well. In the *Dallas Morning News*, the two-paragraph, front-page article was so brief that any reader easily could have missed it. Only the *Los Angeles Times* and the *Miami Herald* had extensive front-page coverage the following morning.

While on a weekend vacation at his residence in Key Biscayne, Florida, Nixon did not release a comment. However, Press Secretary Ron Ziegler, who joined the president in Florida, briefly addressed the incident, dismissing it as "a third-rate burglary and nothing the President would be concerned with."[20] Other members of the administration expressed similar views. Attorney General John N. Mitchell, who was in Beverly Hills raising money for Nixon's reelection campaign, released a statement that the culprits "were not operating either on our behalf or with our consent.... There is no place in our campaign or in the electoral process for this type of activity, and we will not permit or condone it."[21] A Nixon advisor told the Republican National Committee chairman, Bob Dole: "It's got no legs. It'll

Chapter 8. The Caper

blow over.... It'll fade in two or three days."[22] The conventional wisdom among insiders was that the break-in was a "bizarre but isolated political prank of insignificant consequence."[23] But not everyone in DC was convinced.

DNC Chairman Larry O'Brien, in Miami and unaware of the break-in until six hours after the burglars were apprehended, demanded a thorough inquiry, hinting at the involvement of CREEP. As he put it: "Only the most searching professional investigation can determine to what extent, if any, the Committee for the Re-election of the President is involved in this attempt to spy on the Democratic headquarters."[24]

Once the public learned of burglar James McCord and his affiliation with Nixon, "rumors and speculation [circulated] that the Nixon administration, and possibly even the President, had had something to do with it."[25]

***

Frank Wills' friends and family had not even known he had moved to the nation's capital, let alone worked as a security guard, when they learned of his role in what the media called the Watergate Caper.

"What? Frank? They must be kidding," Martez Mims, Wills' second cousin, thought. "I didn't even know where he was. Didn't even know he was in DC."[26]

Pamela Oliver, Mims' sister, was living in New York when she first heard about it. "Oh my god, that's Frank. He was on TV. That was him."[27]

Nat Irvin, Jr., who was attending the University of South Carolina when he heard the news about his father's former student, was in disbelief: "Is that Frank Wills from North Augusta? I know him. He went to school with me."[28] Nat's father, the Reverend Irvin, had tried to reach out to Wills, knowing that this was a lot to handle for the young man he had once mentored. Whether or not he made contact is unknown.

Watergate's Forgotten Hero

Wills' current girlfriend, Marilyn Brown, whom he had met at the Watergate where she worked as a maid, was in shock. "I can't believe it. I can't believe it,"[29] unable to fathom how her quiet, unassuming boyfriend was in the national spotlight.

Like everyone else, Wills' first cousin Eddie Wills heard about it through the news. Of all the possible people involved, Eddie felt it was the most "random"[30] of circumstances for his diffident cousin to play an integral role in such an incident.

For Wills, it may have been random, but he was being hailed a hero.

"[I've] gotten all these letters from people I've never met," Wills said in an interview with reporters from the *Washington Post.* "They really said some nice things about me."[31]

General Security Services, Wills' employer, immediately grasped the importance of what had taken place. Additional publicity could mean more business. Wills was promoted from corporal to sergeant and received a twenty-cent hourly raise, about a 10 percent increase.

Four days after the break-in, America's newest hero received a visit from the FBI.

For the moment, no one (including the White House) knew that Special Agent Angelo J. Lano and his colleagues were combing through the evidence from the scene, trying to piece together the motivation for the robbery attempt. What had initially been deemed a third-rate burglary was turning into a "first-rate mystery."[32] From the desk attendant at the Howard Johnson's across the street to the arresting police officers, the FBI was interviewing anyone linked with the evening's episode. On June 21, Frank Wills joined their growing list.

Wills' story continued to change each time he shared it. He informed agents at this interview, the time between his detection of the tape covering the latch and when he noticed it had been retaped was "approximately ten minutes."[33] Actually, he had first discovered the tape covering the latch at 12:20 a.m., and more than an hour later, detected it had been retaped, and, according to the security

Chapter 8. The Caper

log, called the police at 1:47 a.m. Wills conveniently failed to mention picking up dinner with DNC intern Bruce Givner at the Howard Johnson's restaurant.

In another interview, Wills stated that he contacted the police "between 2:15 a.m. and 2:30 a.m."[34] In the official version of events, the criminals had already been apprehended by 2:20 a.m.

Three days later, when the same agents spoke to Wills, he was "unable to identify photographs of subjects and suspects," whom, in his defense, he had seen for only a few seconds when they were taken through the main lobby in handcuffs.[35]

The FBI agents were not the only ones who caught Wills' inconsistencies. When the police report was taken, Officer Carl Shoffler admitted he had "changed Wills' statement to conform" with the official version of the incident. Shoffler said he did this "because Wills' account of the timing of events just didn't make sense."[36]

While the investigation was under way, the Democrats were determined to exploit the burglary. Larry O'Brien filed a million-dollar lawsuit against the reelection campaign, hoping to keep the break-in as front-page news. But excitement over the incident began to wane. Even presidential candidate Senator George McGovern was reluctant "to make a major issue" of it, instead focusing his attention on Vietnam and brandishing his anti-war credentials.[37] Nor could he be persuaded by the growing suspicions that Nixon and his team "[were] more involved than [they were] admitting." The Democratic candidate stood firm, refusing to capitalize on the break-in, thereby committing a massive political blunder.[38]

Whether or not the attention was shifting elsewhere, the burglars and their accomplices were still facing the possibility of prison. In September 1972, a grand jury indicted all five Watergate burglars and two accomplices (ex–FBI agent G. Gordon Liddy and ex–CIA agent E. Howard Hunt, both affiliated with CREEP) for "conspiracy, burglary, and violation of federal wiretapping laws."[39] Five of the seven indicted men pleaded guilty. Two did not (McCord and Liddy). Their cases would go to trial.

Watergate's Forgotten Hero

Then the caper got more interesting.

On September 29, [Washington, D.C.] *Star-News* reporters Jeremiah O'Leary and Patrick Collins contacted the vice president of General Security Services, F. Kelly Chamberlain, about the possibility that GSS guards colluded with the burglars. Unsure if there was any truth to the accusation, Chamberlain told the *Star-News* reporters he would look into the matter. He immediately informed the FBI of the media inquiry. When agents pressed Chamberlain about it, he maintained he had "no knowledge" that his guards had been bribed to look the other way.[40]

O'Leary and Collins proceeded with their story, "Were Guards Bribed?" which was published on the front page of the October 1, 1972, *Sunday Star* edition.

The journalists revealed that the FBI and GSS were looking into whether any of the "uniformed guards at the Watergate were 'paid off' to permit many nighttime entries of Democratic headquarters."[41] Of the five men arrested at the scene, one had "boasted" to the *Star-News*' reporters of bribing GSS guards so he could gain access to the DNC office.[42] Bearing in mind that the five robbers had over $2,000 in their possession at the time of the arrest, it raised the likelihood that the cash was for bribery purposes. On the night of the break-in, why did a guard leave earlier before his shift and then lie about it on his timecard? Was he cheating his employer? Or was it for other reasons? All eyes were on that GSS guard: Leroy C. Brown.

On the night of June 16, Brown had been scheduled to work from 6:30 p.m. to 1:30 a.m. However, he'd left his post before Wills arrived at midnight. If Brown was somehow linked to the break-in, why did he leave early? It was Brown's presence more than anything else that was needed by the five burglars. After all, his role would be to turn a blind eye once they entered the building.

When the *Star-News* published its story, the FBI identified a glaring mistake. The reporters had misidentified the suspect who had boasted about paying off the guards. They had identified him as Virgilio Gonzalez when it was actually fellow burglar Eugenio Martínez,

Chapter 8. The Caper

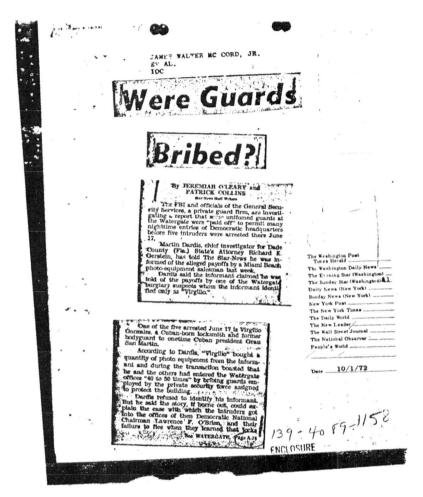

The *Sunday Star*'s October 1, 1972, controversial article, included in the Watergate file of the FBI's investigation (courtesy FBI The Vault).

who recanted his remarks and then denied speaking with reporters. The agents had already interviewed all the Watergate guards (including Brown) and found that none of them were linked to any of the five men arrested.

When television newsman Tom Brokaw asked Wills about the

conspiracy theory, he denied he knew of any corruption. "I don't know anything about that. Nobody paid me or anything like that. I was just a security guard that night."[43]

Regardless, the story was in the public view. Concerned that the allegations could negatively affect General Security Services' reputation and make the firm vulnerable to a lawsuit, Chamberlain ordered the guards present that evening to undergo a polygraph test to see if they were culpable in the alleged bribery scandal.

On October 12, nearly two weeks after the *Star-News* article was published, Frank Wills, Fletcher Pittman (the guard Wills relieved), and three other guards took a polygraph test. The results from the test, which Chamberlain shared with the FBI, proved that these men never had contact with the burglars. Leroy Brown, however, was not listed as one of the guards tested.

Because Brown had reported a previous discovery of a tampered lock at the DNC office to DC police on May 29 and had already been vetted by agents, authorities felt he had no involvement in the caper; in the end, he was disciplined by GSS for leaving his post prematurely. The FBI confirmed Chamberlain's polygraph results, concluding that there was no substance to the article published by O'Leary and Collins. Actually, the *Star-News* reporters always believed that Frank Wills was "not part of the alleged payoff."[44] Yet, in the years to come, this story would be one of many conspiracy theories about Watergate.

***

Less than a month before the presidential election, *Washington Post* reporters Bob Woodward and Carl Bernstein, who had split from their reporting team, were following up on their own leads, determined to solve the mystery behind the break-in. On October 10, they penned an explosive article, "FBI Finds Nixon Aides Sabotaged Democrats." Clearly a preview of what these aggressive investigative journalists would uncover, Woodward and Bernstein—known to colleagues as "WoodStein"[45] because of how much time they were

Chapter 8. The Caper

spending together—argued that the caper was no third-rate burglary. On the *Post*'s front page, they insisted that the break-in had "stemmed from a massive campaign of political spying and sabotage conducted on behalf of President Nixon's re-election and directed by officials of the White House and the Committee for the Re-election of the President."[46]

Because the election was only weeks away and most voters had already made up their minds, the exposé provided minimal help to Senator McGovern's doomed candidacy. Reporters from *Time* magazine stated Nixon's lead was so vast that it wasn't whether he'd win, but by how much. They were right. Nixon trounced McGovern in what was at the time the most lopsided victory in presidential history. With Nixon easily reelected, it appeared the American public wanted to move on from Watergate.

CHAPTER 9

Opportunity Knocks

In 1972, it seemed inconceivable to most Americans that a president could be involved in a criminal investigation. Six months after news reports linked the break-in to the Nixon Administration, nearly half the country refused to recognize the severity of the scandal. "Conventional wisdom," according to *Post* reporter Bob Woodward, "was that Nixon was too smart to be involved."[1] Republican Party insiders either had no idea or refused to believe that Nixon and members of his administration were complicit. Republican National Committee Chairman George H.W. Bush declared: "Watergate was the product of the actions of a few misguided, very irresponsible individuals who violated a high trust and who served neither the President nor the country well."[2]

Nixon had been reelected overwhelmingly, but he had suffered a pivotal defeat—Democrats retained control of both houses of Congress. Privately, many Republicans blamed Nixon for their failure to regain legislative supremacy. Nixon, they argued, with his comfortable lead up to the election, had squandered ample opportunity to offer support to his fellow party candidates, likely costing the GOP a number of races.

Following the election, the Democrats moved their DNC office to the Air Line Pilots Association Building, a more secure location a mile away from the Watergate. Capitalizing on their control of Congress, they wasted no time establishing the Select Committee on Presidential Campaign Activities, commonly known as the Senate Watergate Committee. The Watergate break-in was back on the public's radar. And so was Frank Wills.

Chapter 9. Opportunity Knocks

The Watergate hero was restless. Among his fellow workers, he was teased about the publicity he received, likely out of envy rather than malice. But for Wills, it "got to the point where the joke was too damn much. I was tired of being asked so many questions, of being in the public eye."[3]

In addition to being recognized wherever he went, Wills was "besieged by reporters," who called him around the clock, preventing him from getting a decent sleep.[4] He was the target of gawkers, who came by during his shift, making it difficult to perform his job. "He couldn't take the publicity," his supervisor observed. "Some people can take it in stride. But for him, the people sitting at his door, the telephone ringing, it was all just a little too much."[5]

In December 1972, Wills quit General Security Services, and within a month found a job with Chatham Realty Company, which offered better pay and more accommodating hours. Wills no longer worked the graveyard shift; his schedule was 4:00 p.m. to midnight. When asked why he had left his former employer, he provided differing accounts. He accused General Security Services of passing him over because of his race. When a "white fellow came in after I did," he contended, "they made him a lieutenant. I was a corporal making just $80 a week."[6] In another account, Wills said he left over unfair labor negotiations. When he had been chosen the de facto bargaining representative of the guards, Wills claimed GSS had not met their demands but had offered him "a promotion and a pretty hefty salary package [and] nothing for the others."[7] In response, Wills said, he'd filed a complaint with the National Labor Relations Board. Outraged by the complaint, GSS, which had previously hailed Wills as a hero, now considered him a "union radical" and wanted him out.[8] Wills also maintained that the Watergate management demanded the security agency fire him as a result of "pressure from Washington powers."[9] Whatever the motivation behind Wills' departure, he was well thought of by his superiors. When they were interviewed about the break-in, they mentioned that only the type of guard who was "very observant" and alert would have recognized the reapplied

Watergate's Forgotten Hero

tape.[10] Most of the time, security personnel in Wills' situation would have "let it go by" and not acted on it.[11]

***

On January 16, Frank Wills was scheduled to testify at the Watergate trial of two of the seven men involved. Waiting to be called, Wills was "showing up every day in Judge John Sirica's courtroom," uneasy with so many people looking at him.[12] As it turned out, it was worth the discomfort. When Wills' name was called, the courtroom gave him "a standing ovation."[13]

James McCord and G. Gordon Liddy were found guilty for their roles in the botched break-in. During the sentencing portion of his trial, McCord delivered a letter to Judge Sirica about the "political pressure" from the White House to remain silent.[14] He mentioned that former Attorney General John Mitchell and White House General Counsel John Dean knew in advance about the break-in and were involved in the cover-up. The public and media were aghast. McCord's revelation opened the floodgates and turned the Watergate caper into a full-fledged scandal, giving further justification for lawmakers to proceed with their investigation.

On April 30, 1973, President Nixon delivered a televised address, maintaining his administration's innocence along with his own. The following day, three members of his administration, advisors H.R. Haldeman and John Ehrlichman and Attorney General Richard Kleindienst, resigned. Having refused to step down, White House Counsel John Dean was fired. Hoping his actions had stifled criticism, the President received assurance from House Minority Leader Gerald Ford, who was convinced that Nixon "had nothing to do with this mess." Yet, as *Washington Post* reporters Laurence Stern and Haynes Johnson pointed out, the "ever haunting question of presidential involvement" lingered in the minds of many Americans.[15] Public opinion polls showed that the president's approval ratings were falling, fast.

By the middle of May, media coverage had intensified as seven-

Chapter 9. Opportunity Knocks

teen of Nixon's associates and staff members were under investigation by the Justice Department, the FBI, a federal grand jury, or the U.S. Senate. The Senate hearings had not begun, yet the affair seemed like it was spinning out of the president's control.

As the one-year anniversary of the break-in neared, there was renewed interest in the night watchman. Predictably, Wills' reaction was humble and straightforward. "It was just part of my job," he said. Yet the media, and by extension the public, viewed his actions in more grandiose terms.[16]

Hailed as a "crackerjack detective," as the guard responsible for having "saved his nation," Wills was seen as the tipping point.[17] Without his keen observational skills, wrote the *Washington Post*'s Kenneth Turan, "there would have been no arrests, no prison terms, no resignations, no Senate hearings, no lawsuits and countersuits, [and] no endless newspaper tales."[18] John M. Crewdson in the *New York Times* echoed a similar sentiment. If it weren't "for Mr. Wills' chance encounter with that piece of tape, the world might never have known of the drama—call it that 'Watergate Affair.'"[19]

At the scene of the crime (1973). Photograph by Maurice Sorrell (courtesy Carol McCabe Booker).

On a more personal level, Wills was hearing the same refrain. "My friends think I'm a great celebrity, a great detective," he told a reporter at the *New York Times*. "Down home, I'm big stuff. People I know call me up and say 'How's the hero?'"[20]

As the praise, public and private, continued to pour in, Wills began to wonder why he hadn't been offered more than words. On May 12, according to the *Baltimore Afro-American*, Wills was disenchanted that he had not been offered a job with the FBI or the Secret Service. Wills expressed a similar sentiment to the *Washington Post*, again revealing his abysmal lack of knowledge about securing a position at the Departments of Justice and the Treasury. "People say I really didn't get the benefits I should have," he went on. "Some McGovern aide told me if McGovern got in he'd let me select whatever office I wanted. I told him I wanted to be a Treasury assistant. I like to count money."[21]

Frank Wills appeared on his first and only magazine cover of the May 17, 1973, issue of *JET*. Posing in front of the scene of the crime in his navy-blue guard uniform, he glared at the camera. Simeon Booker, the journalist who had spoken to Wills on the morning of the break-in, penned the featured article, "Untold Story of Black Hero of Watergate."

In the interview for the piece, Wills did not hide his bitterness toward his ex-employer, pointing out that his new job came with a pay increase—and conveniently forgetting that General Security Services had also given him a raise. On the other hand, Wills still seemed ambivalent about his sudden rise to fame. "I want to forget. I hate crowds. I want to be alone. I just like my privacy." When Booker "credited [him] with touching off the century's biggest political scandal," Wills continued to minimize his role, insisting that he did not deserve all the publicity. "Everybody tells me I'm some kind of hero, but.... I did what I was hired to do."[22]

Modest or not, Wills decided it was time to monetize his fame before the saga ran its course. He did what any overnight American folk hero would do in his situation—he hired an agent.

Chapter 9. Opportunity Knocks

In front of the Watergate Complex for a *JET* magazine cover article to commemorate the one year anniversary of the break-in. Photograph by Maurice Sorrell (courtesy Carol McCabe Booker).

***

Born and raised in Kansas City, Kansas, Dorsey Evans, Jr., made his way to the nation's capital after receiving his degree in music (he played the trumpet) from the University of Kansas in 1952 and graduating from Howard University School of Law in 1958. At the time, Howard was one of the few prestigious law schools accessible to African Americans. Settling in DC, Evans practiced law and dabbled in local politics, serving as the region's first Black president of the Young Democrats Club.

Convinced more than ever that everyone was making money off Watergate except him, Wills, through a friend, contacted Evans. After the meeting, Wills hired the forty-three-year-old attorney to handle his business affairs and public appearances.

Watergate's Forgotten Hero

While it took Wills a week to earn $85, Evans promised to secure him events that would net him as much as $300 for a single appearance. Wills agreed to pay Evans 25 percent of his take, regardless of whether the agent was responsible for securing the gig. Evans was also confident that he could line up a book deal and a movie, as well as numerous endorsements similar to those received by Olympic gold medalists.

"Our basic plan at this time," Evans told *JET* in the summer of 1973, "is to take advantage of the kind of attention the public is beginning to focus on Frank to try to turn it into a useful benefit in developing the type of future Frank is interested in."[23] Evans, who had an "unfavorable" reputation for questionable legal ethics in and around Washington, was determined to turn the famous night watchman into a profitable enterprise.[24] Whether it was an interview with a media outlet, a speaking engagement at a Black church, or just having his photograph taken (for a dollar or two) with a random person on the street, anyone who wanted a piece of Frank Wills was now going to pay for it.

As a case in point, when the [Baltimore] *Afro-American News* sought a follow-up interview, the paper's reporter had difficulty reaching Wills. The reporter tracked down Wills' mother, Marjorie, who was in North Augusta. Having received her number from another maid who worked with her, the journalist thought she would connect him to her son. He was surprised by her response, noting:

> The mother apparently had got the word. Her son only wanted to be contacted by certain people and after a few minutes sparring during which she never agreed to know a Frank Wills, Mrs. Wills agreed that she'd take the AFRO telephone number and if she did have a relative by that name, maybe he'd hear from her and call.[25]

Two days later, Wills called back. He spoke to the reporter briefly before scheduling an interview on a later date. When Wills learned the reporter wouldn't pay for the interview, he canceled.

As Americans continued to glue themselves to the televised Watergate hearings, Evans seized the moment in various ways. He

Chapter 9. Opportunity Knocks

booked his client for an appearance on *The Mike Douglas Show* and on the game show *To Tell the Truth*. Wills was also depicted in a comedy sketch on the popular Black humorist Timmie Rogers' 1973 comedy album, *Timmie Rogers as Super Soul Brother Alias "Clark Dark."*

With or without Evans' help, Wills' popularity proved infectious. Country singer and songwriter Ron Turner titled one of his songs "The Ballad of Frank Wills." Popular folk singer and songwriter Harry Nilsson, best known for the 1969 hit song "Everybody's Talkin'," included Wills' photograph on a lapel button attached to his coat for the album cover of *A Little Touch of Schmilsson in the Night*. The authors of *The Watergate File: A Concise, Illustrated Guide to the People and Events*, a team of international journalists, dedicated their book to Frank Wills, whom they described as an "ordinary citizen of the United States, possessing neither high office nor great wealth, [who] made a single call that will echo through the republic as long as it stands."[26] In another book about the affair, the *Washington Post* Managing Editor Ben Bradlee wrote that it was the "the vigilance of an $85-a-week night watchman" that took a presidential administration to task.[27] Frank Wills had gone from American hero to cultural icon.

When he wasn't the subject of a song or comedy skit or book dedication, Wills was the recipient of prestigious honors. Both the NAACP and the National Urban League, the two most prominent African American civic organizations in the country, saluted him at their annual conferences. At the League's reception, following his introduction, there was a "five-minute standing ovation" for the Watergate hero.[28]

As Wills was soaking in the laudatory comments and ovations, however, all was not going well on the job front. Word got out that he had been fired from his security position and was collecting government benefits to offset his loss of pay (apparently, the money his agent had promised was not yet flowing in). Wills' employer had been unwilling to allow the guard time off to further his celebrity status. When Evans set up a meeting with a representative of a "major publishing firm" and ghostwriter to pen *The Frank Wills Story*, Wills took two days off from his job to speak with them in North Augusta.[29] When he returned, he was fired.

Wills' hometown newspaper, the *Augusta Chronicle*, was quick to publish a story focusing on the night watchman's inability either to hold down a job or find a new one. Other newspapers printed similar accounts—"Watergate Hero is Broke and Jobless," "Guard at the Watergate Says He Can't Get a Job." Not for lack of trying, Wills insisted.

"I've looked all over but employers seem afraid to hire me," he complained to a *New York Times* reporter. "Lots of people tell me I should have kept my mouth shut [and not have reported the taped latch]. I'm beginning to think they were right, even though I know I would do the same thing today."[30]

Dorsey Evans believed Wills' hard times weren't about politics; they had to do with race. "If he was white, he'd be a hero and be at the top of his profession."[31]

Evans had a point, at least in terms of endorsements.

Historically, famous whites have always been offered more endorsement opportunities than African Americans. Nowhere is it starker than in professional sports.

Take, for example, the New York Yankees' Mickey Mantle. At the peak of his career, the white slugger was courted by corporations to endorse their products while his Black counterpart, the New York Giants' Willie Mays, attracted far less offers. "[It] threw into sharp relief the different commercial opportunities for white and black athletes," Mays' biographer James S. Hirsch maintains.[32] Throughout most of the twentieth century, it didn't matter whether it was track and field legend Jesse Owens (1930s), boxing great Joe Louis (1930s and '40s), or football icon Jim Brown (1950s and '60s)—Black athletes were not able to monetize their fame the way whites could. And it wasn't just limited to sports. It happened in film, music, literature, and every other industry that allowed for commercial endorsements.

Frank Wills was no exception.

Chapter 9. Opportunity Knocks

Whether it was politics, race, or perhaps Wills' lack of panache, the deal to publish the night watchman's memoir fell through. Undeterred, Evans launched a major campaign.

He booked Wills for a television interview in Boston, a speaking engagement in Milwaukee, and other public appearances throughout the country. Supporters were invited to join the Frank Wills Fan Club, purchase buttons and sweatshirts with a photograph of Frank's face and the words "Watergate Hero" splashed under it, or for two dollars buy a twelve-page color brochure, "The Watergate Hero: An Eyewitness Report by Frank Wills" (fans could send their orders to Evans' law office, where they would be processed).[33]

The agent's best efforts to merchandise his client fell short. Race may have played a minor role, but in truth Wills simply didn't have the wit, intellectual depth, or inviting personality to maintain the public's interest.

On the other hand, Watergate was at the center of the nation's attention, becoming a larger scandal by the day. In July 1973, during the course of congressional testimony, Nixon aide Alexander Butterfield revealed to the American public an Oval Office taping system that would prove critical to the investigation. Adding to the drama, in October, Vice President Spiro Agnew resigned for tax evasion and political corruption. House minority leader and Republican stalwart Gerald Ford was named to replace him. With Agnew gone and a moderate as vice president, lawmakers' thoughts of impeaching Nixon became more palatable.

While the continuing investigation of the break-in and cover-up gained momentum, it did little to enhance Wills' popularity. Whether he or his agent was willing to acknowledge it, their odds of cashing in on the scandal were highly unlikely and slim at best.

CHAPTER 10

Delusions of Grandeur

The trendy bumper sticker on American roadways, "Honk if you think he's guilty," summed up how the majority of Americans felt at the beginning of 1974.[1]

As a result of the televised Senate hearings (the first day drawing one of the "largest audiences in television history"), new admissions of complicity by members of the Nixon Administration, and released excerpts of the soon-to-be-published *All the President's Men* by Bob Woodward and Carl Bernstein (a scathing account of the president's attempted cover-up), Nixon's public trust and support were declining daily.[2]

By late spring, more than two-thirds of Americans believed that the president was involved in or, at the very least, knowledgeable about the break-in. Nixon's antagonists called the approaching season "impeachment summer."[3]

Whether Wills was fully aware of the drama in Washington is unknown, but probably unlikely in view of his own struggles. Now getting by on $65-a-week unemployment benefits, his life was unraveling. Showered with plaques for his role in the affair, enough to leave him "scant wall space" in his one-room apartment, Wills didn't need another award; he needed a job.[4]

After being fired from Chatham Realty, he found another security position that paid more. Concerned that celebrity seekers would find him, he was reluctant to reveal to the media where he was working, except that it was an office building in Virginia. His desire for anonymity was unnecessary; he wasn't on the job long. Wills believed that he was fired because his employer was feared of "get[ting] in

Chapter 10. Delusions of Grandeur

In the months leading up to Nixon's resignation, protests were a regular occurrence in the nation's capital (Mccool/Alamy Stock Photo).

trouble with President Nixon."[5] Dorsey Evans backed him up. He described the situation as the "hot potato" effect. "Firms refused to hire him because they were afraid of government repercussions and the IRS."[6]

Even Howard University was reluctant to offer him a job. Interviewed by television journalist Barbara Walters, Wills claimed: "I was too hot to handle and if the administration had found out [Howard University] had hired me," the college would have lost its federal funding.[7] When the university's chief security officer, Lloyd Lacy, was asked about the reason he did not hire Wills, Lacy said it had nothing to do with Nixon, but with the applicant's lack of qualifications (i.e., no high school diploma).

Ever the publicist, Evans took Wills' assertion further. As he put it: "To hire Frank Wills, is to say, 'Nixon, you're a dirty dog.'"[8]

Race also played a role, an argument previously advanced, but both men raised it anew. "If he was not black, Frank Wills would be

91

a national hero," Evans declared.[9] Comparing Wills to Olympic gold medal swimmer Mark Spitz, Wills' agent couldn't understand why the athlete was treated like a hero—"He gets on television, does commercials, and everyone makes a big deal over him"—while his client, who was involved in the takedown of a corrupt president and his crooked administration, was left with a bunch of plaques to put on his wall and nothing else.[10]

Wills chimed in: "When you're black and do something wrong, everybody's always criticizing loud, but when you're black and you do something good, nobody pays any attention."[11]

While Wills failed to secure steady work, Evans arranged a series of appearances. By delivering a talk at an African American church in DC, for instance, Wills earned $800 (equivalent to about $4,500 today), with a portion of it going to Evans. At other engagements, Wills was usually paid about half that amount, with Evans taking his cut and sometimes more to cover his administrative expenses (the printing of pamphlets and flyers and compensation for his staff, who organized Wills' fan mail).

JET magazine's Simeon Booker continued to write about Wills, keeping him in the public eye. In his columns, Booker chastised organizations like the Congressional Black Caucus and the DNC for failing to find a job for the Watergate hero. Booker's views touched a sympathetic chord with *JET*'s readers, one of whom wrote: "Now that Agnew has resigned from his job as vice president, let's watch to see how long he will be unemployed."[12] (He was right. Agnew never served a day in jail and went on to become a successful businessman in Southern California). Another reader provided food for thought: "[A] few years from now no one will know who Frank Wills was and how he literally changed the whole course of recent American history."[13]

Booker's columns generated an unexpected surprise. After reading about Wills' plight, a white, Milwaukee-based businessman set up a trust fund for the unemployed hero. Donating $500, he asked his fellow citizens to contribute as an expression of gratitude to the

Chapter 10. Delusions of Grandeur

night watchman who saved the United States from "political perversion and corruption [that] could have engulfed us.... Wills was there when we needed him, just as much as Paul Revere was."[14] A retiree from Seattle donated money to the "Frank Wills Fund."[15] A woman from Clayton, Georgia, sent twenty dollars; she would have given more if she could have. In Hemet, California, the Democratic Club took up a collection of twenty-one dollars. Altogether, there were more than 150 contributions totaling $2,000.

Once the United States Supreme Court compelled the President to release recordings in the Oval Office following the break-in, Nixon's days in the White House were numbered. "No one knew when the climax would come," in the words of Secretary of State Henry Kissinger, "but there was no longer any doubt of its imminence or inevitability."[16]

Frank Wills weighed in on the matter:

> I want to see him out, period. He should resign or be impeached.... I pay taxes like anyone else. My taxes pay his salary. And what do we get? Law and order that goes against the little man but means nothing to high government officials.[17]

On July 27, 1974, the House Judiciary Committee voted 27 to 11 in favor of recommending impeachment, passing the first of three articles of impeachment, charging obstruction of justice. Over the next four days, each of the 38 members voiced their opinions about the scandal, how it had reached the highest pinnacles of power, and its impact on the nation.

During the proceedings, two committee members zeroed in on the break-in and reminded their colleagues who was responsible for its detection in the first place. Both members were Democrats. One was an African American from New York City representing Harlem; the other was white, from Greenville, South Carolina.

Harlem's forty-four-year-old Charles Rangel, the first-term, outspoken congressman, made sure that the lone Black figure in this affair was given proper recognition. Mincing few words, Rangel came right to the point. President Nixon had been on track to upend "our

Watergate's Forgotten Hero

democratic system of government ... had it not been for the conscientious performance of his job by Frank Wills, a black, poorly paid night watchman at the Watergate on the night of June 17, 1972. As a black American, I have been especially struck by the poetic justice of the discovery of the Watergate burglars by a black man."[18]

But it was a white lawyer from Greenville who delivered "the most quoted line of the hearings."[19] James Robert Mann, a conservative Democrat whose district voted overwhelmingly for Nixon, credited his fellow South Carolinian for the role he played in the President's downfall:

> Americans revere their President, and rightly they should because they know that by his oath he is supposed to preserve, protect and defend the Constitution, to enforce the Bill of Rights, which is their heritage, your rights and mine, whether I am a Democrat or a Republican, rich or poor, and that he will see that the laws are faithfully executed and that the individual liberties of each of us is protected.... It is not the Presidency that is in jeopardy from us. We would strive to strengthen and protect the Presidency. But, if there be no accountability, another President will feel free to do as he chooses. *But, the next time there may be no watchman in the night* [emphasis added].[20]

On July 30, in a vote of 27 to 11, including an "aye" from Congressman Mann, the House Judiciary Committee adopted the third Article of Impeachment.

Recognizing the inevitable, on August 7, the Republican leadership, headed by Arizona Senator (and former GOP presidential nominee) Barry Goldwater, paid a visit to the White House. The actions of the House Judiciary Committee and the release of the Oval Office recordings (including the one on June 23, 1972, called "the smoking gun," a phrase that henceforth would be used commonly as a reference to a single piece of evidence proving guilt) confirmed unequivocally that Nixon had engaged in obstruction of justice.[21] The leadership informed the president that it no longer had the votes to stop his impeachment and conviction. It was time to step down.

The following day, August 8, more than two years after Frank Wills discovered a piece of gray tape on a basement door latch of the Watergate Office Building, Nixon announced to the world that he

Chapter 10. Delusions of Grandeur

A little more than two years after the break-in, President Richard Nixon announced his resignation (August 8, 1974) (Album/Alamy Stock Photo).

would resign the next day at noon. In an uneventful ceremony, Vice President Gerald R. Ford was sworn in, becoming the only U.S. President not elected to national office.

Wills was back in the spotlight. Not since the immediate aftermath of the break-in had he been in such demand. Less than a week after Nixon's announcement, television talk show host Geraldo Rivera had him on *Good Night America*. Wearing a wide-collar colorful print shirt, Wills received a twenty-two-second-long applause by the studio audience. Appearing pleased by the extended ovation, Wills fielded Geraldo's questions as best he could, particularly one he would hear frequently in the coming months: Did he feel "responsible for the President's humiliation and resignation?" "I think he brought it on his own self," Wills answered, "and hopefully that piece

Watergate's Forgotten Hero

of tape will be a great focus for any other gentleman or whoever it may be to run for president not to use illegal [means] ... to gain office," a theme he would repeat in various ways.[22]

When the *New York Times* asked Wills what he thought of Nixon's resignation, he responded similarly: "No position is too high—if you are wrong, you are wrong, especially if you are elected by a majority of the United States citizens and especially when they elect you to be sincere, honest and forthright."[23] A far more eloquent response (probably drafted by Dorsey Evans) than rendered on Geraldo's show, it was clear that the world's most famous security guard was "not particularly comfortable" talking about political matters.[24] He much preferred topics such as hunting and fishing. This was confirmed by most of his interviews, as the twenty-six-year-old from North Augusta gave the impression of a genuinely nice fellow, charming in many ways, but still an uneducated, unworldly, backwoods Southerner.

When asked by television news broadcaster Tom Brokaw what he deserved for his role in Watergate, Wills said, "a million dollars or a Cadillac."[25]

"Just like the stock market," *New York Times Magazine* writer Sol Stern observed, "Frank Wills' fortunes have fluctuated for the past year and a half, depending on the intensity of Watergate news out of Washington."[26]

Stern's November 10, 1974, article, "A Watergate Footnote*: The Selling of Frank Wills," was the most revealing, in-depth piece ever written about the Watergate hero. For weeks, Stern shadowed Wills and Dorsey Evans, traveled on the road to their public engagements and award banquets, and spent hours chatting with both of them, securing previously unknown details, financial and otherwise, about the client and his agent. At one point, the interviewer thought Wills had revealed a critical piece of information about a "mystery man."[27] Apparently, this figure was the last person Wills had seen before he made his historic phone call to the police. "Wills told me," Stern wrote, "he had no idea who the man was and thought it possible he

Chapter 10. Delusions of Grandeur

might be one of the burglars who was never caught."[28] To the journalist, it was alarming that it had not been mentioned before. Eventually, Stern realized that Wills was putting him on. The so-called "mystery man" was none other than Democratic National Committee intern Bruce Givner, who already had been cleared by the authorities.

Getting to know Wills, Stern was struck by the self-contradictions that plagued the man. On the one hand, Wills said how much fun it was to be famous, making more money at a single public appearance than he did in an entire month working as a guard.On the other hand, he was quick to wallow in self-pity, complaining about the public's lack of appreciation. "Everybody says they are feeling sorry for Richard Nixon but no one is feeling sorry for Frank Wills, who put his life on the line. They make you suffer for doing your job."[29]

Since teaming up with Evans, Wills disclosed to Stern, he had already made over twenty-five paid appearances. Wills' compensation ranged from $200 for an interview to $800 for a single public appearance. The majority of these engagements were hosted by African Americans. At a Southern Christian Leadership Conference event, for example, Stern was impressed by the red-carpet treatment afforded Wills. The Rev. Ralph Abernathy (Martin Luther King, Jr.'s successor) announced that the "highlight of the four-day convention would be an awards dinner at which Frank Wills" would receive the organization's highest honor.[30] He rubbed elbows with some of the leading Black figures of the day, including award-winning actress Cicely Tyson and Southern Poverty Law Center founder Julian Bond. He was then flown to Los Angeles to receive an award from the National Association of Television and Radio Artists, a union representing minorities in the entertainment industry.

What intrigued Stern the most was Wills' relationship with his agent. When the journalist visited Evans at his office, he noticed a picture of President Abraham Lincoln hanging on the wall with a quotation at the bottom that read: "A lawyer's time and advices are his stock in trade."[31] It didn't take long for Stern to conclude that

Wills was Evans' stock in trade. All of Wills' mail and phone calls were dispatched through Evans' office. In short, "Evans completely controls Wills' access to the public."[32]

Evans was more than willing to explain to Stern his role and the opportunities he created for his client (possibly in hopes of recruiting others like Wills). Nor was he reluctant to charge Stern fifty dollars for his two-hour-long interview of Wills. After Evans deducted his 25 percent, the agent proudly pointed out that Wills had earned $37.50, six and a half times the amount he would have earned as an hourly security guard. It was clear to Stern why these two wanted to "play [this] out as long as possible."[33]

Beyond public appearances, Evans informed Stern, he was always on the lookout for additional revenue streams for his client. When he got wind that the DNC received a recent court settlement of $700,000 from the Committee to Re-elect the President, he inquired about receiving a piece of the action. He and Wills were rebuffed. When they solicited the DNC to hire "The Frank Wills Detective Agency," a one-man firm to handle the organization's security needs, the DNC declined.[34] The detective agency never got beyond the idea stage. Evans reminded Stern that the DNC could have been victimized again and again if it were not for his client. All Wills had received was a plaque, a plaque that was returned to the DNC because it had the incorrect date of the break-in.

At the conclusion of the article, Stern expressed reservations about Evans's true intentions: did he really have his client's interest at heart? Others interviewed by Stern questioned whether Wills actually wanted to be in the spotlight or whether Evans was pushing him into it. When Stern raised the issue, he found that Wills was "confused about what he really wants to accomplish out of his temporary fame."[35] In fact, Wills admitted that he was not cut out to be a public figure and longed for a simpler, less demanding lifestyle, where people were friendlier and he could be left alone. "Just give me a glass of lemonade by an oak tree down by the pond, I'll be happy."[36]

Chapter 10. Delusions of Grandeur

Stern couldn't help but notice a sadness that engulfed Wills. When he was not at a public appearance or working at a regular job, Wills spent the majority of his time by himself at his apartment. It appeared the only thing he had to look forward to was the call from Evans about his next assignment.

While Evans steered Wills in a purely monetary direction, others thought about helping him in a more practical way (and in the process, fulfilling their own political agenda).

The plan was the brainchild of strategist Hamilton Jordan, who was working on Georgia Governor Jimmy Carter's campaign to win the Democratic presidential nomination in 1976. Carter needed the support of African American primary voters in the South. What better way to attract this electorate, Jordan thought, than to help a recently minted Black hero to get his life in order? Once Wills was on the straight and narrow, Carter could take credit for the effort and endear himself to the large Black voter base in Dixie.

To put this strategy in motion, Jordan asked a subordinate at the DNC, Paul Brock, who was traveling to Atlanta, to stop off at North Augusta, where Wills was visiting his mother. Upon arrival, he met with Wills and got right to the point. Without a high school diploma, Brock told Wills, he would never get a federal job or any other well-paid position. If he did get a diploma, and if Carter were elected president, there was a strong likelihood his staff would help him get a government job as a security guard. Wills consented to the idea, and Brock put him in touch with the National Urban League's DC branch. Whereas the NAACP focused on ensuring civil rights, the Urban League focused on providing job training and expanding employment opportunities for African Americans.

Before Wills met with Urban League officials, a meeting was arranged between the League's Gerald Donaldson and Dorsey Evans.

When Donaldson spoke with Evans, the agent described his client as "inept, incapable and slow."[37] He said Frank Wills is "like a weed in the garden of life, he is just there, with no direction. He needs somebody to drive him, and I am doing the best I can. If you want him to do anything, let me know, and I will see that it gets done."[38]

Based on Evans' feedback, Donaldson had low expectations of Wills, suspecting that he was mentally challenged. His meeting with Wills left him pleasantly surprised. In Donaldson's judgment, Wills was "not a 'slow' person." Rather, he was "uncomplicated," which some might have mistaken for a learning deficiency.[39]

Having spent an entire day assessing Wills' needs, Donaldson believed firmly that Wills should "replace his present 'agent/lawyer' with a certified attorney."[40]

After Donaldson found out that "Evans was disbarred in the Washington D.C., area several years ago for unprofessional conduct in handling a client's estate," there was no doubt in his mind that Wills had been exploited.[41] In a memo to Urban League officials, Donaldson explained further:

> The method appears to be one of keeping Wills away from other interested parties by presenting himself as Wills [sic] protector and mentor.... Evans gets the payment and then gives Frank his share. Being only twenty-six from a rural background and experience, and having no formal education, all serve to hinder Wills in his relationship with Evans. The quick money and the limelight reinforced by Evans' misguiding have prevented Wills from appreciating the necessity of having a high school diploma for employment purposes.[42]

There was no question in Donaldson's mind that Wills should forgo all public appearances and focus on obtaining his high school diploma, and that the Urban League should support Wills' effort. This was not, he emphasized, "too strong a commitment to make to an individual who deserves the thanks, honor and respect of all black people, and, indeed, the nation."[43] Donaldson's superiors at the Urban League concurred, offering to support Wills' educational efforts as long as he demonstrated a commitment.

Wills agreed to enter the program, although he did not sever business ties with Evans.

Returning to DC, Wills reported to the Armstrong Adult Education Center. Established in 1902 and located in Shaw—a poor,

Chapter 10. Delusions of Grandeur

predominately African American neighborhood that served as ground zero during the King riots—the Armstrong Center helped locals who dropped out of high school earn a General Equivalency Diploma (GED). An instructor assessed Wills' skills and confirmed "Frank was not slow."[44] Aside from needing additional assistance in math, he could easily pass the requirements to obtain a diploma as long as he attended classes regularly.

In the beginning, Paul Brock (the emissary from the DNC who had first conveyed the idea to Wills) picked him up at his apartment and drove him to Armstrong, ensuring he went to class. Brock did it for three weeks until he felt Wills was motivated enough to go on his own. Wills demonstrated that Brock's confidence in him was not misplaced. He attended classes regularly, and the officials at the Urban League's DC branch office took him under their wing. No longer was it an assignment from headquarters; educating Frank Wills had become the branch's mission. Donaldson and his team were committed.

"I have made him understand that the National Urban League, with whatever influence it can muster is deeply committed to his present and future welfare, and that we are prepared to come to his assistance in whatever difficulty he finds himself ... over which he has no control," Donaldson informed the higher-ups in the organization.[45]

On October 31, 1974, Wills' first progress report confirmed that he was attending school regularly, the first step toward earning his diploma. League officials were certain that he "has come to appreciate the fact that Dorsey Evans has been using him and has now decided to devote the major part of his time to preparing for his GED exam."[46] In fact, Wills attended classes at Armstrong five days a week, two more days than he was originally asked, encouraging League staff members to provide further support for him. Anticipating that he would complete the GED, they had developed more ambitious goals for him, focusing on "career development rather than just job placement."[47] Tours of a crime lab at Howard University were planned, in hopes of exposing Wills to criminology, "an area which interests him deeply."[48]

When California Congressman Ron Dellums got wind of what was taking place at the League's DC office, he personally offered to help find a job for Wills upon graduation. It was even mentioned that once Wills finished, he would be offered a scholarship by the Urban League's New Brunswick Chapter, which would cover his room and board for one year if he were willing to relocate to New Jersey and attend Rutgers University.

It seemed as if Wills had finally gotten a solid handle on his life.

Then the bottom fell out.

After sticking out the GED program for several months, his interest waned and his attendance became erratic. At a certain point, Wills was skipping class and not completing his assignments because of last-minute paid engagements arranged by Evans. But not all the blame could be placed on his agent.

"Part of Frank's problem," Donaldson informed his supervisor, was "the cultural shock" of being surrounded by students who were younger, more comfortable in the classroom, and therefore better equipped to navigate the academic setting. Even if Wills had been placed on a vocational track, "he would again have to face the type of social pressures which inhibit him at present."[49]

Lacking the vision and discipline to achieve academic success (not to mention the allure of Evans' enticements), Wills decided to call it quits. Indeed, he was far more complicated than Donaldson had once thought.

In February 1975, back on the circuit, Wills was honored in commemoration of Black History Week at William Paterson College in Wayne, New Jersey, alongside pioneering African American historian John Henrik Clarke. Around the same time, a far more prestigious accolade was in the works. In the U.S. House, Maryland Representative Parren J. Mitchell introduced a resolution honoring Wills. Among the twenty-two supporters were New York City Congresswoman Shirley Chisholm (the first African American woman

Chapter 10. Delusions of Grandeur

elected to Congress and a recent presidential candidate) and Representative Ed Koch, also from Gotham, later its mayor. Not a single supporter hailed from Wills' home state.

"Had it not been for this alert and responsible young man," Mitchell reminded his colleagues, "it is questionable whether or not our government would be intact today as the democracy it was planned to be."[50] In the U.S. Senate, Maryland's Charles Mathias, Jr., a liberal Republican, introduced a similar resolution. With Democratic majorities in both houses of Congress, it was assumed the measure would pass, but it failed to attract the necessary votes, perhaps reflecting the strong bipartisan desire to keep the Watergate nightmare in the past.

JET reporter Simeon Booker had no such intention. On the eve of the three-year anniversary of the break-in, Booker took the opportunity to revisit the man responsible for its detection. Wills held nothing back. Irritated by the concern over Nixon's reported ill health (rumors circulated that the ex-president had suffered a nervous breakdown), Wills for one had no sympathy for him. "He got off scot-free with the pardon, the money, all the benefits—all that goes to the big guys, not the little guys like me."[51]

With dwindling money and no public appearances scheduled, Wills found work as a security guard at Georgetown University. Still, he and Evans remained hopeful that something would turn up, convinced that a pot of gold was at the end of the rainbow.

Maybe that pot of gold was in Hollywood.

In late 1974, Robert Redford—famous for his roles in *Butch Cassidy and the Sundance Kid*, *The Sting*, *The Candidate*, and *The Way We Were*—was lobbying studios to fund a movie about the Watergate cover-up and how *Washington Post* reporters Woodward and Bernstein had exposed it. He had been tracking their progress through the articles they had written for the *Post*. Redford was as intrigued by their partnership as he was by the scandal itself. How could these two unknown, inexperienced reporters who had nothing in common—Bernstein, a Jewish liberal, and Woodward, a "WASPy"

Republican—work so well together that it contributed to the resignation of a president?[52]

Excited about the concept, Redford encountered his first barrier to the project. Neither Bernstein nor Woodward would return his call. At the height of their reporting, they barely had time to shave and shower, let alone follow up with Redford. "We are kind of busy," Woodward later told him when they eventually did make contact.[53] Redford remained persistent and the two reporters relented. But then the actor-turned-director hit another brick wall.

The break-in, the conspiracy, and the eventual demise of Nixon had exhausted Americans. Hollywood wasn't interested in retelling a story that Americans wanted to forget. And certainly no one was interested in a movie about the two journalists. Where was the action? As Redford recalled, it seemed they would rather "film the phonebook" than retell Watergate.[54] The story might make it to the television screen, but not the silver screen.

Convinced of the project's potential, Redford made another pitch. He promised to star in the movie (for no money up-front) and announced that Dustin Hoffman (of *The Graduate* fame) would be his costar. With two box office favorites guaranteed, Warner Brothers signed on.

Soon after, director Alan J. Pakula (best known for producing the 1962 adaptation of *To Kill a Mockingbird* and directing the films *Klute* and *The Parallax View*) committed to the project. By early 1975, casting and preproduction were under way for *All the President's Men*, adapted from Woodward and Bernstein's highly praised book. To Wills' shock, he was invited to join the cast.

The film's producer, Walter Coblenz, wanted the famous security guard to play himself in the movie. Having zero acting experience, Wills was reluctant to accept the role.

"We'll tell you what to do," a production team member informed him.[55] Apparently, that was all Wills needed to hear. He was on board.

Whether it was "a sentimental gesture" or "not entirely devoid of promotional value" is difficult to determine.[56] So what if Robert

Chapter 10. Delusions of Grandeur

Redford couldn't remember his name? It was the biggest invitation to date that either agent or client could have wished for.

During filming, which took place at the actual scene of the crime, Frank Wills' role demanded that he remove the tape from the latch, take his break, walk across the street to the Howard Johnson's restaurant to order an orange juice, return to the basement, discover the door had been retaped, and, finally, call the police. What was a relatively short scene was actually shot "a dozen times from several angles" and in two different cities (he was flown to Los Angles during post-production to reshoot the opening of the door inside a soundstage), leading Wills to believe his role in the movie would be lengthier than what was in the final cut.[57]

In the editing phase, Pakula and Redford were forced to trim the movie's length. Trying to condense the 349-page bestseller into an action-packed political thriller while staying true to the storyline was

Frank Wills portrayed himself in the film *All the President's Men*. He was the first character to appear in the movie, had "one of the biggest close-ups," and was the only person of color in the film. Photograph by Dennis Brack (Danita Delimont/Alamy Stock Photo).

Watergate's Forgotten Hero

no easy task. Much of Wills' screen time ended up on the chopping block, though most agreed that he "handled the assignment with authority."[58] The director felt the burglary was "the least important element" in terms of shaping the film.[59] Even with the cutting of several scenes, *All the President's Men* still clocked in at 138 minutes.

Before the movie was released, there was plenty of buzz surrounding it, as evidenced by the large crowds it attracted while shooting on the streets of downtown DC. Even if it was the twentieth take at four o'clock in the morning, hundreds, if not thousands, of spectators watched closely, hoping to catch a glimpse of Redford or Hoffman.

The movie lived up to expectations. A commercial and critical success, it grossed over $70 million (equivalent to $325 million today) and earned four Oscars. The book *All the President's Men* skyrocketed back to the bestseller list.

For his fifteen seconds of screen time, Wills was paid $1,500, believed to be his largest paycheck for a single assignment. Even though his moment in the sun was minuscule ("If I had yawned, I would have missed it," as Wills put it), he was the first character to appear in the movie, had "one of the biggest close-ups," and was the only person of color in the entire film.[60] Not too shabby for a high school dropout with zero acting experience.

In April 1976, during the film's premiere in DC, Wills' screen presence drew applause from a sympathetic, mostly white liberal audience. Wills was not in attendance. Fearful that he'd lose his guard job at Georgetown if he failed to show up for his shift, he agreed to have Evans go to the premiere in his place. Not pleased with the time allotted Wills in the film, his agent argued that race was the reason. "They treated him in the picture just as the nation has treated him—ignore and neglect a black. This is something that they would much rather forget."[61]

At first glance, Evans' argument could be dismissed as absurd. The premise had merit, but it was misdirected. By focusing on his client's diminished part and arguing that it was a consequence of the

Chapter 10. Delusions of Grandeur

Robert Redford and Dustin Hoffman (left) played the roles of *Washington Post* reporters Bob Woodward and Carl Bernstein in *All the President's Men* (ZUMA PRESS, Inc./Alamy Stock Photo).

racist inclination of the film's director and editor, Evans failed to see that there was something far more revelatory about Wills' role in the movie and in the Watergate scandal itself. Wills was indeed the *only* African American involved, a minimum wage security guard caught up in an unprecedented political upheaval in which the participants, good and bad, were *all* white. The crisis is an indelible reminder that America less than a half century ago had no people of color in any significant number in its corridors of power.

Whatever the underlying racial implications of the movie, Wills was praised for his "admirable poise," although that same critic said he should have "no illusions about an acting career."[62] Nor should he have had any illusions that the movie would lead to renewed interest in his Watergate role. America had moved on.

CHAPTER 11

From Bad to Worse

In June 1977, the media, in print and on the airwaves, reminded the American people that five years had passed since the Watergate break-in—an opportunity to reflect on the event and to provide an update on its participants.

The five burglars as well as accomplice E. Howard Hunt had already served their prison terms (ranging from 4 months for James McCord to 33 months for Hunt). Only G. Gordon Liddy, one of the masterminds behind the scheme, refused to cooperate with authorities and remained in jail (for a total of 52 months).

Members of the Nixon Administration complicit in the scandal were either serving time, released, or awaiting sentencing. Attorney General John Mitchell would receive two and a half to eight years in prison but would be released for medical reasons after serving nineteen months. Bob Haldeman, Nixon's chief of staff, would soon begin his eighteen months in a federal correctional facility. After prison, several of the former administration officials published accounts (a few bestsellers) of their involvement in Watergate, and others went on to lucrative careers in business and other fields.

All the while, Nixon lived comfortably at his estate in San Clemente, California, had written a bestselling memoir, and had been paid $600,000 (equivalent to $2.5 million today) for his television interviews with British journalist David Frost.

Those on the other side of the law had also benefited financially from the scandal. Of course, no one matched the success of Woodward and Bernstein's *All the President's Men*, but trial judge John Sirica and some of the U.S. senators who had served on the select committee had enjoyed fame and profit in the publishing world. In fact, North Carolina Senator Sam Ervin exploited his role as chairman of the investigation committee by generating multiple streams of new income, especially as a spokesman for American Express.

As far as Frank Wills was concerned, he was the only one who had not successfully cashed in on the Watergate story. Sporting a neatly trimmed mustache and dressed in a short-sleeved polo shirt, accentuating his muscular arms, Wills did not hide his bitterness in a mini-interview with Lesley Stahl on *CBS Nightly News*.

The burglars had "gotten more recognition for breaking into Watergate than I have for apprehending them," he said.[1] Within seconds, Stahl moved on to the next interviewee in her anniversary coverage of the scandal, ended the segment, and returned back to her anchor, Walter Cronkite, who closed the show with his signature sign-off, "And that's the way it is."[2]

"Look at how comfortable President Nixon and most all of his men live today," Wills complained to *JET*'s Simeon Booker. "It seems that the bad guys got the good deal. And the good guy got the bad deal."[3] He told the *New York Times*: "John Dean can write a book, Howard Hunt can write a book, all these crooks can write a book. The publicity they received is out of proportion to what I got."[4] The *Chicago Sun-Times* quoted him: "I got truth and honesty and they got the money."[5] Looking back on his actions, Wills confided: "If I had to do it over again, I think I would just pass it by and let it happen because of the response I got."[6]

Venting his frustration might have made Wills feel good, at least for the moment, but was not productive financially. And he needed an income. Having surrendered his security job at Georgetown University, he was totally reliant on public appearances, fundraisers, awards, banquets, and his fan club, none of which could be depended upon for a decent living. Piles of the booklets about his life and the story of the break-in, which were supposed to be sold at events, mostly remained in unopened boxes in Dorsey Evans' office. Of the five thousand copies printed, only fifty were sold. Because his

Chapter 11. From Bad to Worse

agent covered the publishing costs, Wills had his earnings deducted accordingly. It's likely that Wills never saw a penny after the print run. With a book deal that never materialized and the DNC never coming through with a job offer, despite officials—according to agent and client—making "frequent promises of employment," Wills had nothing to show for his national fame.[7] If he had been provided guidance in terms of savings and investments, his financial situation would have been different. But as matters stood, Wills was virtually broke.

Between 1972 and 1977, Wills had made roughly seventy-five public appearances—interviews with the media (some were paid), autograph sessions, award banquets, public talks, and miscellaneous events. His pay ranged from zero to as much as $1,500 (for his movie role). On average, he seems to have made about $300 per appearance, when he was paid.

Ironically, Wills would have been better off financially if he had stuck to his job as a security guard, rather than falling under Dorsey Evans' spell. Assuming that Wills earned $30,000 from public events between the break-in and the five-year anniversary (less 25 percent agent's fee and other deductions Evans levied), he grossed, say, $20,000, or $4,000/year. If Wills hadn't participated in any paid events and had relied solely on a steady paycheck for his guard work, where he was earning $2.50 an hour, forty hours a week, fifty weeks out of the year, taking into account performance-related minimum wage increases, Wills would have probably earned well over $30,000 ($6,000/year) before taxes. In other words, if Wills had worked a normal eight-hour-a-day job (keeping in mind two or three weeks of unpaid vacation or sick leave), he would have earned a third more money than he had on the public circuit.

Sensing he was going nowhere fast in his current situation, Frank Wills finally broke ties with Dorsey Evans, who, under a cloud of questionable ethics, continued to pursue his legal career over the next three decades. In 1990, the DC Court of Appeals Board on Professional Responsibility found he had "engaged in misappropriation" of funds from a client.[8] He was suspended from practicing law for six months. In 2006, he was found guilty by the same body for misrepresenting a client's interests and, again, was suspended for six months for unethical professional behavior. After he complied with the ruling, he was placed on probation for one year. Also in 2006, Evans was suspended for ninety days from the Maryland State Bar Association in a separate matter. These actions triggered a third reprimand in his birth state, Kansas. In 1959, Evans had been admitted to the Kansas State Bar, though he had not practiced law in the state for decades. Since 1987, Evans was already on probation in Kansas for failing to pay his annual dues and not keeping up with his extended legal education units. When the Supreme Court of Kansas got wind of his recent punishments in DC and Maryland, the court agreed to "indefinitely suspend" Evans from practicing law in the state of Kansas.[9] He died in 2010.

Frank Wills went back to work as a security guard, the only occupation he really knew. Fearful he might be recognized and somehow put his job in danger, he tried to keep a low profile. That wasn't difficult for Wills, who was a loner by nature. But if he was going to stay out of the public eye, DC was not the town to live in. Taking stock of where he was and looking for a fresh start, in the summer of 1978, thirty-year-old Frank Wills headed home.

Wills hoped that his return to North Augusta would go largely unnoticed. Moving back in with his mother in her two-bedroom house on Five Notch Road, he was determined to secure a job and put Watergate solidly behind him. After all, North Augusta was a sleepy, slow-moving town where not much ever happened.

True, but Wills had been "at the center of one of the most extraordinary stories in modern American history," as Nat Irvin, Jr., expressed it.[10] If the famous security guard thought he could keep a low profile, it was wishful thinking.

Nearly everyone in town knew about Frank Wills. "There goes the Watergate man," they'd say.[11] Such recognition was not necessarily an expression of pride or friendship. Once he arrived, Wills

112

Chapter 11. From Bad to Worse

encountered an underlying (sometimes overt) climate of hostility. In town, strangers glared at him. Others intentionally ignored him or, worse, expressed their disdain for North Augusta's political pariah. This was a Republican stronghold; for that matter, every county in the state of South Carolina had voted overwhelmingly for Nixon. The "Watergate man"—responsible for the president's demise—was no hero. Hardly surprising that Frank Wills "was not going to find any welcome mats coming back to North Augusta," the Reverend Irvin's son remembered.[12]

Whether he could find a job in this environment was questionable. "Every time" he filled out an application, said William Mims, husband of Wills' cousin Martez, "he was rejected because of his [Watergate] association."[13] Wayne O'Bryant, a North Augusta–based historian, recalled vividly the admonishment: "Don't be seen with Frank Wills. It could affect your employment."[14]

Such talk, neighbors recalled, was hurtful to Wills' mother, Marjorie. In one instance, she was prejudged based on her son's public image. In May 1978, when South Carolina Senator Strom Thurmond's brother, Dr. Allan G. Thurmond, went on trial for filing false Medicaid claims, Marjorie was one of forty-five prospective jurors. When it came time to whittle the pool down to twelve jurors, she did not make the cut for fear that her politics could influence her decision.

To his relief, Wills managed to find work rather quickly. In August 1978, he was hired as a security guard by the Medical College at Augusta University. For the "late-night shift," he was paid $3.50 an hour, more than he had been making in DC.[15] His job entailed "just walking the halls, checking the doors," the same duties he had performed at Watergate.[16] True to form, he didn't last long: a mere three months.

He then worked as a guard at a textile factory but was laid off (as in the previous job, it's not known whether it was due to budgetary cutbacks or performance). Whatever the reason, it would be Wills' final job as a security guard; he would never work again in the profession that had defined his life.

Without a job, Wills spent most of his time at home reading books about mysticism and meditation. To family and his few friends, he announced his belief "in psychic forces," which he said explained his actions on the night of June 17, 1972. "I had vibes something was wrong," compelling him, he insisted, to pay extra attention to the door latch in the basement of the Watergate (failing to remember, intentionally or not, that he had been forewarned about prior break-ins at the start of some of his shifts and this probably put him on heightened alert).[17]

Wills' thinking grew even more bizarre. In a letter to Simeon Booker, he enclosed "decoded" information that only he was able to decipher.[18] Attaching an *Associated Press* newspaper article, "Human Brain Termed a Mystery" (undated), Wills circled words that he felt carried special significance, such as "mystery," "scientist," "decades," "automobile," "computer," and two dozen or so more.[19]

Nonsensical and harmless, perhaps, but Wills' downward spiral had the potential to get him into real trouble. On September 5, 1979, he was arrested in North Augusta for shoplifting a ninety-eight-cent pen from a grocery store. According to Wills, he had purchased the writing instrument from a drug store earlier that day. He kept the pen in his pocket and when he flashed it later at the grocery store, the employees accused him of stealing it from their market. With the assistance of a public defender, he pleaded no contest and was fined $108.25. This was clearly a warning sign, but no one took heed (and it's possible no one knew about it, except Marjorie).

Without full-time employment opportunities, Wills accepted whatever was available. He peddled perfume door-to-door, painted neighborhood homes, mowed lawns, served as a nursing attendant for the elderly, and had other menial jobs that didn't require a car because he couldn't afford to buy one. To get around town, he rode a bicycle. With plenty of free time on his hands, Wills explored the woods, and at home he perfected his cooking skills, especially making cornbread from scratch.

Although he reconnected with his friend Preston Sykes, who

Chapter 11. From Bad to Worse

was now married and raising his own family, for the most part Wills kept to himself. He remained close with his mother, but no one else.

While many dismissed Wills as reclusive, his neighbors often saw a different side. A nearby resident remembered how he would check-in on her elderly mother, even sit and drink coffee with her. He never found it a burden to befriend her. Possibly it helped to distract him from the realization that his prospects for employment and a fuller life remained bleak.

June 1982 marked the ten-year anniversary of the scandal, once again exacerbating Wills' bitterness about his situation and the more favorable outcomes for the Watergate conspirators.

Richard Nixon was living the life of an "elder statesman"—shuttling between his estate in a wealthy New Jersey suburb and his private residence in Washington, D.C., occasionally advising President Ronald Reagan.[20] The government allocated the former president an annual budget of $325,000 to offset costs for a staff, office, and travel. And Nixon's cronies, no longer under a dark cloud of suspicion, were cashing in too. Former White House counsel John Dean raked in half a million dollars traveling the lecture circuit; Nixon's chief of staff H.R. Haldeman earned millions working as a real estate developer in Los Angeles; and political advisor John Ehrlichman and Watergate accomplice G. Gordon Liddy optioned their bestselling memoirs into Hollywood movies. Despite the stigma they would endure for the rest of their lives—Haldeman said "Watergate is like a vulture around your neck"—these men successfully reinvented themselves and made a lucrative living to prove it.[21]

Wills celebrated the anniversary by granting an interview to the only person he trusted in the media, *JET*'s Simeon Booker. The former guard demanded payment for the interview (obviously Evans' influence had rubbed off on him). Wills met the journalist at the magazine's DC bureau office, located blocks away from the White House. The two men strolled to 1600 Pennsylvania Avenue and beyond.

Having known Wills for a decade, Booker was disappointed to

Watergate's Forgotten Hero

On the tenth anniversary of the break-in, *JET*'s Simeon Booker interviewed Wills at the magazine's DC Bureau office. Photograph by Maurice Sorrell (courtesy Carol McCabe Booker).

see the toll Watergate had taken on him. No longer the easygoing Southern country boy, the thirty-four-year-old seemed lost, lonely, and depressed. During their walk, not a single tourist recognized him. Here was a historical figure who, Booker observed, "melted into the crowd like some stranger from the Deep South, moving between the sidewalk crowds." Finally, an acknowledgment of sorts. A homeless, African American veteran approached them. Once he realized who it was, he told Wills, "I guess you feel just like us black Vietnam veterans. Shafted."[22]

After they returned to the *JET* office, Booker conducted a brief interview. Wills appeared, the reporter observed, "uncomfortable, frequently coughing, twisting fingers, and shooting his brown eyes in many directions. His memory is cemented on the limited experience of finding the tape and calling for emergency backup."[23] They then walked over to the Watergate Office Building. Inside the facility, they headed toward the stairwell and walked up to the sixth floor where the burglars were apprehended. It was now vacant. A plaque hung on a wall, acknowledging the break-in. Then they headed to the basement. Workers shuffled by them. None of them had any idea

Chapter 11. From Bad to Worse

Wills at the Watergate Office Building for a photo shoot by *JET* magazine photographer Maurice Sorrell (June 1982) (courtesy Carol McCabe Booker).

who they had passed. Wills pretended it didn't bother him, but it was clear to Booker it did.

Booker was right. Wills refused to let it go. Whoever he spoke to, his argument (which was indeed incontestable) remained the same: "If it wasn't for me there wouldn't have been no Woodward, no Bernstein, no [Judge] Sirica, no Watergate. None of it. I made it all happen."[24]

If Wills thought his anonymity was irreversible, he would soon learn that it was not. Less than three months after the tenth anniversary of the break-in, Wills made national headlines—for all the wrong reasons.

On Wednesday, September 1, 1982, Wills was shopping for a pair

Watergate's Forgotten Hero

of tennis shoes at the Sky City Discount Center in Augusta, Georgia. He was accompanied by his fifteen-year-old son Eugene, whom he saw now and then. Eugene was living in Waynesboro, Georgia, with his mother, Frank's ex-girlfriend from Lucy Craft Laney High School. The extent of Frank's relationship with his son since he'd gone off to Job Corps had been minimal. He sent money occasionally to the boy's mother, but "it was not a lot," he admitted.[25]

Father and son were shopping at the popular (now defunct) Southern chain store for a pair of new athletic shoes that Eugene had expressed interest in. Wanting to "surprise" the boy, Wills went to the shoe department, found what he was looking for (a "certain style tennis shoe") and dropped the twelve-dollar pair of shoes in his hiking bag, which he carried on his shoulder.[26] All the while, he teased Eugene that he wasn't going to buy them for him.

Wills walked toward the cash register and, according to his version of events, was ready to purchase them. The store clerk at the register watched Wills walk "past her with the bag over his shoulder as if he were about to leave."[27] Only a few steps away from the exit doors, a security guard intercepted Wills. The guard checked his knapsack and found the shoes. When the guard asked Wills how he was planning to purchase the items, Wills at first evaded answering the question. Accompanied by the guard, Wills was confronted by the store manager, John Lockhart, who asked similar questions.

"They were a present for my son," Wills responded. "I wanted them to be a surprise so I sought to hide them from him."[28]

There was no question that he was preparing to leave the store with unpaid merchandise, a clear case of attempted theft, store officials argued. Wills was detained.

According to Francis Playford, a nearby cashier, when Wills was confronted about the shoes found in his bag, "he made no attempt to stop in any way." It was then that Wills offered a "$20 bill in hand to pay for the shoes"—after he was caught.[29]

Wills argued he went to the cashier and told her, "[I'd] like to pay for these shoes."[30]

Chapter 11. From Bad to Worse

Playford disagreed: "He wasn't going to pay for the shoes."[31]

"He was treated as any other shoplifter," said Lockhart, who was African American. "We didn't know who he was when he was arrested. He was caught shoplifting. Period."[32] Wills' denial fits the typical profile of a shoplifter. "Most thieves deny they took anything or claim it was a mistake, until the [police] officers show them the tapes or describe what they saw."[33]

The Augusta police were dispatched to Sky City, and when they arrived, Wills was arrested, placed in handcuffs, and taken to the Augusta city jail on a misdemeanor charge. Regardless of Wills' intention, Georgia state law at the time was crystal clear: whenever an individual concealed "items prior to purchase, [it] amounts to shoplifting."[34] He was held on a $1,000 bond. Eugene was separated from Wills and walked from the Sky City Discount Center back to Five Notch Road, which took about forty-five minutes.

"I told the police he had no way to get home," Wills said, "but no one offered to help him get home."[35]

Unable to pay bail, Wills called members of his family to help him. "I called my mother and my uncle to get me out of here, but my own family have turned their backs on me."[36] It's possible that his mother and other family members might not have had the funds to bail him out. According to Augusta Police Chief Danny Philpot, if Wills had been taken to Richmond County Jail, "his family only would have to pay $100 on a $1,000 bond." Since he was brought to a local jail and was an out-of-state resident, family must raise the full $1,000."[37]

When news of Wills' offense was leaked to the media, the police department was bombarded with calls. "I didn't think he'd be in here 15 minutes," a spokesman from the police department said, failing to acknowledge that his bail was $1,000, not $100. "All he needed was somebody to sign for him, but nobody came. Then the media started calling. We had a call from Atlanta, somebody from Chicago, we had Channel 12 up here, we had a station in Columbia [South Carolina]."[38]

Watergate's Forgotten Hero

Overcrowded jails, an inquisitive media, and an inmate who did not pose a public threat led authorities to release Wills on Friday, September 3. He had spent two and a half days behind bars. For once, Wills' fame finally got him something—out of jail.

It was bad enough he had been arrested. It was worse that no one from his family had been willing to post bail for his release. But if Wills thought he had hit rock bottom, he was mistaken.

At first, Wills' arrest attracted local media attention. The area's leading newspapers, the *Augusta Chronicle* and the *Augusta Herald*, published detailed coverage of the event. Inevitably, it was picked up by major news outlets such as the *New York Times*, the *Boston Globe*, the *Washington Post*, and *People* magazine. The entire country soon learned that Wills was a shoplifter and had spent time in jail.

For years, Wills had felt he had not received his fair share of publicity, but this exposure was downright humiliating. It seemed to him that Americans were interested in his life only when it was unraveling. Filled with self-pity and rage, he was overheard grumbling: "If I was a fire, everything would be destroyed by now. That's how angry I am."[39]

Throughout Wills' life, when he was at a low point, he always caught a lucky break. This time it came from an unknown "third party," probably the Augusta-based NAACP branch.[40] It hired John H. Ruffin, Jr., to represent Wills.

Ruffin, a prominent criminal defense attorney, was experienced in dealing with high-profile cases and the media. The son of a shoemaker and a schoolteacher, he was a graduate of Howard University School of Law and was the first African American admitted to the Augusta Bar Association. While serving as the legal plaintiff in a class-action lawsuit to desegregate the local public school system, he had received his fair share of death threats but was not dissuaded from taking on controversial cases. Given his limited resources, Wills could not have had better representation.

Because Southern white conservatives viewed Wills with disdain for his role in Nixon's resignation, Ruffin believed that the

Chapter 11. From Bad to Worse

proposed one-year sentence had more to do with political payback than shoplifting. A trial date was scheduled for Wednesday, December 15, 1982.

For some inexplicable reason, Wills was under the impression it was for Monday, December 13. He spent that day at the courthouse, waiting for his case to be called. Seeing that there was no trial, Wills assumed the date had been changed to "early next year" (but failed to check with Ruffin).[41] The next evening, Tuesday, December 14, Wills went to a friend's house and didn't return to his mother's home until about 1:00 p.m. the following day. Later that morning, on Wednesday, December 15, Wills was supposed to meet Ruffin at the Richmond County Courthouse. At 9:00 a.m., a court official called Wills' mother's house and left a voicemail, notifying the defendant "to be in court at 9:30 a.m."[42]

Presiding over the case was Richmond County State Court Judge James Edward Slaton. A former National Guardsman who rose to the rank of brigadier general and then was appointed to the bench in 1979, Slaton was known to take a hard line against domestic abusers, those driving under the influence, and shoplifters.

At 9:30 a.m., Wills was still a no-show. When Slaton asked for his whereabouts, Ruffin was at a loss for an explanation. He too had called his client, but was unsuccessful in reaching him. Judge Slaton issued a "bench warrant" for Wills, who "blamed his lawyer" later for the miscommunication.[43] Whoever was at fault, Ruffin informed Judge Slaton "there had been a mix-up between him and his client about the court date."[44] Instead of arresting Wills for failing to show up for his appearance, the Court rescheduled his trial for February 14, 1983.

Wills got another break.

The arrest at Sky City should have been his second offense in the past three years; however, the 1979 shoplifting incident in North Augusta had been dropped (it's likely Ruffin had something to do with it). With that previous arrest erased from Wills' criminal record, Ruffin felt it wasn't worth the effort to put up a defense and risk a lengthy trial with the potential for a media circus. If Wills was found guilty, Ruffin believed the worse-case scenario was that his client would likely pay a fine with no time behind bars.

On Monday morning, February 15, 1983, a jury deliberated for about eighty minutes before reaching a verdict: Frank Wills was guilty of shoplifting. The surprise was not the verdict, but the sentence. Judge Slaton had no intention of letting Wills off with a slap on the wrist, ordering him to serve twelve months in the Richmond County Correctional Institution. Attorney and client were aghast. And so was the public.

The news of Wills' yearlong sentence for stealing a pair of twelve-dollar tennis shoes put him back in the headlines. The media instantly highlighted the glaring disparity (and hypocrisy) between the felonies that President Nixon had allegedly committed, for which he never served a day in prison, let alone stand trial; and Frank Wills, who went to jail for petty theft. The message resonated loud and clear within the African American community: racial injustice pure and simple. Georgia's legal system had a long history of applying harsher sentences to people of color than whites for similar offenses. Local African American politicians and civil right activists began lobbying for an appeal on Wills' behalf.

Ben Hasan, an aide to Augusta's first Black mayor, Edward M. McIntyre (elected in 1981), met with Marjorie Wills to discuss the options for getting her son released. Heartbroken over what had transpired, she confided to Hasan that her son was unable to hold down a job and had finally hit rock bottom. She expressed the hope that Mayor McIntyre would step in and use his influence with the state's parole board and Georgia Governor Joe Frank Harris.

In Atlanta, the president of the Georgia State Conference of the NAACP sent a letter to both the parole board and Governor Harris, seeking a commutation of Wills' sentence and emphasizing the historic and ongoing discriminatory sentencing against blacks in Georgia. This was blatantly evident in Wills' case. He should have

Chapter 11. From Bad to Worse

been fined $250, even if it had been his second offense (technically, it was not), and, if it had occurred a third time, received a maximum of thirty days in jail. Obviously, Judge Slaton had ignored the sentencing guidelines and did not take into account Wills' heroic role in Watergate, the NAACP contended. There were calls for Governor Harris to "create a commission to investigate discriminatory sentencing."[45]

Slaton defended his sentencing decision on the legally inaccurate grounds that it was Wills' second offense in three years. When that didn't pass muster, the judge offered a highly peculiar reason: He was "afraid that Wills could not pay a fine," and therefore he put him in jail.[46]

Such ludicrous reasoning served only to highlight the racial discrimination in the state's penal system. "Compare Frank Wills' case," a NAACP official pointed out, "by contrast to the case of a white Cobb County doctor who was charged with writing illegal drug prescriptions to men with criminal records. He [the white doctor] was not imprisoned for so much as a day. Instead, he was channeled to a pretrial diversion program because of what the D.A. called '(his) contribution to the (medical) profession.'"[47] If further evidence was necessary, sheer numbers would suffice. Only a third of Georgia's population was African American, but close to two-thirds of those in prisons and jails throughout the state were Black. Too iniquitous to contain, the issue resonated across the country.

On March 1, 1983, two weeks after Wills was sentenced, New Jersey's East Orange Mayor Thomas Cooke and Newark Mayor Kenneth Gibson got involved in the escalating legal battle. Neither Cooke nor Gibson, both of whom were African American, knew Wills personally, but were sympathetic to his plight, having witnessed many of their own constituents fall victim to a bigoted criminal justice system. The two mayors were also native Southerners—Cooke was born in Camden, South Carolina (only a hundred miles northeast of North Augusta), and Gibson hailed from Alabama. Having risen to heights in their adoptive state that no one could have predicted, both men

Watergate's Forgotten Hero

knew all too well how the Deep South oppressed people of color, especially poor and uneducated ones like Frank Wills.

On the steps of Augusta City Hall, the two mayors declared: "We firmly believe that the treatment of Mr. Wills is grounded in negative racial attitudes toward African Americans, if not outright racism."[48] They demanded a new trial and a new judge. Based on previous rulings rendered by Judge Slaton for similar criminal acts that resulted in lesser punishment, Wills deserved a just sentence, the mayors insisted. Did it have to do with Watergate? Was it racism? If he were white, Mayor Gibson argued, Wills "would have been accorded international fame and fortune."[49]

They put their words into action. Cooke and Gibson handed over $3,000 to Ruffin, who bailed his client out of jail. Wills' appeal was scheduled for April.

Upon leaving jail, Wills expressed his gratitude for the mayors' support. "I think that's a very humanitarian thing that they thought of."[50]

Although supporters praised Cooke and Gibson's generosity, many Augusta residents did not approve of these "carpetbaggers" getting involved in a local matter. "How dare two black Northern mayors question the integrity of our State Court," Augustan Tommy McBride complained in a letter to the editor of the *Augusta Chronicle*.[51] He dismissed the argument that Wills' sentence had been racially inspired. When a local elementary school teacher asked her students to submit letters to the editor either in support of or against Wills' sentence, the majority of youngsters felt he was treated fairly.

Realizing that the New Jersey mayors might have overstayed their welcome, Ruffin made it clear that his client's sentence was not about race. It was purely a legal question of incarceration. Wills backed up his attorney. During his brief stint inside the correctional facility, he had spoken with other inmates, blacks and whites, who "had been given similar sentences by Slaton on the same type of convictions."[52]

Racially instigated or not, the injustice of Wills' sentence served

Chapter 11. From Bad to Worse

as a rallying cry in both the South and the North. The court where Wills was tried was "barraged with letters and phone calls" from supporters throughout the country.[53] In addition, individuals wrote to newspapers, expressing their frustration with the criminal justice system. Mrs. Mims of Edgefield, South Carolina, in a letter to the *Augusta Chronicle*, felt the sentence was "overkill" and didn't understand why the county was focused on locking up a shoplifter while releasing more hardened criminals due to overcrowding.[54] "I'd rather see a shoplifter on the street than a rapist," she added. Hubert W. Merchant of Augusta wrote that Wills' sentence would cost taxpayers $12,000, "[a lot] more than the costs of the shoes involved."[55] In the [Wilmington, North Carolina] *Morning Star-News,* Professor Earl Sheridan reminded his readers that of the twenty people convicted in the Watergate scandal, only four served a year or more in jail. Syndicated columnist Mike Royko of the *Chicago Sun-Times* posed the question: How is it that Vice President Spiro Agnew and President Nixon never saw the inside of a jail cell? With his characteristic wit, Royko added: "The least the rest of the Watergate crowd should do is take up a collection for [Frank Wills]. He helped make most of them rich."[56]

Sensing a story that was not yet ready to fall by the wayside, the *Augusta Chronicle* assigned reporter Mickie Valente to research Judge Slaton's past sentencing practices to determine whether the ruling in Wills' case was consistent with what he had done in the past. Valente found four similar cases where an individual was convicted of shoplifting a second time and the judge had delivered one-year sentences (technically, this was Wills' first offense). In three of those cases, the defendant had served twelve months in prison. The other was behind bars for six months. When Valente interviewed Slaton, he refused to discuss the sentencing guidelines, but explained that he was not opposed to releasing Wills early if "he maintains a good behavior record while incarcerated."[57]

Ruffin wasn't buying it. Employing a new tact, he argued that his client did not receive a fair trial, citing "errors in procedure."[58]

Wills' lawyer requested Slaton to "rectify what he considered 'rubber-stamped' judicial treatment" and throw out the charges against his client.[59]

Two weeks before Wills' April 16 appeal, Ruffin submitted a pretrial legal brief to the state court solicitor, outlining why he felt his client deserved a retrial or, at the very least, a reduced sentence. Ruffin argued that Judge Slaton should not have considered the September arrest a second offense. Furthermore, Ruffin maintained that "Wills' rights had been infringed upon because he and his attorney were not given sufficient notice that the North Augusta conviction would be a factor in the sentence to be imposed."[60]

State Court Solicitor Gayle B. Hamrick denied Ruffin's motions. He ruled that even if Wills' 1979 conviction had been ignored, the judge "had the right to sentence him to the maximum 12-month prison term."[61]

With less than a week until the appeal portion of the trial, the stakes got higher. Disheartened over the "irony of [white] criminals being rewarded and pardoned and [Black] citizen[s] being harassed and made destitute," Newark Mayor Kenneth Gibson took Wills' case all the way to the White House, seeking a presidential pardon from Ronald Reagan.[62] Because a president can issue a pardon only for a federal crime, no doubt it was intended to be a symbolic gesture that would attract more publicity for Wills. Not surprisingly, Gibson never received a response from the President; only Georgia's Democratic Governor Joe Frank Harris had the authority to overturn the conviction.

Though well intentioned, Gibson's actions served only to antagonize some Augustans. "A presidential pardon for a shoplifter? What is this world coming to?" asked Barbara Durland.[63] *Augusta Chronicle* columnist Margaret Twiggs vented her frustration: "[I]sn't it time that black Americans stopped hiding behind the color of their skin? Does Gibson really think if Wills had been white instead of black Judge Slaton would have looked the other way?"[64] Firmly convinced that Slaton took the correct course of action, Twiggs reminded her

Chapter 11. From Bad to Worse

readers: "The sentence may sound harsh on the surface, but it wasn't the first time Wills had been hauled into a local court on a shoplifting charge."[65]

At the April 16 appeals hearing, Ruffin based his argument on process rather than skin color. Realizing this was his only chance for victory, Ruffin maintained that he and his client "did not feel the sentence was racially motivated," but that the punishment did not fit the crime.[66] Once the argument was made, Ruffin requested an extension, hoping that a delay might work in Wills' favor. Judge Slaton agreed to suspend the proceedings until the middle of May. However, when the hearing resumed on May 17, Judge Slaton denied Wills a new trial. No explanation was given. Ruffin and Wills had thirty days to appeal his decision to the Georgia Court of Appeals.

In the midst of all this uncertainty, Wills received a surprise visit from another out-of-towner.

Chapter 12

Downward Spiral

In October 1976, Alex Haley's long-awaited book *Roots* was published. ABC immediately adapted the book, a story of the author's African ancestors, for a television mini-series. When it aired on eight consecutive nights in January 1977, it was an instant hit, each evening attracting more and more viewers. By the final episode, it had the largest television audience ever. The series made Alex Haley the nation's most popular author. His stardom wouldn't last long, but his impact on race relations in America would remain indelible.

In spring 1983, Haley and his lifelong friend and personal assistant, George Simms, were meeting at the author's Burbank, California, office (located at the Warner Brothers studio lot), when their conversation turned to Frank Wills, recently featured in the news because of his shoplifting arrest. How did a low-paid Black security guard go from hero to villain? What had happened to the night watchman after Watergate? Haley was curious. Like any author, he sensed a book in the making.

Having not published a book since *Roots*, Haley was on the lookout for a possible topic. The more he conversed with Simms, the more convinced he was that Wills' story, "if rightly handled, presented a powerful book."[1] When Haley shared the idea with his wife, My Haley, she agreed that the story had enormous potential, comparing Frank Wills to Rosa Parks. Both had committed "a small act, but which changed the course of history."[2]

Later that afternoon, Haley contacted his literary agent, John Hawkins. "Let me throw something at you," Haley began before delving into the topic.

Chapter 12. Downward Spiral

"It could be a fantastic book," Hawkins believed, "if there's enough detail."[3] Was there an adequate amount of material for a book-length story? Instead of guessing blindly, Haley opted to go straight to the source. His next phone call was to Newark Mayor Gibson, whom he knew personally and was aware, based on his reading in *JET*, that Gibson was involved in Wills' case. When Haley called the mayor's office, Gibson, "came right onto the phone," providing the telephone number for Wills' attorney, John Ruffin.[4]

Haley contacted Ruffin, who "was cautious at first."[5] Ruffin explained that he "wasn't any agent, as such, for books, for Wills, that he had represented him in his arrest situation. He said that lawyers should make that distinction, definitely, and not try and double as agents for literary matters." Even still, Ruffin felt the need to protect his client and informed Haley "several approaches had been made to Wills for his story, which had upon his advice been rejected as appearing to be fundamentally exploitive."[6]

But Alex Haley was not just any ordinary writer.

When the author of *Roots* explained to Ruffin that his plan was to "structure" the book in similar fashion to *The Autobiography of Malcolm X*, Haley's other bestseller, Ruffin got interested, barely able to contain his joy.[7]

"*Roots* and *The Autobiography of Malcolm X*," the attorney told Haley, "are two of the books I don't lend."[8]

Ruffin agreed to reach out to Wills and set up a meeting.

On May 23, 1983, Alex Haley flew from his Knoxville, Tennessee, residence to the Augusta airport, where he was picked up by John Ruffin's secretary. Wills had his long-time friend, Preston Sykes, drive him to Ruffin's office. Joining Haley, Ruffin, and Wills was *Augusta News-Review* founder and editor Dr. Mallory Millender, the only reporter present at the meeting. A longtime friend of Ruffin, Millender was grateful to be included, realizing what a scoop this was for his weekly African American newspaper.

When the author and his intended biographical subject met,

Alex Haley (center) meeting with Wills (left) and his attorney John Ruffin in Augusta, Georgia, to discuss the details of their collaborative book, which never came to fruition (photograph by and courtesy of Mallory Millender).

Haley presented Wills with a signed copy of *The Autobiography of Malcolm X*, coauthored with the slain leader and published posthumously.

"I'm sitting here thinking 'Is this a mirage or is this the real thing,'" Wills later confided to Millender. Ruffin facilitated the meeting, but Haley soon took it over, telling those present how "Wills had a story to tell and *he* wanted to tell his story."[9] With pen, pad, and camera, Millender remained quiet, observing, listening, jotting notes, and taking photographs. Wills hadn't said much until he "chimed in" about forty-five minutes into the meeting.[10] As Millender recalled, Wills did not say anything of importance, but there was one takeaway from the meeting: "Alex Haley was very interested in Frank Wills' story."[11]

Haley had already figured out the book's central theme: "Here was a man that set off the whole thing (Watergate).... [It's] a story

Chapter 12. Downward Spiral

of a guy, a so-called little man doing his job, and then it precipitates [into] a huge, huge, literally universal story."[12]

The bestselling author envisioned the book as written in the first person, similar to how he had ghostwritten Malcolm X's story, which explains why he brought a copy of that book instead of *Roots*. The story would begin on the night of the break-in at Watergate, Haley told the group. It was not so much about Watergate, but what happened to Wills afterwards.

For a brief moment, Wills had forgotten about his troubles as he got swept up in Alex Haley's project. The meeting made the front page of the *Augusta News-Review*. When Don Rhodes of the *Augusta Herald* interviewed Wills, he was still in shock that the famous *Roots* author "would be coming to Augusta, Georgia, just to see me."[13] The encounter soon appeared in celebrity gossip columns across the country. Frank Wills may have fallen on "hard times" since Watergate, Millender wrote, but that might have changed thanks to his collaboration with Alex Haley on *The Autobiography of Frank Wills*.[14]

***

On June 14, 1983, Ruffin filed the paperwork with the county clerk's office to appeal the lower court's decision. More than a month later, Ruffin received notice that the Georgia Court of Appeals had docketed the appeal and he had twenty days to submit his legal brief to reverse Wills' conviction.

In his brief, Ruffin argued that Slaton's sentencing of his client was unjust because he did not take his client's personal circumstances into consideration and unfairly included a prior conviction that had been dropped. Ruffin and Wills would have to be patient for the court's ruling, which usually took months.

Meanwhile, an Augusta-based fundraising group formed, calling itself "Friends of Frank Wills Committee."[15] Its purpose was to help Wills in his painting and landscape business by raising money to purchase a pickup truck. (Little did the committee know that Wills had a driver's license, but it had expired.) The committee sought donors from all over the United States, but their efforts fell short.

That fall, Wills was honored by the Georgia State Conference of the NAACP for his Watergate heroism. "The nation should have thanked him instead of mistreating him," a presenter of the award said in his remarks. "It seems as if honesty does not pay anymore. Anyway, we are happy that the NAACP gives him due honor."[16]

On November 23, 1983, the Georgia Court of Appeals three-judge panel upheld Wills' yearlong sentence, finding "no abuse of discretion" by Judge Slaton.[17] The case now entered the next phase of the legal labyrinth, the State Supreme Court of Georgia.

In January of the new year, eighteen months since the arrest, the state's highest court refused to overturn Judge Slaton's decision. Wills had two options: begin serving his sentence or try again to have it reversed by appealing to the United States Supreme Court. It would take months for the court to decide if it even wanted to hear his case.

Before Wills made up his mind, he received a visit from *JET*'s Simeon Booker, one of his most fervent supporters. It was clear to Booker that Wills' legal troubles had taken their toll. Consumed by anxiety, his face was etched with wrinkles, and he seemed to have taken on the "role of a disillusioned hermit."[18]

Wills' neighbors confirmed Booker's assessment, finding that the once-easygoing young man seemed less approachable. "It's a sad commentary on our times," a neighbor told Booker. "[Wills] has needed help for a long time."[19]

Booker agreed but had ambivalent views about Wills' plight. On the one hand, he thought Wills needed to take charge of his own life and stop relying on others. He had "failed to take advantage of the opportunities" that were given to him, and he had to stop blaming society for his current ordeal.[20] On the other hand, make no mistake, Booker painfully acknowledged: Wills' situation of going from national hero to convict—based on "trite and flimsy charges"—was unique and would imperil most people. "It's tragic."[21]

Chapter 12. Downward Spiral

Without a vehicle, Wills had few options to make a living. He picked up local jobs working as a handyman, a landscaper, and a firewood supplier. With time on his hands, he puttered in his mother's garden. But just as Wills' life seemed to be headed for the abyss, as in similar times, help arrived.

***

In August 1984, Wills was out and about when his mother received a telephone call. Marjorie took the message; when Wills returned, she told her son that Dick Gregory had called. Wills figured it was Dick Gregory from the neighborhood and never followed up.

A little while later, Gregory called again. This time Wills was home and quickly realized that it wasn't "Dick-Gregory-from-the-neighborhood."[22] It was *the* Dick Gregory. Having read about Wills' predicament in a *JET* article, the African American comedian and political activist wanted to offer his assistance.

A native of St. Louis, Dick Gregory was born and raised in the age of Jim Crow. Gregory had an innate ability to channel his resentment into humor by poking fun at the absurdity of racism. Coming of age when stand-up comedy was a white-dominated profession, he not only confronted a color barrier, but his material reflected issues of the day, which also challenged tradition. In January 1961, he got his big break at a *Playboy* nightclub, performing in front of a mostly white, Southern male audience. Apprehensive at first, Gregory showed no fear and flourished in his performance. Instead of heckling or hauling him off the stage, the audience laughed along, wanting more. Soon after, Gregory's career took off, and he rose to become one of the leading comedians on the circuit, Black or white.

Comedy wasn't his only passion. A vehement opponent of the war in Vietnam, he fasted in protest. Wanting to lose weight anyway (through years of drinking and poor eating habits, he had ballooned to an unhealthy 280 pounds), Gregory emerged from his protest as a zealous opponent of alcoholic beverages and processed foods. Convinced of the need to cleanse one's body of such toxins, he tried

Watergate's Forgotten Hero

to persuade others to embrace his beliefs, including the 1972 presidential nominee Senator George McGovern. McGovern declined, but Gregory was not deterred. By the 1980s, he was known more for his political activism and nutritional evangelizing than for what had originally catapulted him to fame. Capitalizing on the country's emerging health craze (propelled by fitness icons Jane Fonda and Richard Simmons), he established Dick Gregory Health Enterprises.

It was a research, manufacturing, and distribution company that sold the namesake's branded weight-loss and nutritional products, mainly targeting African Americans. Working with Ohio-based pharmaceutical distributor Cernitin America, Gregory marketed more than a hundred different products. Although he was an effective spokesman, earning as much as a $100,000 a month, he needed help to get the word out. Gregory set his sights on Wills, a nationally known figure and a hero in the Black community. Wasting no time, Gregory made an offer (whether Ruffin was consulted is unknown, but probably not). Wills accepted it, with the understanding that there would be no public announcement of his hiring until the U.S. Supreme Court rendered a decision to hear his case. In the meantime, Gregory and his new employee met secretly in Boston, eating at fancy restaurants and discussing the details of their arrangement.

On October 1, 1984, the U.S. Supreme Court refused to consider Wills' appeal. No explanation was given. Wills had run out of options. Richmond County prosecutors demanded that he begin serving his twelve-month sentence immediately.

Gregory had other plans. The following day at the Watergate Hotel in Washington, D.C., in front of a large gathering of media, Gregory announced the hiring of Frank Wills, America's forgotten hero. Wearing a custom-tailored suit that his new boss had purchased for him, Wills was all smiles and seemed at ease discussing Dick Gregory's Bahamian Diet, the company's newest product. Expected to wear multiple hats in his new position, Wills informed the news outlets that he would work as a company salesman,

Chapter 12. Downward Spiral

spokesman, and author. Gregory would train him to sell the company's product door to door for $19.95. Wills would also serve as a liaison to African American youngsters, advising them about the evils of substance abuse.

"With his wholesome image—both in his personal ideals and in his personal lifestyle," Gregory told the assembled reporters, "Frank Wills will make a perfect representative for educating our youth about the hazards of drug and alcohol abuses and dependency on nicotine and caffeine."[23] Then, with a flair reminiscent of P.T. Barnum, the two announced a plan to coauthor a cookbook called *The Dick Gregory/Frank Wills Watergate Break-In Cook Book.*

Concluding the news conference, Gregory couldn't resist commenting on Wills' actions at Watergate. "Here is the man who has done what the Russians have threatened to do, but he did it without a shot fired," Gregory remarked. Wills should be treated like a hero instead of a felon. "Here is the man who brought the mightiest government in the world to its knees."[24]

Appearing happier than he had been in more than a decade, Wills said that "after twelve frustrating years, someone has exhibited a sincere interest in my welfare."[25]

Wills claimed that he was offered an annual salary of $50,000. But before he could earn that money, he had unfinished business to address.

Shortly after the press conference, Wills began serving his sentence. After three weeks in jail, for unknown reasons (possibly to spare the Georgia state court system from further public exposure), he was released early. After a two-year battle in the courts over a twelve-month sentence for shoplifting a twelve-dollar pair of tennis shoes, Wills ended up spending a fraction of his sentence behind bars. Rather than mull over the ordeal, he put it behind him and went to work for Dick Gregory.

Most of the time, Wills was on the road promoting Gregory's products and speaking to youth groups about the dangers of drugs.

Watergate's Forgotten Hero

When he wasn't working, he was home with his aging mother in North Augusta. But she was not the only woman in his life.

***

JoAnn Hooper was twelve years younger than Frank Wills. She was living on Five Notch Road, only a few houses away from Marjorie's house, when the courtship began. It started, as most do, with some innocent flirtation. "Frank walked right by my house every morning," she recalled.[26] He entered the woods, went for a hike, and when he returned, hung around her house. He would make cracks about her unkempt yard, which needed raking. One morning, Hooper was outside on her porch with her "hair rollers, fluffy shoes and a house coat," and Wills, strolling by, playfully told her "a decent woman wouldn't go out like that."[27]

"I didn't know it at the time, but he was baiting me," she reminisced fondly. "And that was the beginning of our relationship."[28]

Hooper was not aware of Wills' role in Watergate. Only twelve years old when the scandal broke, she had no knowledge of the event. When Hooper found out her new boyfriend was somehow linked to Watergate, she wanted to learn more about it. Years later, she looked back at her very first question and couldn't help but see the humor in it. She asked a neighbor, "What is a Watergate?"[29]

It didn't take long for Hooper to understand Watergate's political significance, but Wills was hesitant to discuss his involvement. "To him, it was negative," Hooper recalled. Still, she was interested in getting to know Frank Wills, not the night watchman. "I liked Frank for being Frank."[30]

When he was home, Wills spent time with Hooper, cooking her salmon croquettes, cleaning her house, and lounging around. Known around the neighborhood as a "fun guy," on one occasion Wills piled a few children in an abandoned shopping cart and pushed them down a steep hill.[31] Wills found it amusing, but Hooper feared for the youths' safety.

"Frank, if you flip these children, somebody is going to get

Chapter 12. Downward Spiral

hurt," she'd yell. He shrugged her off and continued to go up and down the hill. "My heart would almost jump out of my flesh," she remembered.[32]

Wills' romantic relationship did not make him more of a social being. A homebody, he could be found reading books on various topics, playing with his cat, "Happy," or performing household chores. With the exception of Preston Sykes, he had no friends to speak of. His Watergate fame served only to make him more and more suspicious of people. Was someone befriending him because he was a local celebrity? Was it because they wanted to spread rumors? Did he or she have a secret agenda, planning to embarrass him publicly for financial gain? Socially awkward and disposed to conspiracy theories, Wills did not take these concerns lightly.

Within a year of their relationship, Hooper told Wills that she was pregnant. "We talked about getting married and told people we were married," she looked back nostalgically.[33] Wills was excited about having a baby and left no doubt about how much he was going to take care of the child, joking that he would buy him or her a Rolls-Royce. Although Wills maintained his residence at his mother's, he was planning to spend most of his time at his girlfriend's house.

At the beginning of her pregnancy, Hooper remembered that Wills was helpful, offering whatever limited support he could provide. But as the pregnancy grew further along, she realized that Wills would be unable to maintain a consistent presence in his child's life. He was immature and struggling with who he was. How could he put his own troubles aside and take responsibility for a child? Hooper knew her thirty-six-year-old boyfriend was not ready to be a father. "It was one of the reasons we didn't get married," she revealed to the author.[34]

In November 1984, Hooper gave birth to a healthy baby girl, Angel. When Angel was born, her parents were no longer a couple, but they remained friends, and Wills stayed loosely involved in his daughter's life. Busy with Gregory's Health Enterprises, he was frequently out of town on business. He would call from time to time, and when he returned to North Augusta, he always had a gift for Angel.

Aside from Hooper, however, the real constant in Angel's life was Grandma Marjorie. "His mom took up the slack," Hooper recalled. "She was instrumental in helping me [raise Angel]."[35]

During those years, Hooper noted that Angel was the "daughter Margie never had."[36] Grandmother and granddaughter had a special bond. "Angel could do no wrong" in the eyes of her grandmother, who now had another person to pray for when she attended church.[37] Hardly a day went by that Marjorie didn't seize an opportunity to be with Angel.

**

In 1987, another Watergate break-in milestone anniversary was approaching: number fifteen. For Wills, this would be the first time he could report to the media that he was doing reasonably well, assuming that his current situation remained intact.

At a public relations campaign for the "Bahamian Diet Plan" in Fort Walton, Florida, Dick Gregory introduced Wills as one of the plan's counselors (though he had no formal training).[38] During that event, Wills "discovered a nasty side of Mr. Gregory."[39] He would never go into depth about what transpired (he likely signed a nondisclosure agreement), but a falling-out ensued. Gregory bought his once-star employee a one-way ticket to Washington, D.C.

With no reason to stay in the capital, Wills returned to North Augusta. For the moment, he planned to "live off" his soon-to-be exhausted savings.[40] Actually, money was undoubtedly the prime reason for his falling-out with Gregory. In a few years, the health guru would be in hot water with the IRS, who penalized him for over a million dollars in back taxes and fines.

As Wills' job with Health Enterprises came to an abrupt end, his book deal with Alex Haley also collapsed. The author had contact with Wills on at least one occasion after their meeting in Ruffin's office in Augusta. At this particular session, Haley interviewed Wills

Chapter 12. Downward Spiral

for approximately ninety minutes. Light and conversational, Haley, a former journalist who got his start writing for *Reader's Digest* and *Playboy*, was an expert interviewer, making sure the conversation flowed and his subject was relaxed. He jumped around during the interview, trying to cover all aspects of Wills' life: his childhood, his mother, Job Corps, his recent arrest, his son Eugene, episodes of depression, and, of course, the break-in. He never challenged Wills' responses, but it was clear that he was hoping to write another blockbuster, and Wills' life—unlike *Roots'* Kunta Kinte's or Malcolm X's—had neither the drama nor the "action," as Haley put it, that would result in the kind of book he was interested in writing.[41] Overcommitted to other projects to boot, Haley decided to abandon the memoir.

For Wills, these setbacks could not have occurred at a worse time. On the fifteen-year anniversary of Watergate, the media focused on the whereabouts and circumstances of the principals involved in the event, and most were doing better than ever.

After a decade-and-a-half effort to repair his tarnished legacy, Richard Nixon seemed to be well on his way, having recently graced the cover of *Newsweek* and declaring that he was back! His cronies were also doing well. Instead of being shunned, many were living the good life. A few were sought after to fill various positions (especially G. Gordon Liddy, who now had a guest role in the hit television show *Miami Vice*).

When a Duke University political science professor was asked about this change in public opinion, he blamed it on American "amnesia." The entire country had forgotten "what these guys actually did."[42]

To Wills' relief, the media made no mention of his separation from Dick Gregory or the aborted book deal with Alex Haley, although his run-in with the law was often cited. As for his current whereabouts, most of the news outlets were intentionally kept in the dark, as evidenced by the *Augusta Chronicle*, which reported that he was residing in DC. When Marjorie was asked, she responded

Watergate's Forgotten Hero

"she didn't know where he works or lives."[43] Actually, he had been living with her in North Augusta, employed as a gardener and as a part-time hair stylist in Augusta near Paine College, a historical Black university. Apparently, "coeds [were making] a beeline to his workplace."[44]

***

The years had finally caught up to Marjorie. Strong-minded, independent, and committed to her church, at eighty years of age, she still worked regularly as a domestic for wealthy white families. In 1990, she suffered a stroke.

Marjorie had led a simple, uncomplicated life. It revolved around her son, her church, and her granddaughter Angel (why Frank's son Eugene was not in the picture is unclear). Unable to afford a professional caregiver or a nursing facility after her stroke, Wills provided round-the-clock care. In a show of unusual selfless strength that no one who knew him well could have imagined, Wills doted on his mother every day while she remained bedridden. As her caregiver, Wills had to wrestle with the emotional strain, as well as the financial issues, posed by long-term illness.

Wills had been receiving food stamps, but they were discontinued in 1991. When he filed for Social Security Disability Benefits, he was denied. Essentially, mother and son were living on her $450 Social Security income. Wills made the best of it as he rolled up his sleeves, bathed his mother, cooked for her, kept the house in order, and paid the bills.

When neighbors came over, Wills stood by his mother's bedside. "He'd do anything for his mother," a visitor recalled.[45] Hooper helped out too. But the one person who raised Marjorie's spirits the most was her granddaughter Angel. When Hooper brought Angel over to the house, Marjorie's "face would light up like it was Christmas."[46]

As June 17, 1992, approached, Wills, consumed by his duties as a caregiver, hadn't fully prepared for the twentieth anniversary of the break-in. Aside from Attorney General John Mitchell, who had died

Chapter 12. Downward Spiral

in 1988, most of the other Nixon Administration officials were still alive, living comfortably, if not outright lavishly. G. Gordon Liddy and John Dean remained in the public spotlight, while Nixon was beginning to show his age (he was seventy-nine).

More so this time than previous anniversaries, Wills was "besieged" in North Augusta by journalists, news photographers, and television crews. "Vans with satellite dishes," reported the *Augusta Chronicle*'s John Roberts, were parked on Wills' dirt driveway while he fielded phone calls inside his home for interview requests.[47] From *People* to *USA Today*, many of the national media outlets wanted an update about his life. Some went beyond the usual short story.

The *Baltimore Sun* published a lengthy profile piece on the famous night watchman ("Remember Frank Wills?"), while the *Atlanta Journal-Constitution* editors wrote an impressive tribute to him:

> For 20 years we have followed the Watergate break-in story—the investigation, the trials, the prison terms. The guilty gave speeches, wrote books, made career changes, and we devoured it all. Yet very little attention has been paid to Frank Wills, the Watergate security guard who observed an irregularity and performed his job properly. Without the conscientious response of Frank Wills, no further action would or could have taken place to bring to justice a corrupt government.[48]

The *Washington Post*'s Karlyn Barker, who was the first reporter to interview Wills following the break-in, wrote an article about the famous landmarks of the Watergate saga. She even included Wills' apartment building. That once-unimpressive residential structure had become a "fashionable town house," and the night watchman's former apartment was "rented by three friends who were children when the Watergate scandal unfolded and who had no idea of the house's link to Watergate history."[49]

When it came to Watergate coverage, no matter how laudatory, nothing seemed to please Wills. On the one hand, he acknowledged that he "hadn't really thought about it (the anniversary) until they (the media) started calling."[50] Yet, he was obviously focused on

Watergate's Forgotten Hero

the coverage. He dwelled on minor slights, particularly when he was referred to as the "Watergate complex security guard," without mention of his name.[51] He remained adamant that if it weren't for him, there would not have been a Watergate scandal. And the topic of race ignited his usual refrain: "I know if I had a white face things would have been different. Everybody knows that."[52]

When a Virginia-based newspaper reporter came to visit him at his mother's home, his tone was softer and more amendable. Neighbors were over at the time, and Wills cooked "smothered squash with onions, barbecued chicken and cornbread."[53] The reporter described him as chatty and personable, uncharacteristic for Wills, especially in the presence of the media. As he participated in the interview and entertained guests, he spoon-fed his ailing mother.

On November 5, 1992, Marjorie Wills passed away. A memorial service was held for her at Mount Transfiguration Baptist Church in North Augusta, where she regularly attended.

As with so many instances in Frank Wills' life, events took an unexpected turn. When Marjorie's immediate family (with whom she was not exceptionally close) discovered that she had chosen to donate her body to the Medical College of Augusta, they directed blame toward her son. He had nothing to do with the decision, nor was any money exchanged, because federal law prohibits payment for a body donated to science. Marjorie simply did not want any of her meager savings to cover the costs of her burial. Whether it was intentional or not, she had neglected to inform her siblings and other family members of her last wishes. Just at a time when Wills needed all the support available, he was held culpable for the donation, causing an irreversible rift between him and his aunts and uncles, many of whom resided nearby in the Five Notch neighborhood.

In her will, Marjorie had deeded the house and provided a modest sum of money to her son. She also left a small amount of her savings to her granddaughter Angel. While Hooper and Angel

Chapter 12. Downward Spiral

Marjorie Wills' North Augusta home, which Frank inherited in 1992, and occupied until his death eight years later (courtesy Carol McCabe Booker).

had each other for support, Wills was alone. Marjorie was "his backbone, his world," and now she was gone. How could he carry on?

"She supported him in every way," Hooper said. "After she passed, there was not a lot to keep him moving forward."[54]

CHAPTER 13

"I've Done My Work"

Without Marjorie in his life, those who knew Frank Wills believed he would fall further into the depths of loneliness and depression. He proved them wrong.

To keep his grief manageable, he stayed busy repairing his newly acquired house. Having inherited enough funds to purchase the necessary materials, he fixed the leaky roof and the rotted front porch steps and applied a much-needed fresh coat of pink paint to the exterior. Once completed, he took over the master bedroom and decorated it with his awards. In the midst of the repair work, Wills frequently visited Hooper and his daughter Angel.

"Frank was my best friend. We talked every day," Hooper reminisced.[1]

He also kept in touch with his childhood friend Preston Sykes and with other neighbors, who recall a tall, goofy, older man whom all the children enjoyed horsing around with. Wearing his signature white carpenter pants, white tank top, and white Converse shoes, Wills was all smiles around the youngsters, likely because they didn't know about Watergate and wouldn't bombard him with questions.

"He had us laughing all the time," recalled Stephanie Coleman, a nearby resident.[2]

Aside from his playful antics, neighbors enjoyed eating his Southern home-style cooking. Rather than rely solely on a grocery store, Wills gathered some ingredients in the woods near his home to make his specialty, "pork salad," or another one of his favorite dishes, Mexican cornbread.[3]

A frequent patron of the local library, Wills used his bicycle to

Chapter 13. "I've Done My Work"

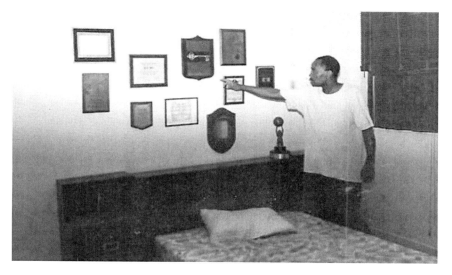

Frank's bedroom, decorated with the awards he had received (courtesy Carol McCabe Booker).

transport himself to the facility. He could be found reading books and writing in his journal in the shaded woods, "leaning against a tree trunk."[4] Friends and family believe he was writing his autobiography, although no one knows how much he wrote or what happened to the pages; some remember that he made notations frequently in a diary (whereabouts unknown). To stay afloat financially, he worked as a gardener, usually for elderly residents who were unable to tend their own yards. For those who employed him (and this applied to friends and neighbors as well), the topic of Watergate was off-limits.

Since everything he did was publicized, Wills remained guarded and few if any people were able to get close to him. That didn't seem to be the case when the media came to town. "Everyone all of a sudden knew Frank," according to resident and local historian Wayne O'Bryant. When the reporters packed up and finally left Wills alone, as O'Bryant put it succinctly, "so did everyone else."[5]

As much as Wills tried to avoid the press corps, he never failed to welcome *JET* magazine's Simeon Booker. His articles were always

One of Frank's pleasures, cooking in his kitchen (1993) (courtesy Carol McCabe Booker).

sympathetic to the famous night watchman, and the one published in March 1993 was no exception: "Frank Wills, Watergate Hero, Tells of Hard Times He Faces."

"Neighbors say the grieving black man is 'at the end of the road' and 'is desperate for a helping hand,'" Booker informed his readers. The neighbors' concerns were not unfounded. Indeed, Wills claimed he was destitute and received government assistance for a "disability," the nature of which he did not specify.[6]

"There are no rugs on the house floor and cold air rushes between cracks of the wooden floor," Booker went on.[7] Wills used a wood-burning stove because the gas and electricity were turned off. For his bathing needs, "water is heated on top of the stove. He hand washes what clothes he has." The only heat he had was from a

Chapter 13. "I've Done My Work"

Mowing the lawn at his home (1993) (courtesy Carol McCabe Booker).

"kerosene heater and they can be very dangerous. He also uses a kerosene lamp for light." During the summer, neighbors would give him ice cubes placed in a Styrofoam chest.

"Frank is in need of glasses," Booker noted. "When reading his Bible, he uses a magnifying glass."

Reading the Bible (1993) (courtesy Carol McCabe Booker).

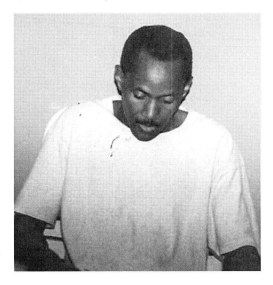

Desperate, Wills expressed the hope that "somebody somewhere will reach down and try to help me."[8]

Booker's account had an immediate impact.

The *Baltimore Sun*'s Liz Atwood reported that the *JET* article resulted in donations of clothing, food, and money. She also stated that Wills was thinking about a return to DC in hopes of securing employment. In nearby Annapolis, a fundraiser for Wills was organized by the nonprofit organization Treat Every American Right (T.E.A.R.). Its founder, James Kilby, believed that Wills was a prime candidate for his organization's mission, "to reach back to those people who have made a contribution to society and didn't get full recognition. Frank is an unsung hero."[9] At $25 a plate, event organizers were hoping to raise $2,000. Fewer than forty people attended, netting only $750.

In the [Washington, D.C.] *Afro-American*, reporter Lawanza Spears characterized Wills as a poor, Black man "that history forgot [and] ... no one seems to be concerned about."[10]

Not everyone agreed with the latter part of the assessment.

Journalist Roger Simon, who had written sympathetically of Wills a decade and a half earlier, had second thoughts. In his editorial, Simon portrayed Wills as a frequent complainer, someone who had been given many opportunities to do something with his life and did not seize them when he had the chance. During a phone interview, Wills complained to Simon. "I laid my life on the line that night. I saved this country from God knows what. I never got the publicity that the others got. I thought I did a million dollars' worth of service for this country."[11] The DNC, he continued his rant, did not give him a job, money, or even a "thank you."[12] Simon reminded him that the Democrats had expressed their gratitude at a banquet, where he received a plaque. "I couldn't eat a plaque!" Wills countered. "I've served my country, and I have been crucified for it!"[13]

Simon decided to pass on this comment, but when it came to Wills' other often-repeated argument—those who were criminally negligent in Watergate had financially benefited while he, the hero,

Chapter 13. "I've Done My Work"

had not—the journalist addressed it head-on: "[The] Watergate criminals who did profit not only had college educations, but lifetimes of powerful contacts in business, government and the media." That fact, Simon argued, "seems to escape Wills."[14]

Simon did his homework. He interviewed the Rev. Alfred Redd of Augusta, who had known Wills since the 1970s. "Frank needs someone to point him in the right direction," Redd told Simon. "A baby will not learn to walk if he continues to crawl. At some point a baby must get off his knees and walk."[15] Simon also interviewed Booker, who remained sympathetic to Wills, but conceded, he has "a feeling that the world owes him something and that isn't true." He's been offered employment and educational opportunities, Booker explained, but Wills did not follow through. "When I heard they were going to give him a fund-raiser.... I said: 'For what?' He doesn't need fund-raisers. He needed guidance."[16]

Over the next four years, Wills continued to live alone on a bare-bones budget in his mother's former home and stay busy by traversing the woods and doing odd jobs for neighbors, earning enough to get by and keep himself from starving.

***

June 1997 marked the silver anniversary of the break-in. With the passage of two and half decades, there were fewer Watergate figures alive. H.R. Haldeman had died in 1993; Nixon a year later. With fewer persons to interview, Frank Wills was the subject of more in-depth stories, no longer relegated to the *whatever happened to ...* section. Greater coverage, however, did little to appease the forty-nine-year-old ex-security guard, who still felt unappreciated.

"Somebody who's doing his job and intercepts a situation should be recognized," he told the *Christian Science Monitor*. "Why couldn't they have a Frank Wills day?"[17]

Of all the interviews Frank Wills participated in over the years, the one conducted by *NBC Nightly News* during the 25th-year-anniversary period attracted the most interest. Anchor

Watergate's Forgotten Hero

Tom Brokaw, from his studio in New York City's Rockefeller Plaza, introduced the segment: "One of the bit players, but an important one in the unfolding drama of Watergate was Frank Wills, the alert security guard who started it all."[18] He then turned it over to Gwen Ifill, one of only a handful of African American reporters at NBC.

On assignment in North Augusta, Ifill was viewed walking slowly in a rural area accompanied by a tall, lean, middle-aged man in a white polo shirt and military camouflage trousers, limping alongside her.

"To find Frank Wills, you have to travel to a dead end of a dirt road," she began her story.[19] Ifill met with Wills at his small, two-bedroom cottage with a front porch and a fully screened entry door to keep out the mosquitoes. The dated interior design and decor were minimal but certainly livable. When television cameras panned his bedroom, the wall was covered with more than a dozen plaques—among them, one from the DNC.

"Frank Wills' fall from the spotlight was swift," Ifill continued. "He never became the national hero he thought he should have been, and he's back home in South Carolina, destitute."

With a national audience tuning in, Wills didn't miss a beat, declaring that he was "used" by both Democratic and African American leaders to further their own goals, not to help a man in need. As hopeless as Wills' comment sounded, Ifill concluded the interview on an upbeat (though curious) point. Frank Wills, she told her viewers, "is convinced that there is another big moment in store for him. He was in the right place at the right time once before. Why not again?"[20]

***

Frank Wills spent the holiday season of 1997 alone and wandering around town. Nat Irvin, Jr. (son of Wills' high school history teacher and advisor, the Rev. Nathaniel Irvin), who was traveling on Five Notch Road on Christmas Eve, would always regret not

Chapter 13. "I've Done My Work"

offering a lift to his father's former student, whom he spotted trudging through the rain, forlorn and barely recognizable.

Around this time, family, friends, and neighbors thought Wills was exhibiting signs of mental health problems, or so it seemed. Wills' complaint about having unshakeable headaches confirmed at the very least a physical disorder. The mother of his daughter, JoAnn Hooper, who ran into him from time to time, noticed that his memory was slipping. When she called him on the phone or spoke with him as he walked by her house, he couldn't recall previous conversations. Hooper suggested that he see a doctor, but he refused because he lacked health insurance.

Popular Augusta–based radio show personality Austin Rhodes recognized something was wrong with the local legend. As host of a live radio show, Rhodes received his fair share of strange callers who seemed a bit unhinged. Wills was one of them.

When he first called Rhodes, Wills identified himself only by his first name. Rhodes didn't think anything of it until another local news broadcaster notified Rhodes that "it was Frank Wills calling the show."[21] When Wills called in again, this time Rhodes was ready. During the commercial break, Rhodes picked up the phone:

> RHODES: "Is this Frank Wills, the Watergate guy?"
> WILLS: "Yes, sir. I thought you knew."
> RHODES: "Frank, you only identified yourself as Frank. How would I know?"
> WILLS: "I guess that's right. Well, I don't want to talk about any of that."
> RHODES: "Okay, well, I understand that. I'm not going to pressure you, but at least it's good to touch base with you and figure out who you are."[22]

Wills continued to call Rhodes, and occasionally made a reference to Watergate, such as "I appreciate you going after these politicians. You gotta be careful because you get on their list, you never get off of it. I oughta know."[23] As he spoke with Wills more, Rhodes realized something was amiss. At first he thought Wills was intoxicated, but after a while he knew that was not the case.

"He was saying crazier and crazier things," Rhodes remembered.

Watergate's Forgotten Hero

"He started talking about the mayor, and Batman would come up." Rhodes estimated that Wills called his 3:00 p.m. show about twenty-five times. "I think he was suffering from his brain tumor years before he died."[24]

In 2000, Frank Wills, 52, was no longer pedaling around town on his black bicycle or pushing a lawn mower. His neighbors grew concerned. Besides the memory lapses, Wills was no longer spending time on his porch or roaming around the woods as they'd see him often. Aside from Hooper, there were only a few who knew the severity of Wills' condition. Martez Mims, Wills' second cousin, recalled an episode when she saw him from her car aimlessly walking around North Augusta like he was a "hobo."

"Frank," she pulled over and yelled, "you need to let someone help you."[25]

He waved her off.

Knowing he was in bad shape, the Reverend Irvin made periodic trips to his former student's home, bringing food and money to help with the bills. Wills, as Irvin recalled, was "disillusioned" over Watergate. "This is what he expressed to me. He felt what he did was not appreciated by people. He felt betrayed."[26] The retired teacher was probably the last person to hear Wills vent about his betrayal, but that did not diminish his pivotal role in Watergate, as far as Irvin was concerned. "I never thought I would teach history to one who would make history."[27]

When neighbors came over to check on him, they saw him gravely sick and in bed. One of them notified Shirley Wills, the wife of Eddie Wills, Frank's cousin, who lived a short walk away. Unaware that he had been suffering, Shirley went over to Wills' house and saw that he was in a near-vegetative state. "I came back and told Eddie, who told me to call the ambulance."[28] When the ambulance arrived, it took Wills to Augusta's University Hospital. Since he was only fifty-two years old, family, friends, and neighbors expected him to pull through. "I didn't think he was going to pass," Hooper recalled sadly.[29]

Chapter 13. "I've Done My Work"

Once he was admitted, however, Wills' condition deteriorated quickly.

On September 27, 2000, Frank Wills, the security guard who alerted police to a break-in at the Watergate Office Building, a singular event that had altered the course of American history and led to the only resignation of a U.S. president, died of an inoperable brain tumor.

For a man who felt he had never received his fair share of the public's attention, news of his passing proved otherwise. The death of America's most famous night watchman prompted obituaries worldwide (Canada, Europe, New Zealand) and in nearly every daily newspaper across the United States. While the headlines varied slightly—"Man Who Discovered Watergate Break-In Dies"; "Guard Who Blew Whistle on Watergate Break-In Dies"; "Man Who Tipped Authorities to Watergate Break-In Dies"—the majority of papers published the same *Associated Press* article. Even the *Savannah Herald*, in the city of Wills' birth, used that piece, mentioning little about Wills' roots in East Savannah. The major papers ran lengthier articles, focusing on the break-in and his decades-long downward spiral.

The *Los Angeles Times* described Wills as "the forgotten hero, the embittered hero.... Nothing in his life had prepared him for the hot lights of fame."[30] Along similar lines, the *New York Times* viewed Wills as a man who "struggled with celebrity and joblessness after being hailed as hero."[31] National Public Radio's Scott Simon summed up Wills' passing best in a truly eloquent sentence: "The man who was in the right place at the right time for his country couldn't seem to find a right place to be after that."[32] The *Washington Post*, which had taken the lead on the Watergate story three decades earlier, ran the most in-depth obituary. Providing a detailed timeline of Wills' life, the *Post* portrayed him as a "bitter" man who "never successfully cash[ed] in on his contribution to the Watergate saga."[33] In a follow-up piece, Bob Woodward, possibly regretting the exclusion of Wills' name from his bestseller *All the President's Men*, set the record straight about the night watchman. "He's the only one in Watergate

Watergate's Forgotten Hero

who did his job perfectly. Calling the police was one of the most important phone calls in American history, and it was so simple and so basic."[34]

***

When it was reported that Frank Wills had died of a brain tumor, the implication was that the tumor was a form of cancer. That was accurate, but it was not the actual cause of his demise. Wills had hidden his true illness from family, friends, and neighbors—he died from complications related to AIDS. On his death certificate, the coroner listed the cause of death as lymphoma, a malignant cancer that commonly develops when a person is infected with AIDS.

Even after NBA superstar Earvin "Magic" Johnson announced publicly that he was HIV positive in 1991 (at the time he was among a growing list of celebrities to be stricken with the disease, including Hollywood icon Rock Hudson and tennis legend Arthur Ashe), AIDS remained a social taboo throughout the 1990s and beyond. AIDS patients were often too embarrassed to admit having the deadly disease because it could lead to the loss of a job as well as being socially ostracized. As a result, aside from a handful of heroic activists, the vast majority of AIDS patients lied about their illness. So did their families—thousands of AIDS victims' obituaries purposely concealed the true cause of their passing. Death was triggered by "heart problems," "sleeping sickness," "liver cancer," or "diabetes."[35] In some cases, a victim simply passed away "after a long illness."

Although the origins of the disease in the United States can be traced to white gay New Yorkers and San Franciscans, by the early 1990s, the fastest-growing number of new cases were African American heterosexuals, and by the middle of the decade, Blacks had "surpassed" whites in "caseloads" even though statistically they made up only 15 percent of the nation's population.[36] By 2000, AIDS had migrated from urban centers to the rural South. Lacking access to medical care and sexual education, many young and middle-aged impoverished African American adults living in the region were

Chapter 13. "I've Done My Work"

the most vulnerable. Usually, all it took was for one sexually active infected person in these insular geographical social networks (Blacks sleeping only with Blacks, whites sleeping only with whites, and so forth) to spread the virus. Since there was little or no testing, most carriers were not aware they were infected until it was too late.

Frank Wills lived in South Carolina, where more than 70 percent of those who suffered from HIV/AIDS were African Americans, one of the highest infection rates of any state. In fact, people of color in Washington, D.C., where Wills also spent a significant amount of time, made up of an even more disproportionate share (82 percent) of AIDS victims—the highest in the nation. Given Wills' age, limited education, economic situation, and location, based on the statistical data his odds of exposure to HIV/AIDS were greatly increased.

It is not known how or when Wills got the disease. There is a possibility that it might have been transmitted by blood transfusion, which Wills received in the early 1980s (before blood banks were required to screen their blood supply). It is more likely, however, that Wills, who was neither gay nor a drug user, acquired AIDS through heterosexual transmission. Since Wills passed away in 2000, it is probable that he contracted HIV/AIDS sometime between 1985 and 1990.

Although he kept his illness a secret, there were indications that something was wrong. In a 1993 *JET* article, for instance, Wills had mentioned he was receiving government assistance for a "disability," but he did not disclose what it was.[37] It is likely that he received subsidies to cover the costs of antiretroviral drugs needed to manage the disease. In that same article, there were photographs of Frank Wills wearing a short-sleeved shirt and shorts. If you compare his somewhat emaciated image here to pictures from a few years earlier, there is a noticeable difference. In March 1994, Wills was cited in *The Advocate*, a national gay magazine, about his plan to blend "herbs, roots and other 'everyday things' into a tonic that will kill HIV."[38] During the first two decades of the disease, it was common to hear about wishful patients creating exotic potions or flying around

Watergate's Forgotten Hero

the world looking for "healers," "psychic surgery," or "snake oil," anything that could lead to a cure.[39]

Radio DJ Austin Rhodes was probably correct when he asserted that Wills was "suffering from his brain tumor years before he died."[40] Given the innumerable drugs AIDS patients ingested, there were often side effects, sometimes mental as well as physical. Journalist Randy Shilts, in his award-winning book *And the Band Played On*, described a patient who was one day "friendly, wonderful, terrific, fun, and caring" and then, as the disease progressed, became "crazy, senile, and psychotic."[41]

Fortunately for Wills, treatment was not too far away. He likely sought it through the federally funded Ryan White Program at University Hospital in Augusta. Named after the famous Indiana teenager who contracted AIDS from an unscreened blood transfusion in 1984, the program provides medical and support services to patients. The treatment Wills received lessened the pain, but it was not enough to keep him alive.

***

Three days following Wills' death, on September 30, a funeral was held for him at his mother's church, Mount Transfiguration Baptist in North Augusta. What was anticipated by many to be a media spectacle turned out to be low-key, described as a "simple, quiet graveside service."[42] Family, friends, and congregants buried him that sunny morning in the cemetery located a short distance from the church. Retired chaplain and civil rights activist Alfred Redd began his eulogy of Frank Wills with the opening verse of the song "I've Done My Work."[43]

Wills was buried next to his mother's gravestone, as well as his cousins, Margie Ann and Josie, and his grandparents, Ida Boeler and Cornelius Wills. The Augusta NAACP branch paid the expenses.

Before leaving the cemetery, several of the mourners voiced frustration over the various Watergate anniversaries, criticizing the

156

Chapter 13. "I've Done My Work"

Frank Wills' gravestone at Mount Transfiguration Baptist Church cemetery in North Augusta, South Carolina (author's photograph).

Watergate's Forgotten Hero

media for having periodically "invaded" their quiet community. But most of all, they expressed sadness that society as a whole did not care enough for the man who saved America.

Five months after he died, a tombstone was unveiled for the forgotten hero. Paid for by relatives and friends, the monument is larger than almost any of the other ones erected at the cemetery and is visible from more than a hundred feet away.

With no one willing to take over the mortgage, Wills' home was foreclosed a year after he died. Hooper tried to purchase it from the bank, but her offer wasn't enough. The house was sold and the new owner tore it down. Although some of Wills' belongings, such as an old passport and his plaques, were given to family and friends, most of what was left (including, perhaps, his diary and partially completed autobiography) was thrown away.

Epilogue

In November 2016, on the final day of my research trip to North Augusta, I scheduled my last interview with Frank Wills' first cousin, Eddie Wills. When I was directed to his home by a neighbor, Eddie's wife, Shirley, greeted me and my father (and traveling companion). Appearing a bit perplexed about why this white, thirty-something male with a man-purse strapped over his shoulder and a seventy-four-year-old, distinguished-looking gentleman with a New York accent were standing on her driveway, she listened as I calmly explained my intentions. She soon relaxed and told me her husband would be home later that evening; we could stop by then.

Although they were blood relatives, grew up in the same neighborhood, and were born on the exact same day and year, Eddie and Frank were on opposite ends of the spectrum. Unlike his introverted cousin, Eddie was an outgoing fellow who graduated from high school, grew up with two loving parents and siblings, raised a family of his own, and was active in the community.

He welcomed me into his house. I sat down on a stool in his kitchen. He stood a few feet away, on the opposite side of the countertop. My father sat nearby. Right away, I sensed this was not Eddie's first interview about his famous cousin, and probably it wouldn't be his last.

To some, it may have seemed Eddie was resentful of Frank receiving all the attention. I admit that was my initial perception too. Aside from his mother, there were few others who knew Frank as long and as well as Eddie. Since he moved to North Augusta at five years of age, Frank had been a part of Eddie's life. They were

Epilogue

never best friends, or very close. But their lives had intersected. They attended the same schools, had the same friends, went to the same family gatherings and the same church, and had similar experiences growing up in the segregated South. Eddie didn't see Frank's life the way most of America did. He saw it through a different set of lenses.

Eddie was wary of the views that neighbors, friends, nosy visitors, relatives, and an intrusive media espoused about his famous cousin: *He did not get the respect he deserved. Everyone involved with Watergate prospered except him. The Democrats should have done more. Black politicians did not do enough for him. Those who befriended him exploited his fame.*

For Eddie, the story of Frank Wills wasn't about politics, money or betrayal. It was simply about a member of his family, who by chance had been involved in a monumental historical event, was ill equipped to cope with it, and in the end it devoured him.

"I frankly wish it had not been him [who detected the Watergate burglars]. I think he probably would have been alive today if it hadn't happened," Eddie said that evening.[1]

Before we left, he showed me one of his cousin's possessions that he still kept: a passport Wills had used to travel to the Bahamas while working for Dick Gregory. I snapped a few photographs of it, thanked him for his time, and left.

I hadn't thought much about that forty-five minute interview beyond the time it took to transcribe the conversation. Then, while working on the first draft of the manuscript, it hit me. I realized that Eddie was right. Eddie was not jealous at all. It was the exact opposite. Filled with compassion for his cousin, Eddie knew Frank better than anyone else, and understood perfectly that he had been in over his head, and that nothing short of a miracle could have rescued him.

In the absence of a miracle, Frank Wills' moment as a global celebrity could not be sustained. As an *Ebony* magazine journalist pointed out, it's astounding that Wills didn't succumb to alcohol or drugs, or get caught up in the black militant movement. This is all the

Epilogue

more surprising as he learned first hand of a "double standard of justice" in the United States.[2]

In Nixonian America, if you were white and powerful, as all the president's men were, you could escape (to a large extent) accountability. Of those tried and found guilty, barring G. Gordon Liddy, none served a full sentence. When Attorney General Richard Kleindienst had his day in court, the judge sentenced him to one month in jail, "noting that he was a family man and a good Christian."[3] Because their crimes were defined as *white-collar*, it was assumed that these men were not hardened criminals. They were not a danger to society; they were *just* being loyal to the president, serving the national interest. Those wielding the gavel failed (or were unwilling) to recognize that the conspirators organized burglaries, committed perjury, violated federal election laws, and misappropriated large sums of money.

On the opposite end of the spectrum was Frank Wills—Black, poor, and uneducated. It didn't matter what crime he committed; he was destined to become a victim of the criminal justice system.

Undoubtedly, race factored into Frank Wills' downfall.

In the second half of twentieth century America, most whites south of the Mason-Dixon Line (and many north of it) shared a common belief: "They start off wanting a pair of tennis shoes and you never know where their lusts and luxurious habits will lead them next."[4] Lock them up! Judge Slaton may not have been motivated by Wills' skin color, but his ruling nonetheless mirrored popular sentiment.

He was raised in a state where African Americans were relegated to second-class citizenship. Certainly, some people of color rose above it, but most, like Frank Wills, were victimized by it. Economically deprived, socially restricted, and relegated to an inferior educational system, the hero of Watergate had neither the background nor the inherent skills to survive his encounter with instant stardom.

Yet his fame remains intact. Frank Wills has been featured in songs, novels, games, a mural (in Tulsa), a comedy skit, and movies,

Epilogue

including more recently Steven Spielberg's film *The Post*, where he's portrayed by actor JaQwan J. Kelly in the final scene. He even has a street ("Frank Wills Place") named after him in Newburg, Maryland. He has been praised in congressional testimony and is regularly mentioned during those routine five-year anniversaries of the break-in. His "semi-literate scrawl" on page 48 of a visitor ledger from the Watergate Office Building is now preserved by the National Archives.[5]

Wills would have been surprised to learn that he is also viewed as a pioneer whistleblower. As is the case with many whistleblowers, "if they could, [they would] go back in time and change their initial decision," Consumer Financial Protection Bureau's Senior Counsel Nina Schichor maintained in a recent study.[6]

Solely focusing on Wills' detection of the break-in obscures some of the key "what ifs" that easily could have derailed the arrests of the perpetrators. What if the burglars' ringleader James McCord had not reapplied the tape on the latch, which was unnecessary since he and his cohorts were already in the building? What if Officer Dennis Stephenson, who first received the burglary call, had responded in his marked police cruiser? The vehicle likely would have been identified by the lookout man in the Howard Johnson's motel. What if intern Bruce Givner had left earlier in the evening, allowing more time for the burglars to case the DNC office and escape undetected? Or, what if CREEP hadn't been formed with the intention of sabotaging their opponents' operation and had focused on what reelection committees normally do—raising money?

But suppose the only change in the course of events was Frank Wills.

If Wills hadn't made that historic phone call to DC Metro Police, President Nixon might have escaped scrutiny and would instead be regarded as one of the most successful modern presidents. According to presidential chronicler Theodore White, Nixon was on track to become "one of the major Presidents of the twentieth century, in a rank just after Franklin Roosevelt."[7] Presidential rankings aside, if

Epilogue

the conspirators were not held accountable, the very fabric of our constitutional system would have been irreparably damaged. Princeton historian Sean Wilentz explains it best: "Had Nixon succeeded in evading detection or frustrating his accusers, he would have fundamentally changed the character of the federal government, vaunting the White House over Congress and the courts ... [i]n flagrant contradiction of the framers' conception of divided power and of checks and balances as the surest guarantees against tyranny...."[8]

On a lighter side, without Watergate the political lexicon would be less colorful today. Phrases such as "deep-six," "smoking gun," "stonewalling," and "enemies list," or the "gate" suffix that's added to every political scandal, would not exist.[9]

As for the fate of Frank Wills, what if he did not perform his job properly, and failed to check those basement doors? He could have gone on to lead an uneventful existence, working as a private security guard similar to what Roderick Warrick at Brookings had done. Wills was lavishly praised by his superiors for his excellent observational skills, a key trait in the profession—a profession he had entered just as it was rapidly expanding, offering him the opportunity for seniority and upward mobility. In addition, he might have been able to have a family of his own, be a loving husband and an attentive father.

But he couldn't lead a normal life. He lived in the shadow of Watergate, plagued by massive regrets over the action he had taken on the morning of June 17, 1972. For the remainder of his life, he missed no opportunity to express his bitterness and disappointment.

Yet, this should not distract us from the indisputable fact that Frank Wills was an American hero. He deserves to be remembered.

Chapter Notes

Introductory Quote

1. "Frank Wills: The Watergate Break-In, 17 June 1972," 1989, Box 1, File 31, John B. Sanford/Robert W. Smith Collection. Mss 34. Department of Special Collections, Davidson Library, University of California, Santa Barbara.

Chapter 1

1. "Conversation No. 533-1," Nixontapes.org, June 30, 1971, http://nixontapeaudio.org/chron1/rmn_e533a.mp3. For this chapter, I relied heavily on material derived from an email interview of Bruce Givner, February 15–16, 2018, and the court transcript of United States District Court for the District of Columbia, Watergate in Court: The Official Transcripts of the Court Proceedings of the Four Major Watergate Trials Including Indictments and Exhibits. United States of America v. George Gordon Liddy, et. al., Criminal No. 1827–72, Reel 1, January 16, 1973 (Arlington, VA: A Microfilm Project of University Publications of America, Inc., 1975).

2. Don Oldenburg, "No Leaks in This Think Tank," *Washington Post*, November 23, 1996.

3. Johanna Neuman, "Brookings Guard Who Foiled Burglars Dies," *Los Angeles Times*, March 1, 2003. See also Oldenburg, "No Leaks in This Think Tank"; and Justin Vaïsse, "In Memoriam: Henry Owen, Director of Foreign Policy at Brookings, 1969–1977," November

21, 2011, https://www.brookings.edu/blog/up-front/2011/11/21/in-memoriam-henry-owen-director-of-foreign-policy-at-brookings-1969-1977/.

4. Neuman, "Brookings Guard Who Foiled Burglars Dies."

5. "R. Warrick, Brookings Guard at Start of Watergate Scandal," [Long Island, New York] *Newsday*, March 2, 2003.

Chapter 2

1. Simeon Booker, "Untold Story of Black Hero of Watergate," *JET*, May 17, 1973. For Frank Wills' Christmas trek in the rain, see Nat Irvin, "Homespun: Little House Is Filled with Big Memoires," *Winston-Salem Journal*, January 4, 1998.

2. *Ibid.* There is a discrepancy over which guard—Fletcher Pittman or Leroy Brown—left his shift early. Author Jim Hougan said it was Brown. See his *Secret Agenda: Watergate, Deep Throat and the CIA* (New York: Random House, 1984), p. 190. Special Agent Angelo J. Lano stated it was Pittman who left prematurely. In Bob Woodward and Carl Bernstein's "Frank Wills" file, which is located in their Watergate papers housed at the Harry Ransom Center, University of Texas at Austin, there is an undated memo (likely written sometime within months of the break-in) that may have the answer. In their notes, Wills' supervisor, Major Ira O'Neal, was asked about the guard who left his shift early. At the bottom of the

Notes—Chapter 3

page, Woodward wrote: "Leroy Brown, guard who [*sic*] not there."

3. Bruce Givner with Cherie Kerr, *My Watergate Scandal Tell-All: How I Unwittingly Caused This Historic Event* (Santa Ana, CA: ExecuProv Press, 2019), p. 98.

4. Bruce Buschel, Albert Robbins, William Vitka, and edited by Rod Nordland, *The Watergate File: A Concise, Illustrated Guide to the People and Events* (New York: Flash Books, 1973), p. 11.

5. "Security Officer's Log of the Watergate Office Building Showing Entry for June 17, 1972," National Archives Identifier: 304970; Collection RN-SMOF: White House Staff Member and Office Files (Nixon Administration), 01/20/1969–08/09/1974; Records of the Watergate Special Prosecution Force, 1971–1977; Record Group 460; National Archives and Records Administration. https://www.archives.gov/historical-docs/todays-doc/?dod-date=617.

6. Hougan, *Secret Agenda*, p. 193.

7. "Interview Report," Watergate Part 87, p.179, Federal Bureau of Investigation Records: The Vault (Watergate Collection), https://vault.fbi.gov.

8. Givner, *My Watergate Scandal Tell-All*, p. 99.

9. "Bruce Givner's My Watergate Scandal Tell-All: How I Unwittingly Caused This Historic Event," https://www.youtube.com/watch?v=TmjwY6lzYtY, June 10, 2019. Accessed on May 23, 2020.

10. Givner, *My Watergate Scandal Tell-All*, p. 159.

11. *Ibid.*, p. 117.

12. *Ibid.*

13. *Ibid.*, p. 122.

14. "Howard Johnson's Motor Lodges and Restaurants advertisement," *Time*, November 6, 1972.

15. Givner, *My Watergate Scandal Tell-All*, p. 125.

16. "Security Officer's Log of the Watergate Office Building."

Chapter 3

1. Associated Press, "Marshall to Ask for Another Billion," *Savannah Morning News*, February 5, 1948. The same publication provided weather conditions for the day Wills was born. Interestingly, four months later and eleven miles down the road, in Pin Point, Georgia, another African American boy was born, Clarence Thomas, the future United States Supreme Court justice.

2. Calvin Kytle, "A Long, Dark Night for Georgia?" *Harper's Magazine*, September 1948.

3. Andrew Billingsly, *Mighty Like a River: The Black Church and Social Reform* (New York: Oxford University Press, 1999), p. 53. For the history of twentieth century black Savannah, see Stephen G.N. Tuck, *Beyond Atlanta: The Struggle for Racial Equality in Georgia, 1940–1980* (Athens: University of Georgia Press, 2001); Charles J. Elmore, *Black America Series: Savannah, Georgia* (Charleston, SC: Arcadia Publishing, 2000); Charles L. Hoskins, *Out of Yamacraw and Beyond: Discovering Black Savannah* (Savannah, GA: Gulah Press, 2002); and Townsend Davis, *Weary Feet, Rested Souls: A Guided History of the Civil Rights Movement* (New York: W.W. Norton & Company, 1998). For more about the history of blacks in Georgia, see Asa Gordon, *The Georgia Negro: A History* (Ann Arbor, MI: Edwards Brothers, Inc., 1937).

4. 1948 Savannah City Directory, accessed at Georgia Historical Society in Savannah, Georgia. Although I was successful in obtaining a copy of Frank Wills' Social Security application card, the names of his parents were redacted. After petitioning the governing agency to undo the redaction by providing evidence of his mother's death, Marjorie's name was cleared, but the agency would not release the father's name. I would later learn from a promotional pamphlet, *The Watergate Hero: An Eyewitness Report by Frank Wills* (Washington, D.C.: Wil-Van, Inc., 1973),

Notes—Chapter 4

that Frank's father's first name or surname was "Oliver."

5. Author's interview of Walter B. Simmons, July 15, 2017.

6. *The Watergate Hero: An Eyewitness Report by Frank Wills* (Washington, D.C.: Wil-Van, Inc., 1973), p. 3. Wills never mentioned his deceased brothers in another interview or publication. In fact, in the pamphlet, *The Watergate Hero: An Eyewitness Report by Frank Wills*, there is no mention of siblings. For infant and youth mortality in the African American community, see "Exploring the Racial Gap in Infant Mortality Rates, 1920–1970," [research paper] William J. Collins and Melissa A. Thomasson, [September 2001: Preliminary], National Bureau of Economic Research; and Michael Haines, "Fertility and Mortality in the United States," EH.Net Encyclopedia, edited by Robert Whaples. March 19, 2008. http://eh.net/encyclopedia/fertility-and-mortality-in-the-united-states/.

7. Arthur Gordon, *How Sweet It Is: The Story of Dixie Crystals and Savannah Foods* (Savannah: Savannah Food Industries, 1992), p. 10. In various interviews, Wills mentioned that his mother worked for a sugar refinery while living in Savannah.

8. Clive Webb, "A Tangled Web: Black-Jewish Relations in the Twentieth-Century South," in Marcie Cohen Ferris and Mark I. Greenberg, editors, *Jewish Roots in Southern Soil: A New History* (Waltham, MA: Brandeis University Press, 2006), p. 193. See also Marcie Cohen Ferris, "From the Recipe File of Luba Cohen: A Study of Southern Jewish Foodways and Cultural Identity," *Southern Jewish History: Journal of the Southern Jewish Historical Society* (1999), Volume 2.

9. Eli N. Evans, *The Provincials: A Personal History of Jews in the South* (New York: Simon & Schuster, 1992), p. 256.

10. Author's interview of Lee Shonfield, May 22, 2019. I became aware of Margie's employment by the Shonfield family as a result of Alex Haley's interview of Wills in 1983. See "Frank Wills, 1983," Box Number 24, Audio Cassette Tape 15, Side 2, NAM MSS 16, Alex Haley Manuscript Collection, Manuscripts/Archive Collection, National Afro-American Museum and Cultural Center, Wilberforce, Ohio.

11. *Ibid.*

12. *Ibid.*

13. *Ibid.*

14. Author's interview of Lee Shonfield, June 15, 2019.

15. Lee Shonfield to author, May 26, 2020. Unbeknownst to Margie, when she had chosen to donate her body to the Medical College of Georgia, it was the same institution where Lee Shonfield studied medicine. When Frank passed away, he died at University Hospital, the medical institution where Shonfield trained to become a physician. Indeed, Lee and Frank's paths intersected again, but not in the way that either could have imagined.

Chapter 4

1. John W. White, "Managed Compliance: White Resistance and Desegregation in South Carolina, 1950–1970," Ph.D. Dissertation, University of Florida (2006), p. 127.

2. James O. Farmer, Jr., "A Collision of Cultures: Aiken, South Carolina Meets the Nuclear Age," *The Proceedings of the South Carolina Historical Association*, South Carolina Historical Association (Columbia: University of South Carolina, 1995), p. 40.

3. "More Tourists Than Ever This Winter," *Augusta Chronicle*, July 5, 1903. For the history of North Augusta, see Jeanne McDaniel, *North Augusta: James U. Jackson's Dream* (Charleston, SC: Arcadia Publishing, 2005); *History of North Augusta, South Carolina* (North Augusta, SC: North Augusta Historical Society, 1980); and League of Women Voters of South Carolina, *Survey of the town of North Augusta, South Carolina*. South

Notes—Chapter 5

Carolina: League of Women Voters of South Carolina, 1959.

4. Author's email interview of Wayne O'Bryant, May 14, 2019.

5. *Ibid.*

6. Author's interview of Nathaniel (Nat) Irvin Jr., January 27, 2017.

7. Tom Mack, *Hidden History of Aiken County* (Charleston, SC: History Press, 2012), p. 118.

8. Author's interview of JoAnn Hooper, November 4, 2016.

9. Author's interview of Eddie Wills, November 4, 2016.

10. Margaret N. O'Shea, "Watergate Guard Led Quiet Life," *Augusta Chronicle*, September 30, 2000.

11. Author's interview of Pamela Oliver, July 15, 2017.

12. Author's interview of Martez Mims, November 2, 2016. The importance of baseball in the region during that time was provided by Dr. Martha Keber in an interview on May 31, 2017.

13. Frank G. Roberson, *Over a Hundred Schoolhouses: A Historical Account of Public Education in Aiken County Before and After Consolidation and Integration* (Aiken, SC: Aiken County Consolidated School District, 2000), p. 252. For South Carolina's education practices in the 1930s–1950s, see Walter Edgar, *South Carolina: A History* (Columbia: University of South Carolina Press, 1998); "South Carolina," *Southern School News*, September 3, 1954; and Allen Riddick, *Aiken County Schools: A Pictorial History and More* (Aiken, SC: Rocket Publishing, 2003).

14. Author's interview of Eddie Wills, November 4, 2016. Frank Wills described his educational experience in an interview conducted by Alex Haley, which can be accessed in: "Frank Wills, 1983," Box Number 24, Audio Cassette Tape 15, Side 2, NAM MSS 16, Alex Haley Manuscript Collection, Manuscripts/Archive Collection, National Afro-American Museum and Cultural Center, Wilberforce, Ohio.

15. Author's interview of Pamela Oliver, July 15, 2017.

16. Author's interview of Nathaniel Irvin, Jr., January 27, 2017. Dr. Nathaniel Irvin II (or Jr.), currently a professor of business at Louisville University, had taken part in one of the first integration experiments in North Augusta in 1965, when he was enrolled at Paul Knox Middle School. Despite requiring a police escort throughout the fall semester of his first term, Irvin's efforts ultimately proved successful. Within three years, all schools in North Augusta had been integrated.

17. *Ibid.*

18. Author's interview of Martez Mims, November 2, 2016.

19. Author's interview of Nathaniel Irvin, Jr., January 27, 2017.

20. Nathaniel Irvin, Jr. "Escape from Boggy Branch: The True Story of How Reverend Nathaniel Irvin, Sr., found his way to heaven 1929–2016," *A Service of Life and Legacy of the Reverend Dr. Nathaniel Irvin, Sr. 1929–2016*, October 8, 2016 (privately printed).

21. *Ibid.*

22. Author's interview of Nathaniel Irvin, Jr.

23. Author's interview of Stephanie Coleman, November 4, 2016. I obtained information about the property history of Wills' home from the Aiken County Assessor's Office.

24. Author's interview of Carrie Williams, November 4, 2016.

25. "Frank Wills, 1983," Box Number 24, Audio Cassette Tape 15, Side 2, NAM MSS 16, Alex Haley Manuscript Collection, Manuscripts/Archive Collection, National Afro-American Museum and Cultural Center, Wilberforce, Ohio.

Chapter 5

1. Sar A. Levitan and Benjamin H. Johnston, *The Job Corps: A Social Experiment That Works* (Baltimore: Johns Hopkins University Press, 1975), p. 28.

2. John M. Berry and Art Pine, "19 Years of Job Programs—Question Still Is

Notes—Chapter 6

'What Works?'" *Washington Post*, April 24, 1979.

3. Records of the Community Services Administration, National Archives (Record Group 381), 1963–81, 381.3.135 Records of the Job Corps History. https://www.archives.gov/research/guide-fed-records/groups/381.html#page-header.

4. Levitan and Johnston, *The Job Corps*, p. 21. For Battle Creek's African American heritage, see Sonya Bernhard-Hollins, *Here I Stand: A Musical History of African Americans in Battle Creek, Michigan* (Kalamazoo, MI: Fortitude Graphic Design & Publishing, 2003).

5. Simeon Booker, "Untold Story of Black Hero of Watergate," *JET*, May 17, 1973. Also helpful was "With Thanks to Frank Wills," *Ebony*, June 1973.

6. Levitan and Johnston, *The Job Corps*, p. 8.

7. Booker, "Untold Story of Black Hero of Watergate." For Wills' motor assembly experience, see "Frank Wills, 1983," Box Number 24, Audio Cassette Tape 15, Side 2, NAM MSS 16, Alex Haley Manuscript Collection, Manuscripts/Archive Collection, National Afro-American Museum and Cultural Center, Wilberforce, Ohio.

8. Sol Stern, "A Watergate Footnote*: The Selling of Frank Wills," *New York Times Magazine*, September 10, 1974.

9. "Frank Wills, 1983," Box Number 24, Audio Cassette Tape 17, Side 5, NAM MSS 16, Alex Haley Manuscript Collection.

10. *Ibid.* Information about his first trip to DC and subsequent move can also be found in this collection on Tape 15, Side 1. For Washington, D.C., in the post–King assassination years, see Harry S. Jaffe and Tom Sherwood, *Dream City: Race, Power, and the Decline of Washington, D.C.* (New York: Simon & Schuster, 1994).

11. James S. Kakalik and Sorrel Wildhorn, *The Private Police: Security and Danger* (New York: Crane, Russak, & Company, 1977), pp. 121–122.

12. Richard L. Worsnop, "Guards Are Underpaid,'" *Augusta Chronicle*, May 19, 1973.

13. Kakalik and Wildhorn, *The Private Police*, p. 184.

14. *Ibid.*

Chapter 6

1. Ada Louise Huxtable, "Controversy Widens on Design of Development in Washington," *New York Times*, April 29, 1962. It took forty-years, but now we have an authoritative history of the Watergate Complex thanks to Joseph Rodota, *The Watergate: Inside America's Most Infamous Address* (New York: William Morrow, 2018). For additional information on the Watergate Complex, see Mike Livingston, "Watergate: The Name That Branded More Than a Building," *Washington Business Journal*, June 17, 2002; United States Department of the Interior National Park Service: National Register of Historic Places, Watergate, Washington, DC, October 12, 2005; and the following *Washington Post* articles: John B. Willmann, "Foggy Bottom Gas House Site to get Facelift," October 22, 1961; Willard Clopton, "Board Opposition Rises to Watergate Apartment Project," December 24, 1961; Laurence Stern, "White House Acts to Cut Height of Huge Watergate Development," May 5, 1962; "High-Rise Watergate Towne Given Final D.C. Approval," July 14, 1962; "Towne Plan Stirs Row by Protestants," November 17, 1962; Jean M. White, "Woes Stall Watergate Project," October 18, 1963; "Development of Watergate Towne Gets Go-ahead on Ground Breaking," January 25, 1964; "Watergate East Gets First Tenants," October 24, 1965; "Watergate Apartment Hotel Opens," April 1, 1967; "Democrats to Take New Headquarters," April 26, 1967; "Watergate Selling in Fourth Building," October 7, 1967; "Watergate Plans Reaffirmed," November 16, 1967; "Compromise Plan Ends Watergate Controversy," August 9, 1968; "Watergate Complex Spreads Out," August 17, 1968.

2. David Lindsay, "The Watergate: The Building That Changed Washington," *Washingtonian*, October 1, 2005;

Notes—Chapter 7

Huxtable, "Controversy Widens on Design of Development in Washington."

3. John B. Willmann, "Watergate's Architect Shudders at Conformity," *Washington Post,* February 25, 1965.

4. Lindsay, "The Watergate: The Building That Changed Washington."

5. Philip D. Carter, "Watergate: Potomac Titanic," *Washington Post,* May 3, 1970.

6. Lindsay, "The Watergate: The Building That Changed Washington."

7. *Ibid.*

8. "Watergate Noses Up," *Washington Post,* October 3, 1964.

9. Carter, "Watergate: Potomac Titanic."

10. Myra MacPherson, "Watergate, Where Republicans Gather," *Washington Post,* February 25, 1969. Ironically, the first publicized burglary at the newly opened Watergate Complex involved Nixon's longtime secretary, Rose Mary Woods, who was the victim of a home invasion when robbers stole her jewelry, worth thousands of dollars. See David Lindsay, "The Watergate: The Building That Changed Washington," *Washingtonian,* October 1, 2005.

11. Carter, "Watergate: Potomac Titanic."

12. *Ibid.*

13. "Problems of Watergate 'In' Place of the Capital, Anger Many Residents," *New York Times,* March 12, 1972. In the end, SGI, the builder, filed a "counterclaim of $4 million for 'malicious embarrassment.'" After five years of legal battles, SGI agreed to pay a settlement of $600,000. See Mike Livingston, "Watergate: The Name That Branded More Than a Building," *Washington Business Journal,* June 17, 2002.

14. MacPherson, "Watergate, Where Republicans Gather."

15. Transcript, Lawrence F. O'Brien Oral History Interview XXVIII, 9/24/87, by Michael L. Gillette, Internet Copy, LBJ Library, p. 14.

16. Richard Nixon, *RN: The Memoirs of Richard Nixon* (New York: Simon and Schuster, 1990), p. 497.

17. Fred Emery, *Watergate: The Corruption of American Politics and the Fall of Richard Nixon* (New York: Random House, 1994), p. 32.

18. Transcript, Lawrence F. O'Brien Oral History Interview XXXI, 12/10/87.

19. *Ibid.*, p. 9.

20. Stephen E. Ambrose, *Nixon: The Triumph of a Politician 1962–1972* (New York: Simon and Schuster, 1989), Vol. 2, p. 558.

21. Transcript, Lawrence F. O'Brien Oral History Interview XXXI, 12/10/87. Although they might have been relaxed when it came to security, the DNC staff was hardly a band of misfits. The Democratic nominee's campaign team was known as McGovern's Army and included Bill Clinton, Hillary Rodham Clinton, future Secretary of Labor Robert Reich, and future U.S. Senator Gary Hart.

Chapter 7

1. Fred Blumenthal, "Watergate: How It All Started," *Washington Post,* August 26, 1973. Officer Dennis P. Stephenson's role in the Watergate story remains unresolved. The official version, which was published in the *Washington Post* ("An Unmarked Car Watergate Break," May 13, 1973) a year after the incident, was that Stephenson was low on gas and waived the call. In 2007, though, Stephenson, then living in Rolla, Missouri, and working as a bus driver, was interviewed by Karen (Cox) Bliss, a Rolla High School reporter for her school newspaper, *ECHO.* In the interview, Stephenson claimed he and his partner were in their patrol car "taking a break in an alley, drinking coffee and eating a pizza." When the call came in from the dispatcher, the two officers "threw their coffees out the window and folded the pizza up" and were just about to respond when Leeper's unit took the call, and the rest is history. Bliss' interview was eventually published, "A Tribute to Dennis Stephenson." (It was later republished online, https://www.rhsecho.

Notes—Chapter 7

com/news/2015/09/02/a-tribute-to-dennis-stephenson/, on September 2, 2015, following Stephenson's death). It's possible that this account might be true, but it has never been confirmed or mentioned by the arresting officers or anyone else investigating the case. When I reached out to the school's journalism department for a Stephenson interview transcript, I received no response. In 2012, Ronald Reagan biographer Craig Shirley was working on *Reagan Rising*, his fourth book about the Gipper, when he inadvertently discovered new evidence that may have contradicted the original version and Bliss' account. Shirley interviewed Bill Lacey, co-owner of a D.C. bar, PW's Saloon. Popular among politicos as well as men in blue, Lacey told Shirley that Stephenson was at the Saloon that evening when the call came in from the dispatcher. He was inebriated to the point he "could barely walk." Supposedly, Stephenson asked Lacey's brother, Richard, who was working the bar, "How the hell am I going to investigate a burglary? I can't even stand." Richard suggested telling the dispatcher that his vehicle was out of gas. Stephenson did so. This account is riddled with problems. Given the level of public scrutiny surrounding the break-in, it's surprising that this story was never shared before. Second, according to a PW Saloon fan tribute website, which is currently online, http://pwssaloon.com/default.htm, the site's author claims the bar opened its doors in August 1972, which meant that it could not have been the pub that Stephenson had visited since the break-in occurred in June 1972. In his "The Bartender's Tale: How the Watergate Burglars Got Caught," *Washingtonian*, June 20, 2012, Shirley never referred to Stephenson by name, perhaps a sign that he had doubts about his source.

2. *Ibid.*

3. "Truth and Lies: Watergate," *20/20*, American Broadcasting Company, aired June 16, 2017.

4. Karlyn Barker and W. Pincus, "Watergate Revisited: 20 Years After the Break-In, the Story Continues to Unfold," *Washington Post*, June 14, 1992.

5. Walter Rugaber, "Motive Is Big Mystery in Raid on Democrats," *New York Times*, June 26, 1972.

6. "Testimony of Carl M. Shoffler, officer, Metropolitan Police Department, Washington, D.C., Hearings Before the Select Committee on Presidential Campaign Activities of the United States," Senate Ninety-third Congress First Session: Watergate and Related Activities, Phase I: Watergate Investigation, *Presidential Campaign Activities of 1972 Senate Resolution 60*, Book 1 (U.S. Government Printing Office: Washington, D.C., 1973), pp. 118–125.

7. *Ibid.*

8. *Ibid.*

9. *Ibid.*

10. *Ibid.*

11. "Still Living It After 25 Years: Officer Who Caught Watergate Burglars Will Never Forget," *Pittsburgh Post–Gazette*, June 15, 1997.

12. Barker and Pincus, "Watergate Revisited: 20 Years After the Break-In, the Story Continues to Unfold." Little did Wills or the intern, Bruce Givner, know that this same man, Alfred Baldwin, a retired FBI agent working for Nixon's re-election campaign, was a few flights above them when they ordered their late-night snacks at the Howard Johnson's restaurant. Baldwin spotted Wills leaving the complex, which is probably when the burglars made their way inside and to the sixth floor.

13. "Still Living It After 25 Years: Officer Who Caught Watergate Burglars Will Never Forget."

14. "Watergate 20th Anniversary," television interview on C-SPAN aired June 18, 1992. http://www.c-span.org/video/?26646-1/watergate-20th-anniversary&start=NaN.

15. "Testimony of Paul W. Leeper, Sergeant, Metropolitan Police Department, Washington, D.C., Hearings Before the Select Committee on Presidential Campaign Activities of the United States," pp. 95–105.

Notes—Chapter 8

16. "Truth and Lies: Watergate," *20/20*, ABC. In *A Piece of Tape: The Watergate Story, Fact and Fiction* (Rockville, MD: Washington Media Services), p. 32, burglar James McCord wrote: "[H]ad the police search not been as thorough as it was, we might have escaped detection. Had they only opened the glass door into the reception room, and had seen no one, then moved on, we would not have been found. But they were too well trained."

17. Bruce Buschel, Albert Robbins, William Vitka, and edited by Rod Nordland, *The Watergate File: A concise, illustrated guide to the people and events* (New York: Flash Books, 1973), p. 13.

18. Barker and Pincus, "Watergate Revisited: 20 Years After the Break-In, the Story Continues to Unfold."

19. Bob Woodward and Carl Bernstein, *All the President's Men* (New York: Simon & Schuster, 2012, republished) p. 18.

20. Martin Weil, "DNC's Stanley Greigg Dies; Signed Watergate Complaint," *Washington Post*, June 16, 2002.

21. Joseph A. Califano, Jr. *Inside: A Public and Private Life* (New York: Public Affairs, 2004), p. 267.

22. "Sgt. Paul Leeper's Watergate Experience," *The West Virginia News Video*, posted December 7, 2012. https://www.youtube.com/watch?v=l6aGRtEmwTE.

23. *Ibid.*

24. *Ibid.*

25. "Still Living It After 25 Years: Officer Who Caught Watergate Burglars Will Never Forget." Buschel, Robbins, et. al., *The Watergate File*, p. 13.

Chapter 8

1. Jim Shaw, "But for Him, Nixon Might Sill Be President," *Columbia Law School Observer*, February 24, 1975. For Special Agent Lano's role, see Barker and Pincus, "Watergate Revisited: 20 Years After the Break-In, the Story Continues to Unfold."

2. *Ibid.*

3. *The Presidents: Nixon*, PBS American Experience, aired October 15, 1990, http://www.pbs.org/wgbh/americanexperience/films/nixon/.

4. Alfred E. Lewis, "5 Held in Plot to Bug Democrats' Office Here," *Washington Post*, June 18, 1972.

5. *Ibid.*

6. Carol McCabe Booker to author, January 25, 2019. Simeon Booker's widow, Carol McCabe Booker, provided invaluable assistance reconstructing these events.

7. Emily Langer, "Simeon Booker, Intrepid Chronicler of Civil Rights Struggle for *Jet* and *Ebony*, Dies at 99," *Washington Post*, December 10, 2017.

8. *Ibid.*

9. Simeon Booker, *Shocking the Conscience: A Reporter's Account of the Civil Rights Movement* (Jackson: University Press of Mississippi, 2013), p. 294. Booker held on to those two door hinges for years. It was a reminder of what the Nixon years represented to him, "a presidency unhinged."

10. "Frank Wills, 1983," Box Number 24, Audio Cassette Tape 16, Side 3, NAM MSS 16, Alex Haley Manuscript Collection, Manuscripts/Archive Collection, National Afro-American Museum and Cultural Center, Wilberforce, Ohio.

11. *Ibid.*

12. Sue A. Pressley, "Man Who Made Watergate Call Mourned," *Washington Post*, October 1, 2000.

13. Kenneth Turan, "Opening of Watergate Dam No Act of Heroism to the Guard," *Pittsburgh Press* in *Washington Post*, May 14, 1973.

14. Karlyn Barker, "Intruders Foiled by Security Guard, *Washington Post*, June 19, 1972.

15. *Ibid.*

16. *Ibid.*

17. *The Watergate Hero: An Eyewitness Report by Frank Wills*, p. 8.

18. Douglas Brinkley, *Gerald R. Ford* (New York: Henry Holt and Company, 2007), p. 44.

19. "5 Charged with Burglary at

Notes—Chapter 9

Democratic Quarters," *New York Times,* June 18, 1972.

20. *The Presidents: Nixon*, PBS American Experience.

21. Barker and Pincus, "Watergate Revisited: 20 Years After the Break-In, the Story Continues to Unfold."

22. Richard Ben Kramer, *What It Takes* (New York: Vintage Books, 1993), p. 606.

23. Justin P. Coffey, "Watergate and the Committee to Reelect the President," MA Thesis, University of Wyoming (1998), p. 13.

24. "Appendix: Statement of Lawrence O'Brien June 18, 1972," Lawrence O'Brien, *No Final Victories: A Life in Politics from John F. Kennedy to Watergate* (New York: Doubleday & Company, 1974), p. 369.

25. Brinkley, *Gerald R. Ford*, p. 44.

26. Author's interview of Martez Mims, November 2, 2016.

27. Author's interview of Pamela Oliver, July 15, 2017.

28. Author's interview of Nathanial Irvin, Jr., January 27, 2017.

29. "Frank Wills, 1983," Box Number 24, Audio Cassette Tape 16, Side 4, NAM MSS 16, Alex Haley Manuscript Collection, Manuscripts/Archive Collection, National Afro-American Museum and Cultural Center, Wilberforce, Ohio.

30. Author's interview of Eddie Wills, November 4, 2016.

31. "Wills, Frank." Watergate Collection.

32. Walter Rugaber, "Motive Is Big Mystery in Raid on Democrats," *New York Times*, June 26, 1972.

33. Watergate Part 17, p. 11, Federal Bureau of Investigation Records: The Vault (Watergate Collection), https://vault.fbi.gov.

34. *Ibid.*

35. "General Investigative Division Summary," Watergate Part 4, p. 82, Federal Bureau of Investigation Records: The Vault (Watergate Collection), https://vault.fbi.gov.

36. Hougan, *Secret Agenda*, p. 196.

37. Califano Jr. *Inside: A Public and Private Life*, p. 263.

38. Barker and Pincus, "Watergate Revisited: 20 Years After the Break-In, the Story Continues to Unfold."

39. *Ibid.*

40. "Memo," Watergate Part 37, p. 32. Federal Bureau of Investigation Records: The Vault (Watergate Collection), https://vault.fbi.gov.

41. Jeremiah O'Leary and Patrick Collins, "Were Guards Bribed?" [Washington, D.C.] *Sunday Star*, October 1, 1972.

42. *Ibid.*

43. "Frank Wills Interviewed by Bill Monroe," June 17, 1974, sound recording, G. Robert Vincent Voice Library, Gerald Kline Digital and Multimedia Center at Michigan State University Library. Voice #6608. http://catalog.lib.msu.edu/record=b8534230~S39a

44. O'Leary and Collins, "Were Guards Bribed?" Another of the many conspiracy theories involved DNC Chairman O'Brien, who political opponents claimed had known in advance about the June 17 break-in and made a calculated decision not to report it, with the hope that the arrests (and fallout) would sway the election to McGovern. Even DNC intern Bruce Givner was a target of a conspiracy theory. Because he graduated from the University of California, Los Angeles, the same university as Nixon's chief of staff, H.R. Haldeman, there were those who thought he was working as a mole, passing along highly secretive material to high-level Nixon staff members. Givner, a self-described "liberal Democrat," has emphatically denied the allegation. See also Jim Shaw, "But for Him, Nixon Might Sill Be President."

45. Bill Straub, "Following the Watergate Scandal's Key Players," *San Francisco Chronicle*, June 14, 2002.

46. Carl Bernstein and Bob Woodward, "FBI Finds Nixon Aides Sabotaged Democrats," *Washington Post*, October 10, 1972.

Chapter 9

1. Bob Woodward, *The Last of the President's Men* (New York: Simon & Schuster, 2015), p. 145.

Notes—Chapter 9

2. Kramer, *What It Takes*, p. 612. For the DNC's change of locations, see Clay F. Richards, "Democrats to Have Permanent Home After 200 Years," United Press International Archives, April 19, 1983, https://www.upi.com/Archives/1983/04/19/-Democrats-to-have-permanent-home-after-200-years/2748419576400/.

3. Kenneth Turan, "Opening of Watergate Dam No Act of Heroism to the Guard," *Pittsburgh Press* in *Washington Post*, May 14, 1973.

4. Marlene Cimons, "Whatever Happened to—Frank Wills," *Toledo Blade*, January 6, 1974.

5. Turan, "Opening of Watergate Dam No Act of Heroism to the Guard."

6. Booker, "Untold Story of Black Hero of Watergate."

7. Leonard E. Colvin, "Frank Wills: Forgotten Hero of Watergate," [Norfolk, Virginia] *New Journal & Guide*, June 24-June 30, 1992.

8. "Frank Wills, 1983," Box Number 24, Audio Cassette Tape 16, Side 3, NAM MSS 16, Alex Haley Manuscript Collection, Manuscripts/Archive Collection, National Afro-American Museum and Cultural Center, Wilberforce, Ohio.

9. *Ibid.*

10. Turan, "Opening of Watergate Dam No Act of Heroism to the Guard."

11. *Ibid.*

12. Stern, "A Watergate Footnote*: The Selling of Frank Wills." John Sirica was one of the only chroniclers involved with the scandal who acknowledged Wills by name in his post–Watergate memoir. "Had Frank Wills, the night guard at the Watergate complex, not found the telltale on the door," he wrote, "the whole business might have gone undetected." John J. Sirica, *To Set the Record Straight: The Break-Ins, the Tapes, the Conspirators, the Pardon* (New York: W.W. Norton & Company, 1979), p. 302.

13. Simeon Booker, "Ticker Tape USA," *JET*, August 23, 1973.

14. Barker and Pincus, "Watergate Revisited: 20 Years After the Break-In, the Story Continues to Unfold."

15. Laurence Stern and Haynes Johnson, "3 Top Nixon Aides, Kleindienst Out; President Accepts Full Responsibility; Richardson Will Conduct New Probe," *Washington Post*, May 1, 1973.

16. Associated Press, "NA Native Triggered Watergate Alarm,'" *Augusta Chronicle*, April 26, 1973.

17. "Watergate Guard Bailed Out; Seeks New Trial," [Baltimore] *Afro-American*, May 8, 1973.

18. Turan, "Opening of Watergate Dam No Act of Heroism to the Guard."

19. John M. Crewdson, "Who Called the Signals," *New York Times*, March 18, 1973.

20. James F. Clarity, "Notes on People: Watergate Produces One Hero," *New York Times*, April 28, 1973.

21. Turan, "Opening of Watergate Dam No Act of Heroism to the Guard."

22. Booker, "Untold Story of Black Hero of Watergate."

23. "Watergate Hero Attempts to Cash In on His Fame," *JET*, July 5, 1973. For background information about Wills' agent, Dorsey Evans, see Wilma F. Bonner, et al., *The Sumner Story: Capturing Our History, Preserving Our Legacy* (Garden City, NY: Morgan James Publishing, 2011) and "Interview with Dorsey Evans by Chuck Stanley and Earl Ofari," KPFK radio broadcast, 1974, Call#BC 1912. https://www.pacificaradioarchives.org/recording/bc1912?nns=dorsey%2Bevans.

24. "Memorandum: From Gerald Donaldson to Emory N. Jackson, Subject: Frank Wills' 2nd Progress Report," October 31, 1974. File: Wills, Frank, 1974, Box III: 329, National Urban League Records, Manuscript Division, Library of Congress, Washington, D.C. http://rs5.loc.gov/service/mss/eadxmlmss/eadpdfmss/1997/ms997012.pdf.

25. "The $80-a-Week Guard Who 'Blew the Whistle' on Watergate," [Baltimore] *Afro-American News*, May 12, 1973.

26. Buschel, Robbins, Vitka, and edited by Nordland, *The Watergate File*, Introduction.

Notes—Chapter 10

27. William B. Dickinson Jr., editor, and introduction by Ben Bradlee, *Year of Scandal: How the* Washington Post *Covered Watergate and the Agnew Crisis* (Washington, D.C.: Washington Post Company, 1973).

28. Booker, "Ticker Tape USA," *JET,* August 23, 1973.

29. "Watergate Hero is Broke and Jobless," *JET,* September 20, 1973.

30. "Guard at the Watergate Says He Can't Get a Job," *New York Times,* September 21, 1973.

31. "Watergate Hero is Broke and Jobless."

32. James S. Hirsch, *Willie Mays: The Life, The Legend* (New York: Simon and Schuster, 2010), p. 241.

33. Cimons, "Whatever Happened to—Frank Wills."

Chapter 10

1. Mike Feinsilber, "Watergate was Big Show 10 Years Ago," *Augusta Chronicle,* August 14, 1983.

2. *The Presidents: Nixon,* PBS American Experience. Among the millions of viewers was a ten-year-old from Hawaii who years later would be the forty-fourth President of the United States.

3. Barry Werth, *31 Days: The Crisis That Gave Us the Government We Have Today* (New York: Doubleday, 2006), p. 3.

4. "Happenings," *Augusta Chronicle,* February 25, 1974.

5. Associated Press, "Watergate Guard Can't Find a Job," *The Charleston* [West Virginia] *Daily Mail,* October 25, 1973.

6. "Happenings," *Augusta Chronicle,* February 25, 1974.

7. "Frank Wills Interviewed by Bill Monroe," June 17, 1974.

8. "Happenings," *Augusta Chronicle,* February 25, 1974.

9. Sol Stern, "A Watergate Footnote*: The Selling of Frank Wills."

10. Cimons, "Whatever Happened to—Frank Wills."

11. *Ibid.*

12. Randal L. Key, "Readers Rap: Plight of Frank Wills," *JET*, November 22, 1973.

13. Alfred Baker Lewis, "Our Readers Say: Little Wrote about Frank Wills," [Washington, D.C.] *Afro-American,* May 28, 1974.

14. "Watergate Guard Gets Trust Fund," *Milwaukee Sentinel,* November 15, 1973.

15. "Watergate Guard a Hero to Many," *Milwaukee Journal,* February 18, 1974.

16. Henry Kissinger, "Years of Upheaval: Watergate," *Time,* March 8, 1982.

17. Cimons, "Whatever Happened to—Frank Wills." In view of Wills' less polished comments delivered previously and Dorsey Evans' penchant for politically charged rhetoric, it's likely that the agent helped his client prepare this statement.

18. "Separate and Additional Views of Mr. Rangel, Concerning Articles of Impeachment Against the President of the United States, Richard M. Nixon," *The Impeachment of Richard M. Nixon President of the United States the Final Report of the Committee of the Judiciary House of Representatives* (New York: Viking Press, 1975), p. 314.

19. William Grimes, "James Mann, 90, Dies; Worked on Nixon Impeachment," *New York Times,* December 23, 2010.

20. Debate on Articles of Impeachment: Hearings of the Committee of the Judiciary House of Representatives (U.S. Government Printing Office: Washington, D.C., 1974), p. 428. The italics are mine.

21. Hugh Rawson, "The Words of Watergate: An Anniversary Look Back at the Biggest Presidential Scandal Ever, Through the Changes It Wrought in the Language," *American Heritage* (October 1997), 24–42.

22. "Frank Wills On Watergate Burglary," *Good Night America,* aired August 15, 1974, https://www.youtube.com/watch?v=aFS497TYZRY.

23. "Watergate Guard Says No Position Is Too High," *New York Times,* August 9, 1974.

Notes—Chapter 11

24. Cimons, "Whatever Happened to—Frank Wills."

25. "Frank Wills Interviewed by Bill Monroe."

26. Stern, "A Watergate Footnote*: The Selling of Frank Wills."

27. *Ibid.*

28. Sol Stern, "Letters: Watergate Update," *New York Times*, December 1, 1974.

29. Stern, "A Watergate Footnote*: The Selling of Frank Wills."

30. "Guard at Watergate to get S.C.L.C Honor," *New York Times*, August 14, 1974.

31. Stern, "A Watergate Footnote*: The Selling of Frank Wills."

32. *Ibid.*

33. *Ibid.*

34. *Ibid.*

35. *Ibid.*

36. *Ibid.*

37. "Letter from Gerald Donaldson to Emory N. Jackson, October 31, 1974, "Frank Wills' First Progress Report," in "Wills, Frank, 1974, [file]," Box III: 329, National Urban League Records, Manuscript Division, Library of Congress, Washington, D.C.

38. *Ibid.*

39. *Ibid.*

40. *Ibid.*

41. *Ibid.*

42. *Ibid.*

43. *Ibid.*

44. *Ibid.*

45. *Ibid.*

46. Gerald Donaldson to Emory N. Jackson, October 31, 1974, "Frank Wills' 2nd Progress Report," in "Wills, Frank, 1974, [file]," Box III: 329, National Urban League Records, Manuscript Division, Library of Congress, Washington, D.C.

47. Gerald Donaldson to Emory N. Jackson, November 1, 1974, "Memorandum: Frank Wills' 3rd Progress Report," in "Wills, Frank, 1974, [file]," Box III: 329, National Urban League Records, Manuscript Division, Library of Congress, Washington, D.C.

48. Donaldson to Jackson, "Frank Wills' 2nd Progress Report," October 31, 1974.

49. *Ibid.*

50. "Mitchell Seeks National Honor for Watergate Guard," [Baltimore] *Afro-American*, February 18, 1975.

51. "Watchman at Watergate Has Troubles," *Augusta Chronicle*, December 15, 1974.

52. Alicia Shepard, "Woodward and Bernstein Uncovered," *Washingtonian*, September 1, 2003.

53. *Ibid.*

54. Jon Boorstin, "On Its 40th Anniversary: Notes on the Making of All the President's Men," *Los Angeles Review of Books*, March 25, 2016.

55. "Frank Wills, 1983," Box Number 24, Audio Cassette Tape 17, Side 5, NAM MSS 16, Alex Haley Manuscript Collection, Manuscripts/Archive Collection, National Afro-American Museum and Cultural Center, Wilberforce, Ohio.

56. Jack Hirshberg, *Redford/Hoffman: A Portrait of All the President's Men* (New York: Warner Books, 1976), p. 143.

57. *Ibid.*

58. *Ibid.*

59. *Ibid.*, p. 99.

60. Simeon Booker, "Watergate Is Revisited in Film, but Still No Glory for Frank Wills," *JET*, April 22, 1976. Boorstin, "On Its 40th Anniversary: Notes on the Making of All the President's Men."

61. Booker, "Watergate Is Revisited in Film, but Still No Glory for Frank Wills."

62. Hirshberg, *Redford/Hoffman*, p. 143.

Chapter 11

1. "Watergate: 5 Years Ago," CBS News, June 17, 1977, Episode #252652, Vanderbilt Television News Archive. https://tvnews.vanderbilt.edu/broadcasts/252652

2. *Ibid.*

3. Booker, "Watergate Is Revisited in Film, but Still No Glory for Frank Wills."

4. "Guard Who Caught Burglars Is Bitter," *New York Times*, June 17, 1977.

Notes—Chapter 11

5. Roger Simon, "Watergate Hero's Note," *Chicago Sun-Times*, October 26, 1977.

6. *Ibid.*

7. "Things Looking Up for Frank Wills, the Watergate Hero," [Fredericksburg, Virginia] *Free Lance-Star*, July 29, 1977.

8. D.C. Attorney Discipline System: District of Columbia Court of Appeals Board of Professional Responsibility, "Disciplinary Action," July 24, 1990. For information about Dorsey Evans' other professional legal troubles, see D.C. Attorney Discipline System: District of Columbia Court of Appeals Board of Professional Responsibility, "Disciplinary Action," April 27, 2006 and "Attorney Grievance Commission of Maryland v. Dorsey Evans, Jr." Court of Appeals of Maryland, Misc. Docket AG No. 14, September Term 2006.

9. Supreme Court of Kansas. IN RE: Dorsey EVANS, Respondent. No. 98,842. Decided: October 26, 2007 https://caselaw.findlaw.com/ks-supreme-court/1142406.html

10. Author's interview of Nathaniel Irvin Jr., January 27, 2017.

11. Stern, "A Watergate Footnote*: The Selling of Frank Wills."

12. Author's interview of Nathaniel Irvin Jr., January 27, 2017.

13. Author's interview of William Mims, November 2, 2016.

14. Author's interview of Wayne O'Bryant, November 4, 2016.

15. "Scandal's Cop Works, Meditates in South; No Fond Memories of D.C." *Washington Post*, October 22, 1978.

16. *Ibid.*

17. "Young Frank Wills, Unsung Watergate Hero, Changed U.S. History," *JET*, August 22, 1974.

18. Frank Wills to Simeon Booker, November 19, 1979, Simeon Booker Papers, in possession of Carol McCabe Booker.

19. Jack Stillman, "Human Brain Termed a Mystery," (undated press clipping), Simeon Booker Papers.

20. Paul L. Montgomery, "10 Years Later: Watergate Figures Recall Turning Point in Their Lives," *New York Times*, June 17, 1982.

21. "A Decade Later, Watergate's Veterans Are Winners, Losers—and Everything in Between," *People*, June 14, 1982.

22. Simeon Booker, "Special Report on Black Hero of Watergate," *JET*, June 21, 1982.

23. *Ibid.*

24. Mike Royko, "Fame Hasn't Done a Thing for Frank Wills," [Prescott, Arizona] *Courier* in *Chicago Sun-Times*, March 9, 1983.

25. "Frank Wills, 1983," Box Number 24, Audio Cassette Tape 16, Side 4, NAM MSS 16, Alex Haley Manuscript Collection, Manuscripts/Archive Collection, National Afro-American Museum and Cultural Center, Wilberforce, Ohio.

26. Pat Powers, "Watergate Break-In Discoverer Arrested for Shoplifting Shoes'" *Augusta Chronicle*, September 4, 1982. "WILLS v. THE STATE," 169 Ga. App. 260 (1983) 312 S.E.2d 367 67148. Court of Appeals of Georgia, Decided November 23, 1983, Rehearing Denied December 12, 1983.

27. "Court Upholds Conviction of Former Watergate Guard," *Augusta Chronicle*, October 2, 1984.

28. Leonard E. Colvin, "Frank Wills: Forgotten Hero of Watergate," [Norfolk, Virginia] *New Journal & Guide*, June 24–June 30, 1992.

29. Don Rhodes, "Wills Convicted of Shoplifting, Given 1-Year Prison Term," *Augusta Herald*, February 15, 1983.

30. "Frank Wills, 1983," Box Number 24, Audio Cassette Tape 16, Side 3 and 4, NAM MSS 16, Alex Haley Manuscript Collection.

31. *Ibid.*

32. Ben Bradlee, Jr., "Watergate Celebrity No More," *Boston Globe*, April 30, 1983.

33. Brad Kava, "The 'Eye in the Sky' Sees It All," *Gilroy* [California] *Dispatch*, December 15, 2016.

34. Pat Powers, "Watergate Break-In Discoverer Arrested for Shoplifting

Notes—Chapter 11

Shoes,'" *Augusta Chronicle*, September 4, 1982.

35. Don Rhodes, "Guard Who Touched Off Watergate in Jail," *Augusta Herald*, September 3, 1982.

36. Henry Allen, "Fame and the Freedom of Wills; Watergate Guard Released After Shoplifting Arrest," *Washington Post*, September 4, 1982.

37. Rhodes, "Guard Who Touched Off Watergate in Jail."

38. Allen, "Fame and the Freedom of Wills; Watergate Guard Released After Shoplifting Arrest."

39. Powers, "Watergate Break-In Discoverer Arrested for Shoplifting Shoes.'" For more on Wills' legal battles, see the following articles (all published in the *Augusta Chronicle*): "Ex-guard who Discovered Watergate Draws Jail Term," February 16, 1983; Mickie Valente, "Wills Release from Prison Pending Retrial Pushed Back," March 2, 1983; Mickie Valente, "Request to Pardon Wills Misdirected," April 6, 1983; Mike Vogel, "Slaton Refuses New Trial for Wills," May 17, 1983; "Watergate Guard Readies Appeal of Judge's Ruling," May 18, 1983; "Watergate Guard Appeals Termed as 'Probable,'" May 18, 1983; "Wills Seeks to Have Conviction Overturned," June 16, 1983; "Former Guard's Appeal Docketed," July 30, 1983. "Shoplifting Sentence Appealed by Wills," March 22, 1984. For details of the case, see "WILLS v. THE STATE," 169 Ga. App. 260 (1983) 312 S.E.2d 367 67148. Court of Appeals of Georgia, Decided November 23, 1983, Rehearing Denied December 12, 1983.

40. Kathleen Sterritt and John Kennedy, "Personalities," *Washington Post*, September 11, 1982.

41. Don Rhodes, "Wills Claims Not Informed About Court Date for Shoplifting Trial," *Augusta Herald*, December 16, 1982.

42. Chris Peacock, "Unaware of Court Date, Watergate Guard Says" *Augusta Chronicle*, December 16, 1982.

43. *Ibid.* Rhodes, "Wills Claims Not Informed About Court Date for Shoplifting Trial." For Frank Wills' 1979 shoplifting arrest, see Don Rhodes, "Record Shows Previous Shoplifting Charge Brought Against Wills," *Augusta Herald*, September 7, 1982.

44. "Wills' Trial to Be Held in February," *Augusta Chronicle*, December 17, 1982.

45. "Wills Out on Bond," *Augusta Herald*, March 2, 1983.

46. "Frank Wills Case 1981," Folder 5, Box 178, *Voter Education Project Organizational Records*, Atlanta University Center Robert W. Woodruff Library. For the verdict, see Don Rhodes, "Wills Convicted of Shoplifting, Given 1-year Prison Term," *Augusta Herald*, February 15, 1983.

47. "Frank Wills Case 1981," Folder 5, Box 178, Voter Education Project Organizational Records.

48. Associated Press, "Watergate Guard," *Beaver* [Pennsylvania] *County Times*, March 1, 1983.

49. Ken Denney, "Presidential Pardon for Wills Doubted by Justice Department," *Augusta Herald*, April 5, 1983.

50. Associated Press, "Watergate Guard Free with Help of Mayors," [Wilmington, North Carolina] *Morning Star-News*, March 3, 1983.

51. Tommy McBride, "Letters to the Editor: Opposes Mayors' Interference,'" *Augusta Chronicle*, March 3, 1983.

52. Mickie Valente, "Wills Posts Bond, Freed from Prison," *Ibid.*, March 3, 1983.

53. "Ex-Watergate Guard's Sentence Routine Policy," *Ibid.*, March 6, 1983.

54. Mrs. BL Mims, Jr., "Letters to the Editor: Finds 'Justice' Gets 'Curiouser,'" *Ibid.*, February 20, 1983.

55. Hubert W. Merchant, "Letters to the Editor: Claims He's Not Liberal, Just Mad,'" *Ibid.*, March 10, 1983.

56. [Prescott, Arizona] *Courier* in *Chicago Sun-Times*, March 9, 1983.

57. Mickie Valente, "Ex-Watergate Guard's Sentence Routine Policy."

58. "Wills Appeals One Year Shoplifting Sentence," *JET*, March 7, 1983.

Notes—Chapter 12

59. Mickie Valente, "Wills' Attorney Cites Errors, Requests New Trial," *Augusta Chronicle*, April 22, 1983.

60. *Ibid.*

61. *Ibid.*

62. "Newark Mayor Asks Reagan to Pardon Frank Wills," *JET*, April 4, 1983.

63. Barbara Durland, "Letters to the Editor: Opposes Pardon for Shoplifter," *Augusta Chronicle*, April 11, 1983.

64. Margaret Twiggs, "Ridiculous Aspects to Wills Case," *Ibid.*, April 10, 1983.

65. *Ibid.*

66. Mickie Valente, "Presidential Pardon Sought for Wills," *Ibid.*, April 5, 1983.

Chapter 12

1. "Frank Wills: Chronology," Box Number 7, Folder 21, NAM MSS 16, Alex Haley Manuscript Collection, Manuscripts/Archive Collection, p. 1.

2. *Ibid.*, p. 3.

3. *Ibid.*, p. 2.

4. *Ibid.*

5. *Ibid.*

6. *Ibid.*, p. 3.

7. *Ibid.*, p. 2.

8. *Ibid.*

9. Mallory Millender, "Alex Haley in Augusta, Starts Autobiography of Frank Wills," *Augusta News-Review*, May 28, 1983. Author's interview of Mallory Millender, November 2, 2016. In *Secret Agenda: Watergate, Deep Throat and the CIA*, Jim Hougan made an observation about Haley's commitment to the project: "[O]ne can only wonder at author Alex Haley's intention to write Wills' biography."

10. Author's interview of Mallory Millender, November 2, 2016.

11. *Ibid.*

12. Millender, "Alex Haley in Augusta, Starts Autobiography of Frank Wills."

13. Don Rhodes, "Life Takes a Positive Turn; *Roots'* Author Alex Haley to Tell About Former Watergate Guard in a New Book," *Augusta Herald*, May 27, 1983.

14. Millender, "Alex Haley in Augusta, Starts Autobiography of Frank Wills."

15. "Group Continues Push to Buy Truck for Wills," *Augusta Chronicle*, October 7, 1983.

16. Dorethea H. Kitchen, "NAACP on the Move," *Columbus* [Georgia] *Times*, October 26, 1983.

17. Mike Vogel, "Conviction, Jail Sentence of Wills Upheld by Court," *Augusta Chronicle*, November 29, 1983.

18. Simeon Booker, "Frank Wills, 10 Years After Watergate, Faces Dismal Future," *JET*, September 10, 1984.

19. *Ibid.*

20. *Ibid.*

21. *Ibid.*

22. Lloyd Grove, "Gregory's New Diet: He Mixes Watergate with Health Promotion," *Washington Post*, October 3, 1984.

23. "Watergate Hero Wills to Help Gregory Promote Diet Product," *Washington Informer*, Oct 10, 1984.

24. Grove, "Gregory's New Diet."

25. "Watergate Hero Wills to Help Gregory Promote Diet Product."

26. Author's interview of JoAnn Hooper, November 2, 2016.

27. *Ibid.*

28. *Ibid.*

29. *Ibid.*, November 4, 2016.

30. *Ibid.*, November 2, 2016.

31. *Ibid.*

32. *Ibid.*

33. *Ibid.*

34. *Ibid.*

35. *Ibid.*

36. *Ibid.*, November 4, 2016.

37. *Ibid.*, November 2, 2016.

38. Colvin, "Frank Wills: Forgotten Hero of Watergate."

39. *Ibid.*

40. In *Defining Moments in Black History: Reading Between the Lies* (New York: Amistad, 2017), p.1 22, Dick Gregory said he paid Wills $2,500 a week (which comes out to $130,000 annually, equivalent to $315,000 in todays dollars). Wills said it was $1,500 a month plus commission, which was probably more accurate.

41. "Frank Wills, 1983," Box Number

Notes—Chapter 13

24, Audio Cassette Tape 17, Side 5, NAM MSS 16, Alex Haley Manuscript Collection.

42. Nicholas D. Kristof, "The Success of the 'President's Men,'" *New York Times*, July 13, 1986.

43. Associated Press, "Road to Nixon's downfall began 15 years ago today," *Augusta Chronicle*, June 17, 1987.

44. Booker, "Ticker Tape, USA."

45. Author's interview of Cathy Grant, November 3, 2016.

46. Author's interview of JoAnn Hooper, November 2, 2016.

47. John Roberts, "Watergate Security Guard Now N. Augustan," *Augusta Chronicle*, June 17, 1992.

48. Susan K. Tauber, "We Owe Much to Frank Wills," *Atlanta Journal and Constitution*, June 23, 1992.

49. Karlyn Barker and Vivien Lou Chen, "Landmarks Tell Lore of Watergate; Scandal Unfolded at Many Addresses," *Washington Post*, June 17, 1992.

50. Roberts, "Watergate Security Guard Now N. Augustan."

51. Colvin, "Frank Wills: Forgotten Hero of Watergate."

52. Richette Haywood, "Frank Wills, Reflects on Discovery of Watergate Break-In 20 Years Later," *JET*, June 22, 1992.

53. Colvin, "Frank Wills: Forgotten Hero of Watergate."

54. Author's interview of JoAnn Hooper, November 2, 2016.

Chapter 13

1. Author's interview of JoAnn Hooper, November 2, 2016.

2. Author's interview of Stephanie Coleman, November 4, 2016.

3. *Ibid.*

4. O'Shea, "Watergate Guard Led Quiet Life."

5. Author's interview of Wayne O'Bryant, November 3, 2016.

6. Simeon Booker, "Frank Wills, Watergate Hero, Tells of Hard Times He Faces," *JET*, March 8, 1993.

7. *Ibid.*

8. Simeon Booker, "Draft of Article," Simeon Booker Papers.

9. Roger Simon, "Watergate 'Hero' Has Let Opportunities Pass Him By," *Baltimore Sun*, October 25, 1993. Also helpful is Liz Atwood, "Fund-Raiser Conducted for Man Who Helped Unseat a President," *Baltimore Sun*, October 14, 1993.

10. Lawanza Spears, "20 Years After Watergate, Hero Lives in Poverty," [Washington, D.C.] *Afro-American and the Washington Tribune*, April 24, 1993.

11. Roger Simon, "Former Watergate Guard's Complaints Lack Conviction," *Baltimore Sun*, October 24, 1993.

12. Roger Simon, "Watergate 'Hero' Has Let Opportunities Pass Him By."

13. *Ibid.* Decades earlier, another famous African American made a similar statement. After winning four gold medals in the 1936 Olympics in Berlin, Jesse Owens came home only to be a victim of racism. Owens had few options to earn a living as a professional athlete, so he was willing to accept whatever was available. On one occasion he was taken to task for it. "People say it was degrading for an Olympic champion to run against a horse, but what was I supposed to do? I had four gold medals, but you can't eat four gold medals." ("From horse-racer to speech writer: Jesse Owens' life after the Olympic Games," Olympic.org, March 31, 1980.) https://www.olympic.org/news/-from-horse-racer-to-speech-writer-jesse-owens-life-after-the-olympic-games.

14. Roger Simon, "Watergate 'Hero' Has Let Opportunities Pass Him By."

15. *Ibid.*

16. Roger Simon, "Former Watergate Guard's Complaints Lack Conviction."

17. Abraham T. McLaughlin, Whatever Happened to...?" *Christian Science Monitor*, January 25, 1996. Also helpful was John Aloysius Farrell, "Watergate's Hero Forgotten, Alone Former Guard Broods in a Cabin in the Woods," *Boston Globe*, June 15, 1997.

18. "In Depth: Watergate 25th Anniversary," NBC Evening News, June 17,

180

Notes—Epilogue

1997, Episode #618825, Vanderbilt Television News Archive. https://tvnews.vanderbilt.edu/broadcasts/618825

19. *Ibid.*

20. *Ibid.*

21. Author's interview of Austin Rhodes, November 3, 2016.

22. *Ibid.*

23. *Ibid.*

24. *Ibid.*

25. Author's interview of Martez Mims, November 2, 2016.

26. Elaine Woo, "Frank Wills; Guard Discovered Watergate Break-In," *Los Angeles Times*, September 29, 2000.

27. Sue A. Pressley, "Man Who Made Watergate Call Mourned," *Washington Post,* October 1, 2000.

28. Author's interview of Shirley Wills, November 4, 2016.

29. Author's interview of JoAnn Hooper, November 2, 2016.

30. Woo, "Frank Wills; Guard Discovered Watergate Break-In." See also Harold Jackson, "Obituary: Frank Wills, Security Guard in Watergate Crisis," *The* [London] *Guardian*, October 22, 2000.

31. Adam Clymer, "Frank Wills, 52: Watchman Foiled Watergate Break-In," *New York Times*, September 29, 2000.

32. "Watergate Guard Frank Wills," Weekend Edition, National Public Radio, September 30, 2000.

33. Adam Bernstein, "Frank Wills: Detected Watergate Break-In," *Washington Post*, September 29, 2000.

34. Pressley, "Man Who Made Watergate Call Mourned."

35. Randy Shilts, *And the Band Played On: Politics, People, and the AIDS Epidemic* (New York: St. Martin's Press, 1988), p. 178.

36. Stephen Inrig, *North Carolina and the Problem of AIDS: Advocacy, Politics, and Race in the South* (Chapel Hill: University of North Carolina Press, 2011). For additional statistical data on AIDS and African Americans, see Kai Wright, ed., "AIDS and Black America," in *AIDS in Blackface: 25 Years of an Epidemic* (Los Angeles: Black AIDS Institute, June 2006).

37. Booker, "Frank Wills, Watergate Hero, Tells of Hard Times He Faces."

38. "Which Watergate Figure Believes," *The Advocate*, September 20, 1994.

39. Shilts, *And the Band Played On*, pp. 241, 353.

40. Author's interview of Austin Rhodes, November 3, 2016.

41. Shilts, *And the Band Played On*, p. 353.

42. Margaret O'Shea, "Watergate Guard Led Quiet Life," *Augusta Chronicle*, September 30, 2000.

43. Pressley, "Man Who Made Watergate Call Mourned."

Epilogue

1. Author's interview of Eddie Wills, November 4, 2016.

2. "Speaking Out: Frank Wills Must Not Be Forgotten," *Ebony*, June 1976.

3. Charles J. Helm , "A Modest Proposal for the Fostering of Acquiescence in the Republic, or Frank Wills, and a 'Sensitive Due Regard for Our Betters': Notes on the Language of Equality ," *Crime and Social Justice*, No. 20 (1983), pp. 78.

4. *Ibid.*

5. Harold Jackson, "Obituary: Frank Wills, Security Guard in Watergate Crisis."

6. Nita Schichor, "Does Sarbanes-Oxley Force Whistleblowers to Sacrifice Their Reputations?: An Arugment for Granting Whistleblowers Non-Pecuniary Damages," *Business Law Journal*, University of California, Davis, 272 (Spring 2008).

7. Theodore H. White, *The Making of the President 1972* (New York: Atheneum Publishers, 1973), p. 386.

8. Sean Wilentz, *The Age of Regan: A History, 1974–2008* (New York: Harper, 2008), p. 17.

9. Hugh Rawson, "The Words of Watergate: An Anniversary Look Back at the Biggest Presidential Scandal Ever, Through the Changes It Wrought in the Language," *American Heritage* (October 1997), 24–42.

Bibliography

Archives

Alex Haley Manuscript Collection, Manuscripts/Archive Collection, National Afro-American Museum and Cultural Center, Wilberforce, Ohio.

Augusta University, Special Collections Library.

Davidson Library, Department of Special Collections, University of California, Santa Barbara.

Georgia Historical Society.

Georgia State Office of Vital Records.

The Irvin Department of Rare Books and Special Collections, South Carolina Political Collections, University of South Carolina.

Lawrence F. O'Brien Oral History Interview, Lyndon Baines Johnson Presidential Library, University of Texas at Austin.

National Urban League Records, Manuscript Division, Library of Congress, Washington, D.C.

Nixontapes.org.

Pacifica Radio Archives.

Paine College, Special Collections.

Simeon Booker Papers, in possession of Carol McCabe Booker.

Southern Oral History Program Collection, University of North Carolina, Chapel Hill.

"Student Protests at Northern Michigan University," Central Upper Peninsula and Northern Michigan University Archives.

University of Kansas Special Collections.

Vanderbilt Television News Archive.

Voter Education Project Organizational Records, 1962–1992, Archives Research Center, Robert W. Woodruff Library, Atlanta University Center.

Watergate Collection, Harry Ransom Center, University of Texas at Austin.

Books, Dissertations and Theses

Ambrose, Stephen E. *Nixon: The Triumph of a Politician 1962–1972.* Volume 2. New York: Simon & Schuster, 1989.

Bernhard-Hollins, Sonya. *Here I Stand: A Musical History of African Americans in Battle Creek, Michigan.* Kalamazoo, MI: Fortitude Graphic Design & Publishing, 2003.

Bibliography

Billingsly, Andrew. *Mighty Like a River: The Black Church and Social Reform.* New York: Oxford University Press, 1999.

Bonner, Wilma F., et al. *The Sumner Story: Capturing Our History, Preserving Our Legacy.* Garden City, NY: Morgan James Publishing, 2010.

Booker, Simeon. *Shocking the Conscience: A Reporter's Account of the Civil Rights Movement.* Jackson: University Press of Mississippi, 2013.

Brinkley, Douglas. *Gerald R. Ford.* New York: Henry Holt and Company, 2007.

Budiansky, Stephen. *The Bloody Shirt: Terror After Appomattox.* New York: Viking Press, 2008.

Buschel, Bruce, and Albert Robbins, William Vitka, edited by Rod Nordland. *The Watergate File: A Concise, Illustrated Guide to the People and Events.* New York: Flash Books, 1973.

Califano, Joseph A., Jr. *Inside: A Public and Private Life.* New York: PublicAffairs, 2004.

Chester, Lewis, and Cal McCrystal, Stephen Aris, William Shawcross. *Watergate: The Full Inside Story.* New York: Ballantine Books, 1973.

Coffey, Justin P. "Watergate and the Committee to Reelect the President." University of Wyoming, MA Thesis, 1998.

Davis, Townsend. *Weary Feet, Rested Souls: A Guided History of the Civil Rights Movement.* New York: W.W. Norton & Company, 1998.

Dickinson, William B., Jr. *Year of Scandal: How the* Washington Post *Covered Watergate and the Agnew Crisis.* Washington, D.C.: Washington Post Company, 1973.

Elmore, Charles J. *Black America Series: Savannah, Georgia.* Charleston, SC: Arcadia Publishing, 2000.

Emery, Fred. *Watergate: The Corruption of American Politics and the Fall of Richard Nixon.* New York: Random House, 1994.

Evans, Eli N. *The Provincials: A Personal History of Jews in the South.* New York: Simon & Schuster, 1992.

Ferris, Marcie Cohen, and Mark I. Greenberg, editors. *Jewish Roots in Southern Soil: A New History.* Waltham, MA: Brandeis University Press, 2006.

Givner, Bruce, with Cherie Kerr. *My Watergate Scandal Tell-All: How I Unwittingly Caused This Historic Event.* Santa Ana, CA: ExecuProv Press, 2019.

Gordon, Arthur. *How Sweet It Is: The Story of Dixie Crystals and Savannah Foods.* Savannah, GA: Savannah Food Industries, 1992.

Gregory, Dick. *Defining Moments in Black History: Reading Between the Lies.* New York: Amistad, 2017.

_____. *Dick Gregory's Natural Diet for Folks Who Eat: Cookin' with Mother Nature.* New York: Harper & Row, 1973.

Hirsch, James S. *Willie Mays: The Life, the Legend.* New York: Simon & Schuster, 2010.

Hirshberg, Jack. *Redford/Hoffman: A Portrait of All the President's Men.* New York: Warner Books, 1976.

History of North Augusta, South Carolina. North Augusta, SC: North Augusta Historical Society, 1980.

Hoskins, Charles L. *Out of Yamacraw and Beyond: Discovering Black Savannah.* Savannah, GA: Gulah Press, 2002.

Hougan, Jim. *Secret Agenda: Watergate, Deep Throat and the CIA.* New York: Random House, 1984.

Bibliography

Inrig, Stephen. *North Carolina and the Problem of AIDS: Advocacy, Politics, and Race in the South.* Chapel Hill: University of North Carolina Press, 2011.

Irvin, Nat, II. "Escape from Boggy Branch: The True Story of How Reverend Nathaniel Irvin, Sr. Found His Way to Heaven 1929–2016," *A Service of Life and Legacy of the Reverend Dr. Nathaniel Irvin, Sr. 1929–2016,* October 8, 2016 (privately printed).

Jaffe, Harry S., and Tom Sherwood. *Dream City: Race, Power, and the Decline of Washington, D.C.* New York: Simon & Schuster, 1994.

Kakalik, James S., and Sorrel Wildhorn. *The Private Police: Security and Danger.* New York: Crane, Russak & Company, 1977.

Kramer, Richard Ben. *What It Takes.* New York: Vintage Books, 1993.

League of Women Voters of South Carolina. *Survey of the Town of North Augusta, South Carolina.* South Carolina: League of Women Voters of South Carolina, 1959.

Levitan, Sar A., and Benjamin H. Johnston. *The Job Corps: A Social Experiment That Works.* Baltimore: Johns Hopkins University Press, 1975.

Mack, Tom. *Hidden History of Aiken County.* Charleston, SC: History Press, 2012.

McCord, James W., Jr. *A Piece of Tape: The Watergate Story, Fact and Fiction.* Rockville, MD: Washington Media Services, 1974.

McDaniel, Jeanne. *North Augusta: James U. Jackson's Dream.* Charleston, SC: Arcadia Publishing, 2005.

Nixon, Richard. *RN: The Memoirs of Richard Nixon.* New York: Simon & Schuster, 1990.

O'Brien, Lawrence F. *No Final Victories: A Life in Politics from John F. Kennedy to Watergate.* New York: Doubleday & Company, 1974.

Riddick, Allen. *Aiken County Schools: A Pictorial History and More.* Aiken, SC: Rocket Publishing. 2003.

Roberson, Frank G. *Over a Hundred Schoolhouses: A Historical Account of Public Education in Aiken County Before and After Consolidation and Integration.* Aiken, SC: Aiken County Consolidated School District, 2000.

Rodota, Joseph. *The Watergate: Inside America's Most Infamous Address.* New York: William Morrow, 2018.

Shilts, Randy. *And the Band Played On: Politics, People, and the AIDS Epidemic.* New York: St. Martin's Press, 1988.

Sirica, John J. *To Set the Record Straight: The Break-Ins, the Tapes, the Conspirators, the Pardon.* New York: W.W. Norton & Company, 1979.

Sussman, Barry. *The Great Cover-Up: Nixon and the Scandal of Watergate.* New York: Signet, 1974.

Tuck, Stephen G. N. *Beyond Atlanta: The Struggle for Racial Equality in Georgia, 1940–1980.* Athens: University of Georgia Press, 2001.

The Watergate Hero: An Eyewitness Report by Frank Wills. Washington, D.C.: Wil-Van, Inc., 1973.

Werth, Barry. *31 Days: The Crisis That Gave Us the Government We Have Today.* New York: Doubleday, 2006.

White, John W. "Managed Compliance: White Resistance and Desegregation in South Carolina, 1950–1970." Ph.D. Dissertation, University of Florida; 2006.

Wilentz, Sean. *The Age of Regan: A History, 1974–2008* New York: Harper, 2008.

Woodward, Bob. *The Last of the President's Men.* New York: Simon & Schuster, 2015.

Bibliography

Woodward, Bob, and Carl Bernstein. *All the President's Men.* New York: Simon & Schuster, 2012 (republished).

Wright, Kai, editor. "AIDS and Black America," in *Aids in Blackface: 25 Years of an Epidemic.* Los Angeles: Black AIDS Institute, June 2006.

Government and Judicial Documents

Aiken County Assessor's Office.

Court of Appeals of Maryland, Misc. Docket AG No. 14, September Term 2006.

D.C. Attorney Discipline System: District of Columbia Court of Appeals Board of Professional Responsibility, "Disciplinary Action," July 24, 1990 and April 27, 2006.

Federal Bureau of Investigation (FBI) Records: The Vault (Watergate Collection), Washington, D.C., https://vault.fbi.gov.

National Archives and Records Administration,
- Records of the Job Corps History
- Records of the Watergate Special Prosecution Force, 1971–1977

Report of the Committee of the Judiciary House of Representatives, August 20, 1974. Debate on Articles of Impeachment: Hearings of the Committee of the Judiciary House of Representatives. Washington, D.C.: US Government Printing Office, 1974.

Senate Ninety-third Congress First Session: Watergate and Related Activities, Phase I: Watergate Investigation, *Presidential Campaign Activities of 1972 Senate Resolution 60,* Book 1. Washington, D.C.: U.S. Government Printing Office, 1973.

Supreme Court of Kansas. IN RE: Dorsey EVANS, Respondent. No. 98,842. Decided: October 26, 2007, https://caselaw.findlaw.com/ks-supreme-court/1142406.html.

United States Census, 1950 Population General Characteristics, Georgia.

United States Department of the Interior National Park Service: National Register of Historic Places, Watergate, Washington, D.C., Section 7, Page 6, October 12, 2005.

United States District Court for the District of Columbia, Watergate in Court: The Official Transcripts of the Court Proceedings of the Four Major Watergate Trials Including Indictments and Exhibits. United States of America v. George Gordon Liddy, et. al., Criminal No. 1827–72, Reel 1, January 16, 1973. Arlington, VA: A Microfilm Project of University Publications of America, Inc., 1975.

"WILLS v. THE STATE," 169 Ga. App. 260 (1983) 312 S.E.2d 367 67148. Court of Appeals of Georgia, Decided November 23, 1983, Rehearing Denied December 12, 1983.

Interviews

Paul Brock, February 23, 2017.
Stephanie Coleman, November 4, 2016.
Bruce Givner, February 15, 16, 2018.
Cathy Grant, November 3, 2016.
Reco Grant, November 3, 2016.

Bibliography

JoAnn Hooper, November 2, 4, 2016, July 7, 2018, November 10, 2018.
Nathaniel Irvin, Jr., January 27, 2017.
Dr. Martha Keber, May 31, 2017.
Mallory Millender, November 2, 2016.
Martez Mims, November 2, 2016.
William Mims, November 2, 2016
Mary Newsome, November 3, 2016.
Wayne O'Bryant, November 2, 3, 2016.
Pamela Oliver, July 15, 2017.
Austin Rhodes, November 3, 2016.
Don Rhodes, November 8, 2016.
Lee Shonfield, May 22, June 15, 2019, May 26, 2020.
Walter B. Simmons, July 15, 2017.
Preston Sykes, November 2, 2016.
Carrie Williams, November 4, 2016.
Eugene Williams, November 3, 2016.
Eddie Wills, November 4, 2016.
Shirley Wills, November 4, 2016, April 25, 2019.

Magazines

EBONY

"With Thanks to Frank Wills," June 1973.
"Speaking Out: Frank Wills Must Not Be Forgotten," June 1976.

JET

Booker, Simeon. "Untold Story of Black Hero of Watergate," May 17, 1973.
"Watergate Hero Attempts to Cash In on His Fame," July 5, 1973.
Booker, Simeon. "Ticker Tape USA," August 23, 1973.
"Watergate Hero Is Broke and Jobless," September 20, 1973.
Key, Randall L. "Readers Rap: Plight of Frank Wills," November 22, 1973.
"Young Frank Wills, Unsung Watergate Hero, Changed U.S. History," August 22, 1974.
Booker, Simeon. "Watergate Is Revisited in Film, but Still No Glory for Frank Wills," April 22, 1976.
_____. "Special Report on Black Hero of Watergate," June 21, 1982.
"Wills Appeals One Year Shoplifting Sentence," March 7, 1983.
"Newark Mayor Asks Reagan to Pardon Frank Wills," April 4, 1983.
Booker, Simeon. "Frank Wills, 10 Years After Watergate, Faces Dismal Future," September 10, 1984.
_____. "Ticker Tape, USA," September 23, 1985.
Haywood, Richette. "Frank Wills, Reflects on Discovery of Watergate Break-in 20 Years Later," June 22, 1992.
Booker, Simeon. "Frank Wills, Watergate Hero, Tells of Hard Times He Faces," March 8, 1993.

Bibliography

Time

"Howard Johnson's Motor Lodges and Restaurants Advertisement," November 6, 1972.

Kissinger, Henry. "Years of Upheaval: Watergate," March 8, 1982.

Washingtonian

Shepard, Alicia. "Woodward and Bernstein Uncovered," September 1, 2003.

Lindsay, David. "The Watergate: The Building That Changed Washington," October 1, 2005.

Shirley, Craig. "The Bartender's Tale: How the Watergate Burglars Got Caught," June 20, 2012.

Miscellaneous Magazines

Kytle, Calvin. "A Long, Dark Night for Georgia?" *Harper's Magazine*, September 1948.

Stern, Sol. "A Watergate Footnote*: The Selling of Frank Wills," *New York Times Magazine*, September 10, 1974.

"A Decade Later, Watergate's Veterans Are Winners, Losers—and Everything in Between," *People*, June 14, 1982.

"Which Watergate Figure Believes...," *The Advocate*, September 20, 1994.

Newspapers

Augusta Chronicle

"More Tourists Than Ever This Winter," July 5, 1903.

Associated Press, "NA Native Triggered Watergate Alarm," April 26, 1973.

Worsnop, Richard L. "Guards Are Underpaid," May 19, 1973.

"Watergate Guard Wishes He Wasn't Man on Spot," June 17, 1973.

"Happenings," February 25, 1974.

"Watchman at Watergate Has Troubles," December 15, 1974.

"Testimony Will Begin in Thurmond's Trial," May 23, 1978.

Powers, Pat. "Watergate Break-in Discoverer Arrested for Shoplifting Shoes," September 4, 1982.

Peacock, Chris. "Unaware of Court Date, Watergate Guard Says," December 16, 1982.

_____. "Wills' Trial to Be Held in February," December 17, 1982.

"Ex-guard Who Discovered Watergate Draws Jail Term," February 16, 1983.

Mims, Mrs. BL, Jr., "Letters to the Editor: Finds 'Justice' Gets 'Curiouser,'" February 20, 1983.

Valente, Mickie. "Wills Release from Prison Pending Retrial Pushed Back," March 2, 1983.

McBride, Tommy. "Letters to the Editor: Opposes Mayors' Interference," March 3, 1983.

Valente, Mickie. "Wills Posts Bond, Freed from Prison," March 3, 1983.

Bibliography

_____. "Ex-Watergate Guard's Sentence Routine Policy," March 6, 1983.

Merchant, Herbert W. "Letters to the Editor: Claims He's Not Liberal, Just Mad," March 10, 1983.

Valente, Mickie. "Presidential Pardon Sought for Wills," April 5, 1983.

_____. "Request to Pardon Wills Misdirected," April 6, 1983.

Twiggs, Margaret. "Ridiculous Aspects to Wills Case," April 10, 1983.

Durland, Barbara. "Letters to the Editor: Opposes Pardon for Shoplifter," April 11, 1983.

Valente, Mickie. "Wills' Attorney Cites Errors, Requests New Trial," April 22, 1983.

Vogel, Mike. "Slaton Refuses New Trial for Wills," May 17, 1983.

"Watergate Guard Readies Appeal of Judge's Ruling," May 18, 1983.

"Watergate Guard Appeals Termed as 'Probable,'" May 18, 1983.

"Wills Seeks to Have Conviction Overturned," June 16, 1983.

"Former Guard's Appeal Docketed," July 30, 1983.

Feinsilber, Mike. "Watergate Was Big Show 10 Years Ago," August 14, 1983.

"Group Continues Push to Buy Truck for Wills," October 7, 1983.

Vogel, Mike. "Conviction, Jail Sentence of Wills Upheld by Court," November 29, 1983.

"Shoplifting Sentence Appealed by Wills," March 22, 1984.

"Court Upholds Conviction of Former Watergate Guard," October 2, 1984.

Associated Press. "Road to Nixon's Downfall Began 15 years Ago Today," June 17, 1987.

Roberts, John. "Watergate Security Guard Now N. Augustan," June 17, 1992.

O'Shea, Margaret. "Watergate Guard Led Quiet Life," September 30, 2000.

Augusta Herald

Rhodes, Don. "Guard Who Touched Off Watergate in Jail," September 3, 1982.

_____. "Record Shows Previous Shoplifting Charge Brought Against Wills," September 7, 1982.

_____. "Wills Claims Not Informed About Court Date for Shoplifting Trial," December 16, 1982.

_____. "Wills Convicted of Shoplifting, Given 1-year Prison Term," February 15, 1983.

"Wills Out on Bond," March 2, 1983.

Denney, Ken. "Presidential Pardon for Wills Doubted by Justice Department," April 5, 1983.

Rhodes, Don. "Life Takes a Positive Turn; Roots' Author Alex Haley to Tell About Former Watergate Guard in a New Book," May 27, 1983.

[Baltimore] *Afro American*

"Watergate Guard Bailed Out; Seeks New Trial," May 8, 1973.

"The $80-a-Week Guard Who 'Blew the Whistle' on Watergate," May 12, 1973.

"Mitchell Seeks National Honor for Watergate Guard," February 18, 1975.

Baltimore Sun

Atwood, Liz. "Fund-Raiser Conducted for Man Who Helped Unseat a President," October 14, 1993.

Bibliography

Simon, Roger. "Former Watergate Guard's Complaints Lack Conviction," October 24, 1993.
Simon, Roger. "Watergate 'Hero' Has Let Opportunities Pass Him By," October 25, 1993.

Boston Globe

Bradlee, Ben Jr. "Watergate Celebrity No More," April 30, 1983.
Farrell, John Aloysius. "Watergate's Hero Forgotten, Alone Former Guard Broods in a Cabin in the Woods," June 15, 1997.

Chicago Sun-Times

Simon, Roger. "Watergate Hero's Note," October 26, 1977.
Royko, Mike. "Fame Hasn't Done a Thing for Frank Wills," March 9, 1983.

Los Angeles Times

Woo, Elaine. "Frank Wills; Guard Discovered Watergate Break-In," September 29, 2000.
Neuman, Johanna. "Brookings Guard Who Foiled Burglars Dies," March 1 2003.

Milwaukee Journal

"Watergate Guard a Hero to Many," February 18, 1974.
"Expo Guest Bitter About Watergate," September 21, 1974.

New York Times

Huxtable, Ada Louise. "Controversy Widens on Design of Development in Washington," April 29, 1962.
"Problems of Watergate 'In' Place of the Capital, Anger Many Residents," March 12, 1972.
"5 Charged with Burglary at Democratic Quarters," June 18, 1972.
Rugaber, Walter. "Motive is Big Mystery in Raid on Democrats," June 26, 1972.
Crewdson, John M. "Who Called the Signals," March 18, 1973.
Clarity, James F. "Notes on People: Watergate Produces One Hero," April 28, 1973.
"Guard at the Watergate Says He Can't Get a Job," September 21, 1973.
"Watergate Guard Says No Position Is Too High," August 9, 1974.
"Guard at Watergate to Get S.C.L.C. Honor," August 14, 1974.
"Guard Who Caught Burglars Is Bitter," June 17, 1977.
Montgomery, Paul L. "10 Years Later: Watergate Figures Recall Turning Point in Their Lives," June 17, 1982.
Kristof, Nicholas D. "The Success of the 'President's Men,'" July 13, 1986.
Clymer, Adam. "Frank Wills, 52; Watchman Foiled Watergate Break-In," September 29, 2000.
Grimes, William. "James Mann, 90, Dies; Worked on Nixon Impeachment," December 23, 2010.

Bibliography

[Washington, D.C.] *Afro American*

Baker Lewis, Alfred. "Our Readers Say: Little Wrote About Frank Wills," May 28, 1974.

Spears, Lawanza. "20 Years After Watergate, Hero Lives in Poverty," April 24, 1993.

Washington Post

Willmann, John B. "Foggy Bottom Gas House Site to Get Facelift," October 22, 1961.

Clopton, Willard. "Board Opposition Rises to Watergate Apartment Project," December 24, 1961.

Stern, Laurence. "White House Acts to Cut Height of Huge Watergate Development," May 5, 1962.

"High-Rise Watergate Towne Given Final D.C. Approval," July 14, 1962.

"Towne Plan Stirs Row by Protestants," November 17, 1962.

White, Jean M., "Woes Stall Watergate Project," October 18, 1963.

"Development of Watergate Towne Gets Go-Ahead on Ground Breaking," January 25, 1964.

"Watergate Noses Up," October 3, 1964.

Willmann, John B., "Watergate's Architect Shudders at Conformity," February 25, 1965.

"Watergate East Gets First Tenants," October 24, 1965.

"Watergate Apartment Hotel Opens," April 1, 1967.

"Democrats to Take New Headquarters," April 26, 1967.

"Watergate Selling in Fourth Building," October 7, 1967.

"Watergate Plans Reaffirmed," November 16, 1967.

"Compromise Plan Ends Watergate Controversy," August 9, 1968.

"Watergate Complex Spreads Out," August 17, 1968.

"Watergate, Where Republicans Gather," February 25, 1969.

"Watergate: Potomac Titanic," May 3, 1970.

Lewis, Alfred E. "5 Held in Plot to Bug Democrats' Office Here," June 18, 1972.

Barker, Karlyn. "Intruders Foiled by Security Guard," June 19, 1972.

Bernstein, Carl and Bob Woodward. "FBI Finds Nixon Aides Sabotaged Democrats," October 10, 1972.

Stern, Laurence, and Haynes Johnson. "3 Top Nixon Aides, Kleindienst Out; President Accepts Full Responsibility; Richardson Will Conduct New Probe," May 1, 1973.

Lewis, Alfred E. "An Unmarked Car Watergate Break?" May 13, 1973.

Turan, Kenneth. "Opening of Watergate Dam No Act of Heroism to the Guard," May 14, 1973.

Blumenthal, Fred. "Watergate: How It All Started," August 26, 1973.

Raspberry, William. "Frank Wills—and Attorney," March 1, 1974.

"Scandal's Cop Works, Meditates in South; No Fond Memories of D.C.," October 22, 1978.

Berry M., John and Art Pine. "19 Years of Job Programs—Question Still Is 'What Works,'" April 24, 1979.

Allen, Henry. "Fame and the Freedom of Wills; Watergate Guard Released After Shoplifting Arrest," September 4, 1982.

Bibliography

Sterritt, Kathleen and John Kennedy. "Personalities," September 11, 1982.

Grove, Lloyd. "Gregory's New Diet; He Mixes Watergate with Health Promotion," October 3, 1984.

Barker, Karlyn and W. Pincus."Watergate Revisited: 20 Years After the Break-in, the Story Continues to Unfold," June 14, 1992.

Barker, Karlyn and Vivien Lou Chen. "Landmarks Tell Lore of Watergate; Scandal Unfolded at Many Addresses," June 17, 1992.

Oldenburg, Don. "No Leaks in This Think Tank," November 23, 1996.

Bernstein, Adam. "Frank Wills; Detected Watergate Break-In," September 29, 2000.

Pressley, Sue A. "Man Who Made Watergate Call Mourned," October 1, 2000.

Weil, Martin. "DNC's Stanley Greigg Dies; Signed Watergate Complaint," June 16, 2002.

Shapiro, T. Rees. "Dick Gregory, Cutting-Edge Satirist and Uncompromising Activist, Dies at 84," August 20, 2017.

Langer, Emily, "Simeon Booker, Intrepid Chronicler of Civil Rights Struggle for *Jet* and *Ebony,* Dies at 99," December 10, 2017.

Miscellaneous Newspapers

Associated Press. "Marshall to Ask for Another Billion," *Savannah Morning News,* February 5, 1948.

_____. "Watergate Guard Can't Find a Job," *Charleston* [West Virginia] *Daily Mail,* October 25, 1973.

_____. "Watergate Guard," *Beaver County* [Pennsylvania] *Times,* March 1, 1983.

_____. "Watergate Guard Free with Help of Mayors," [Wilmington, North Carolina] *Morning Star-News,* March 3, 1983.

Boorstin, Jon. "On its 40th Anniversary: Notes on the Making of All the President's Men," *Los Angeles Review of Books,* March 25, 2016.

Cimons, Marlene. "Whatever Happened to—Frank Wills," *Toledo Blade,* January 6, 1974.

Colvin, Leonard E. "Frank Wills: Forgotten Hero of Watergate," [Norfolk, Virginia] *New Journal & Guide,* June 24-June 30, 1992.

Eidson, Stacy. "Opening Doors: 60 Years After Brown v. Board of Education," [Augusta, Georgia] *Metro Spirit,* May 19, 2014.

Irvin, Nat. "Homespun: Little House Is Filled with Big Memoires," *Winston-Salem Journal,* January 4, 1998.

Jackson, Harold. "Obituary: Frank Wills: Security Guard in Watergate Crisis," *The* [London] *Guardian,* October 22, 2000.

Kitchen, Dorethea H. "NAACP on the Move," *Columbus* [Georgia] *Times,* October 26, 1983.

Livingston, Mike. "Watergate: The Name That Branded More Than a Building," *Washington* [D.C.] *Business Journal,* June 17, 2002.

McLaughlin, Abraham T. "Whatever Happened to...?" *Christian Science Monitor,* January 25, 1996.

Millender, Mallory. "Alex Haley in Augusta, Starts Autobiography of Frank Wills," *Augusta News-Review,* May 28, 1983.

Bibliography

O'Leary, Jeremiah and Patrick Collins. "Were Guards Bribed?," [Washington, D.C.] *Sunday Star*, October 1, 1972.

"R. Warrick, Brookings Guard at Start of Watergate Scandal," [Long Island, New York] *Newsday*, March 2, 2003.

Richards, Clay F. "Democrats to Have Permanent Home After 200 Years," United Press International Archives, April 19, 1983, https://www.upi.com/Archives/1983/04/19/Democrats-to-have-permanent-home-after-200-years/2748419576400/.

Shaw, Jim. "But for Him, Nixon Might Sill Be President," *Columbia Law School Observer*, February 24, 1975.

"Still Living It After 25 Years: Officer Who Caught Watergate Burglars Will Never Forget," *Pittsburgh Post–Gazette*, June 15, 1997.

Stillman, Jack. "Human Brain Termed a Mystery," undated newspaper clipping, Simeon Booker Collection in the possession of Carol McCabe Booker.

Straub, Bill. "Following the Watergate Scandal's Key Players," *San Francisco Chronicle*, June 14, 2002.

Tauber, Susan K. "We Owe Much to Frank Wills," *Atlanta Journal and Constitution*, June 23, 1992.

"Things Looking Up for Frank Wills, the Watergate Hero," [Fredericksburg, Virginia] *Free Lance-Star*, July 29, 1977.

"Watergate Guard Gets Trust Fund," *Milwaukee Sentinel*, November 15, 1973.

"Watergate Hero Wills to Help Gregory Promote Diet Product," *Washington Informer*, Oct 10, 1984.

Radio and Television

"Bruce Givner's *My Watergate Scandal Tell-All: How I Unwittingly Caused This Historic Event*," https://www.youtube.com/watch?v=TmjwY6lzYtY, June 10, 2019.

"In Depth: Watergate 25th Anniversary," *NBC Evening News*, June 17, 1997, Episode #618825, Vanderbilt Television News Archive. https://tvnews.vanderbilt.edu/broadcasts/618825

The Presidents: Nixon, PBS American Experience, aired October 15, 1990, http://www.pbs.org/wgbh/americanexperience/films/nixon/.

"Sgt. Paul Leeper's Watergate Experience," *The West Virginia News Video*, posted on YouTube December 7, 2012. https://www.youtube.com/watch?v=l6aGRtEmwTE

"Truth and Lies: Watergate," *20/20*, American Broadcasting Company, aired June 16, 2017.

"Watergate: 5 Years Ago," *CBS News*, June 17, 1977, Episode #252652, Vanderbilt Television News Archive. https://tvnews.vanderbilt.edu/broadcasts/252652

"Watergate Guard Frank Wills," Weekend Edition, National Public Radio, September 30, 2000.

"Watergate 20th Anniversary," C-SPAN, aired June 18, 1992. http://www.c-span.org/video/?26646-1/watergate-20th-anniversary&start=NaN

Bibliography

Statistical Studies

William J. Collins and Melissa A. Thomasson, "Exploring the Racial Gap in Infant Mortality Rates, 1920–1970" [research paper], [September 2001: Preliminary], National Bureau of Economic Research.

Haines, Michael. "Fertility and Mortality in the United States," EH.Net Encyclopedia, edited by Robert Whaples. March 19, 2008. http://eh.net/encyclopedia/fertility-and-mortality-in-the-united-states/

Index

Numbers in ***bold italics*** indicate pages with illustrations

Aaron, Hank 37
Abernathy, Ralph 97
The Advocate 155
AEC (Atomic Energy Commission) 33, 36
African Americans: AIDS 154–155; Atlanta, Georgia 21; baseball 37; Battle Creek, Michigan 44; Georgia 21; Hamburg Massacre 35; health disparity 24; North Augusta, South Carolina 34–36; relationship with Jews in South 26–28; Savannah, Georgia 21–26; second-class status 25, 26; South Carolina schools 37–38; Tybee Island, Georgia 31; *see also* racism
Afro-American (Baltimore) 69, 84, 86
Afro-American (Washington, D.C.) 148
Agnew, Spiro 89, 92
AIDS 154–156
Aiken, South Carolina 34
Aiken County schools 38
Air Line Pilots Association Building 80
Ali, Muhammad 3
All the President's Men (film) 103–108, ***105, 107***
All the President's Men (Woodward and Bernstein) 90, 106
And the Band Played On (Shilts) 156
Angel (Wills' daughter) 137–138, 140, 142–144
Armstrong Adult Education Center (Armstrong Center) 100–101
Ashe, Arthur 154
Associated Press 114, 153
Atlanta, Georgia 21
Atlanta Journal-Constitution 141
Atomic Energy Commission (AEC) 33, 36
Atwood, Liz 148
Augusta, Georgia: history 34; Lucy Craft Laney High School 39, 41, 118; Wills'

shoplifting arrest 117–127, 131, 132, 134, 135, 161
Augusta Chronicle: Watergate anniversaries 139, 141; Wills' death 158; Wills' employment problems 88; Wills' shoplifting arrest 120, 124, 125, 126–127
Augusta Herald 120, 131
Augusta News-Review 129–131
Aunt Sadie 37
The Autobiography of Frank Wills (proposed Haley book) 3–4, 128–131, ***130,*** 138–139, 179*n*9
The Autobiography of Malcolm X (Haley) 129, 130, 131

Bailey, John M. 55
Baldwin, Alfred 171*n*12
"The Ballad of Frank Wills" (song) 87
Baltimore Afro-American 69, 84, 86
Baltimore Sun 141, 148
Barker, Bernard L. 64, 75
Barker, Karlyn 70–72, 141
Barrett, John 59–64
baseball 37
Battle Creek, Michigan 43, 44
Bay of Pigs invasion 64
Bernstein, Carl: *All the President's Men* (film) 104; *All the President's Men* (with Woodward) 90; papers 4, 165*n*2; Watergate break-in reports 68, 78–79, 103–104; Wills interview 23–24
Berry, John M. 43
Bettis Academy 39
Bliss, Karen (Cox) 170*n*1
Bohler, Mary 23, 156
Bond, Julian 97
Booker, Carol McCabe 11, 83, 85, 116, 117, 143, 145, 146, 147
Booker, Simeon ***68***; background 4, 69; door hinges 70, 172*n*9; Watergate anniversaries

195

Index

103, 110, 115–117, *116, 117*; Watergate break-in story 68–70, 84; Wills' employment and finances 92, 145–148, 149; Wills' mental state 114, 132
Boston Globe 72, 120
Brack, Dennis, photograph by *105*
Bradlee, Ben 87
Brock, Paul 99, 101
Brokaw, Tom 77–78, 96, 150
Brookings Institution 7–9, 163
Brown, Angel (Wills' daughter) 137–138, 140, 142–144
Brown, Jim 88
Brown, Leroy C. 13, 76, 78, 165*n*2
Brown, Marilyn 74
Brown v. Board of Education (1954) 37–38
Bush, George H.W. 80
Butterfield, Alexander 89

Camp Custer/Fort Custer 43, 44
Carter, Jimmy 99
Castro, Fidel 68
CBS Nightly News 110
CCC (Civilian Conservation Corps) 42
Central Colored School playground, North Augusta 39–40
Central Intelligence Agency (CIA) 68
Cernitin America 134
Chamberlain, F. Kelly 76, 78
Chatham Realty Company 81, 90
Chicago Seven 53
Chicago Sun-Times 110, 125
Chicago Tribune 72
childhood of Frank Wills: North Augusta, South Carolina 31–33, 36–37, 39–41; Savannah, Georgia 20, 23–31, *29*
Chisholm, Shirley 102–103
Christian Science Monitor 149
Chrysler Motors 45
civil rights movement 21–22 *see also* King, Martin Luther, Jr.; National Association for the Advancement of Colored People
Civilian Conservation Corps (CCC) 42
Clarke, John Henrik 102
Clinton, Bill 170*n*21
Clinton, Hillary Rodham 170*n*21
Cobb, Ty 33
Coblenz, Walter 104
Coleman, Stephanie 144
Collins, Patrick 76–78
Committee to Re-elect the President (CREEP) 57–58, 65, 73, 75, 78–79, 162
conspiracy theories 73, 76–80, *77*, 173*n*44
Cooke, Thomas 123–124
Cranston, Alan 53
CREEP *see* Committee to Re-elect the President

Crewdson, John M. 83
Cronkite, Walter 110

Dallas Morning News 72
Davis, Miles 3
DC Court of Appeals Board on Professional Responsibility 111–112
DC Metropolitan Police Department (DC Metro Police) 18, 59–67, 170*n*1, 172*ch*7*n*16
Dean, John 82, 110, 115, 141
Dellums, Ron 102
Democratic Club (Hemet, California) 93
Democratic National Committee (DNC): conspiracy theories concerning 173*n*44; CREEP settlement 98; first break-ins 57–58; headquarters in Air Line Pilots Association Building 80; headquarters in Watergate Office Building 12, 54–55; hyperactivity 13; Wills banquet and plaque 148, 150; Wills job prospects with 98, 111; *see also* Watergate Office Building break-in
Democratic National Convention (1968) 53
Democratic National Convention (1972) 13, 15
Detroit, Michigan 12, 45–46
Dick Gregory Health Enterprises 134–135, 137–138, 160, 179*n*40
DNC *see* Democratic National Committee
Dole, Bob 72–73
Donaldson, Gerald 99–102
Douglass, Frederick 44
Durland, Barbara 126

Ebony magazine 160–161
Ehrlichman, John 82, 115
elections 7, 55–56, 99
Ellsberg, Danie l 7
Ervin, Sam 110
Evans, Dorsey, Jr.: background 85; death 112; ethical problems 86, 100, 111–112; exploitation of Wills 100, 101; polishing Wills' statements 96, 175*n*17; on racism 88, 91–92, 106–107; as Wills' agent 84–89, 91–92, 96–103, 106–107, 110–111
Evans, Eli 27

Federal Bureau of Investigation (FBI) 56, 67, 74–77
Federal Reserve Board 17, 61
finances of Wills: *All the President's Men* wages 106; appearance fees 86, 92, 97, 111; Booker's reports on 92, 145–149; Dick Gregory Health Enterprises salary 135, 179*n*40; donations and fundraisers

196

Index

148; employment problems 87–88, 90–91, 113, 114; Evans contract 86, 110–111; Friends of Frank Wills Committee 131–132; government assistance 90, 140, 146, 155; interview fees 97, 98, 115; security guard wages 4, 48, 81, 86, 111, 113; spending habits 11; trust fund 92–93
Firestone, Harvey 33
Fonda, Jane 134
Ford, Gerald 82, 89, 95
Ford Motor Company 45
Fort Custer/Camp Custer 43, 44
The Frank Wills Detective Agency 98
Frank Wills Fan Club 89
Frank Wills Fund 92–93
Friends of Frank Wills Committee 131–132
Frost, David 109

Gandhi, Mahatma 20
General Equivalency Diploma (GED) 99–102
General Security Services (GSS): conspiracy theories concerning 76–78, **77**; hiring Wills 12, 48; praise for Wills 74, 81–82; Wills as hero 74; Wills quitting his job 81; *see also* Watergate Office Building break-in
Georgetown University 103, 106, 110
Georgia: Court of Appeals 131, 132; Jim Crow laws 20–21; State Supreme Court 132
Giant Island Films 1
Gibson, Kenneth 123–124, 126, 129
Gilbert, Ralph Mark 22
Givner, Bruce 14–16, 67, 75, 97, 171*n*12, 173*n*44
Goldwater, Barry 94
Gonzalez, Virgilio R. 64, 75, 76–77
Good Night America 95–96
Gregory, Dick: background 133; finances 138; Wills as spokesman for 134–135, 137–138, 160, 179*n*40
Greigg, Stanley L. 65
GSS *see* General Security Services

Haldeman, H.R. 7, 82, 109, 115, 149, 173*n*44
Haley, Alex: *The Autobiography of Malcolm X* 129, 130, 131; background 139; *Roots* 128, 129; Wills book project 3–4, 128–131, **130**, 138–139, 167*n*10, 179*n*9
Haley, My 128
Halperin, Morton 7–8
Hamburg, South Carolina 34–35
Hamburg Massacre 35
Hamrick, Gayle B. 126
Harding, Warren G. 33
Harris, Joe Frank 122–123, 126

Harry Ransom Center, University of Texas at Austin 4
Hart, Gary 170*n*21
Hasan, Ben 122
Hawkins, John 128–129
He, the People (film) 1
Hellams, Walter 17, 61
Hemet, California 93
Highsmith, Carol M., photograph by **53**
Hirsch, James S. 88
HIV/AIDS 154–156
Hoffman, Dustin 104, 106, **107**
Hooper, Angel *see* Brown, Angel
Hooper, JoAnn 136–137, 140, 142–144, 151, 158
Hoover, J. Edgar 56
Hougan, Jim 165*n*2, 175*n*9
House Judiciary Committee 93–94
Howard Johnson's Motor Lodge & Restaurant 16, 62, 75, 162, 171*n*12
Howard University 85, 91, 101
Hudson, Rock 154
Hughes, Mary Margaret 48
Humphrey, Hubert 55
Hunt, E. Howard 75, 109, 110

Ifill, Gwen 150
impeachment 89, 93–94
infant mortality rate 24
Internal Revenue Service (IRS) 57, 138
Irvin, Leroy 40, 43
Irvin, Nathaniel 40, 41, 73, 152
Irvin, Nathaniel (Nat), Jr.: on Ku Klux Klan 35–36; school integration 168*n*16; on Wills and Watergate break-in 73; on Wills' childhood 40; Wills' Christmas Eve walk 150–151; on Wills' return to North Augusta 112, 113

Jackson, Bobby 14, 16, 18
Jackson, James Urquhart 33–34
Jackson, Walter 33
Jefferson High School 39, **39**, 40
JET magazine: Evans' plans 86; Watergate anniversaries 103, 110, 115–117, **116**, **117**; Watergate break-in story 68–69, 84; Wills cover 84, **85**; Wills' finances 145–148, 155; *see also* Booker, Simeon
Jews, relationship with African Americans 26–28
Jim Crow laws 20–21, 31
Job Corps 42–49
Johnson, Earvin "Magic" 154
Johnson, Haynes 82
Johnson, Lyndon B. 7, 42, 44, 47, 55
Jordan, Hamilton 99

197

Index

Kansas State Bar Association 112
Kelly, JaQwan J. 1–2, 162
Kennedy, John F. 50, 55
Kennedy, Robert F. 55
Kennedy Center 50
Kilby, James 148
King, Martin Luther, Jr. 3, 47, 97, 101
Kissinger, Henry 8, 93
KKK (Ku Klux Klan) 22, 35–36
Kleindienst, Richard 82, 161
Koch, Ed 103
Ku Klux Klan (KKK) 22, 35–36

Lacey, Bill 171*n*1
Lacey, Richard 171*n*1
Lacy, Lloyd 91
Lano, Angelo J. 67, 74–75, 165*n*2
Lasky, Victor 53
Leeper, Paul 59–65, 170*n*1
Lena (African American maid) 28
Lewis, Alfred 68, 70, 71
Liddy, G. Gordon 75, 82, 109, 115, 139, 141, 161
Lincoln Memorial 50, 51
A Little Touch of Schmilsson in the Night (Nilsson album) 87
Lockhart, John 118–119
Los Angeles Times 72, 153
Louis, Joe 88
Lucy Craft Laney High School, Augusta, Georgia 39, 41, 118

Malcolm X 129, 130, 131
Mann, James Robert 93–94
Mantle, Mickey 88
Marshall, George C. 20
Martínez, Eugenio R. 64, 75, 76–77
Maryland State Bar Association 112
Mathias, Charles, Jr. 103
Mays, Willie 37, 88
McBride, Tommy 124
McCord, James: arrest and aftermath 64, 65, 75, 82, 109; CREEP 65, 73; Watergate break-in 162, 172*ch7n*16
McGovern, George 57, 75, 79, 134, 170*n*21
McIntyre, Edward M. 122
Medical College of Georgia 32, 113, 142, 167*n*15
Merchant, Hubert W. 125
Metropolitan Police Department *see* DC Metropolitan Police Department
Miami, Florida 13, 15
Miami Herald 72
Miami Vice (television show) 139
"midnight rides" 35
midterm elections (1970) 55–56
The Mike Douglas Show 87

Millender, Mallory 129–131
Mims, Martez 37, 40, 73, 152
Mims, Mrs. 125
Mims, William 113
Mitchell, John 52, 57–58, 72, 82, 109, 140–141
Mitchell, Martha 52
Mitchell, Parren J. 102–103
Moretti, Luigi 50–51, 52
Morse, Wayne 53
Mosbacher, Emil "Bus" 53
Mount Transfiguration Baptist Church 36, 142, 156, *157*

National Afro-American Museum and Cultural Center 4
National Association for the Advancement of Colored People (NAACP) 21–22, 87, 99, 120–123, 132, 156
National Association of Television and Radio Artists 97
National Cultural Center (Kennedy Center) 50
National Public Radio 153
National Urban League 87, 99–102
NBC News 68
NBC Nightly News 149–150
New York Times: Watergate break-in coverage 72, 83–84, 110; Wills' employment problems 88; Wills' obituary 153; Wills on Nixon's resignation 96; Wills' shoplifting arrest 120
New York Times Magazine 96
Newsweek 139
Nilsson, Harry 87
Nixon, Richard: approval rating 56, 82; Brookings Institution break-in 7–8; death 149; election (1968) 55; election (1972) 7, 56, 79, 80; "Enemies List" 8, 56–57; health issues 103; impeachment 89, 93–94; Job Corps cuts 44; Oval Office taping system 89, 93, 94; post–Watergate life 109, 115, 139, 141; protests against *91*; resignation 94–96, *95*; South Carolina supporters 113; staff with Watergate apartments 52–53; "Tricky Dick" nickname 56; Vietnam War 7–8; Watergate break-in, involvement in 73, 78–79, 80, 82, 90; "what ifs" 162–163; *see also* Committee to Re-elect the President
North Augusta, South Carolina: African Americans 34–36; Central Colored School playground 39–40; history 33–35; hostility toward Wills 112–113; Ku Klux Klan 35–36; location 23; Mount Transfiguration Baptist Church 36, 142, 156, *157*; school integration 168*n*16; segregation

198

Index

35; West Five Notch Road home 41, 112, 142–147, ***143, 145, 146, 147,*** 150, 158; Wills' childhood 31–33, 36–37, 39–41; Wills family background 23; Wills' later life 19–20, 150–152; Wills' return to 112–113; Wills' shoplifting arrest 114, 121
North Augusta High School 39

Obama, Barack 175*n*2
O'Brien, Lawrence 55–57, 62–63, 65, 73, 75, 173*n*44
O'Bryant, Wayne 113, 145
O'Leary, Jeremiah 76–78
Oliver, Pamela 37, 39, 73
Oliver (Wills' father) 23, 166*ch*3*n*1
O'Neal, Ira 14, 165*n*2
Oval Office taping system 89, 93, 94
Owens, Jesse 88, 180*n*13

Pakula, Alan J. 104–106
Paul Knox Middle School, North Augusta 168*n*16
Pentagon Papers 7–8
People magazine 120
Philpot, Danny 119
Pin Point, Georgia 166*n*1
Pine, Art 43
Pittman, Fletcher 13, 17–18, 78, 165*n*2
Playford, Francis 118–119
police *see* DC Metropolitan Police Department
The Post (film) 1, 162
The Presidents (PBS American Experience) 175*n*2
private security industry 47–48
The Provincials (E. Evans) 27
PW's Saloon, Washington, D.C. 171*n*1

"Queen for a Day" (radio program) 31

racism: endorsement opportunities 88, 180*n*13; health disparities 24; hero status 91–92; justice system 122–125, 161; second-class status of African Americans 25, 26; United Automobile Workers 45
Rangel, Charles 93–94
Reagan, Ronald 115, 126, 171*n*1
Redd, Alfred 149, 156
Redford, Robert 103–106, ***107***
Reich, Robert 170*n*21
Rhodes, Austin 151–152, 156
Rhodes, Don 131
Richmond County Correctional Institution 122
Rivera, Geraldo 95–96
Roberts, John 141
Robinson, Jackie 37

Rockefeller, John D. 33
Rogers, Timmie 87
Rolla High School, Missouri 170*n*1
Roosevelt, Franklin D. 20, 42
Roots (ABC mini-series) 128
Roots (Haley) 128, 129
Royko, Mike 125
Ruffin, John H., Jr.: Wills book project (Haley) 129–130, ***130***; Wills' shoplifting case 120–122, 124–127, 131, 132
Rutgers University 102
Ryan White Program 156

Sadie, Aunt 37
Sanford, John B. viii
Savannah, Georgia: African Americans 21–26; civil rights movement 21–22; segregation 21–22, 26; Wills' birth and childhood 20, 23–31, ***29***
Savannah Herald 153
Savannah River Site (nuclear power facility) 33, 36
Savannah Sugar Refinery 26
Schichor, Nina 162
Schofield High School, Aiken, South Carolina 39
schools: integration 168*n*16; quality of black schools 37–38; Wills' education 39, ***39,*** 40, 41
Second District Police Headquarters 67
security industry 47–48
segregation: medical facilities 24; North Augusta, South Carolina 35; public schools 37–38; Savannah, Georgia 21–22, 26; Tybee Island 31
Select Committee on Presidential Campaign Activities (Senate Watergate Committee) 80, 90, 109–110
SGI (Watergate builder) 170*n*13
Sheridan, Earl 125
Shilts, Randy 156
Shirley, Craig 171*n*1
Shoffler, Carl 59–64, 75
Shonfield, Henry 27–28, 30, ***30***
Shonfield, Lee 27–31, ***30,*** 32, 167*n*15
Shonfield, Sayde 27, 28, ***30***
shoplifting arrests 114, 117–127, 131, 132, 134, 135, 161
Shriver, Sargent 42
Simmons, Richard 134
Simmons, Walter B. 23
Simms, George 128
Simon, Roger 148–149
Simon, Scott 153
Sirica, John 82, 109, 174*n*12
Sky City Discount Center, Augusta, Georgia 118–122

199

Index

Slaton, James Edward 121–127, 131, 132, 161
Sorrell, Maurice: photographs by *11, 83, 85, 116, 117*; Wills interview 68–70
South Carolina schools 37–38
Southern Christian Leadership Conference 97
Southern Dining Room, Washington, D.C. 10–11
Spears, Lawanza 148
Spielberg, Steven 1, 162
Spitz, Mark 92
sports, racism in 88, 180*n*13
Stahl, Lesley 110
Stans, Kathleen 52
Stans, Maurice 52
Steinbrenner, George 55
Stephenson, Dennis P. 59, 162, 170*n*1
Stern, Laurence 82
Stern, Sol 96–99
Sturgis, Frank 64, 75
Supreme Court *see* U.S. Supreme Court
Sykes, Preston 40, 41, 114–115, 129, 137, 144

Taft, William Howard 33
Talmadge, Eugene 20–21
tape recordings 89, 93, 94
T.E.A.R. (Treat Every American Right) 148
Thomas, Clarence 166*n*1
Thompson, Melvin E. 20–21
Thurmond, Allan G. 113
Thurmond, Strom 38
Timmie Rogers as Super Soul Brother Alias "Clark Dark" (album) 87
To Tell the Truth 87
Treat Every American Right (T.E.A.R.) 148
trials and sentencing of Watergate burglars 82, 109, 161
Truman, Harry S. 20, 56
Turan, Kenneth 83
Turner, Ron 87
Twiggs, Margaret 126–127
Tybee Island, Georgia 29–31
Tyson, Cicely 97

United Automobile Workers 45
U.S. State Department 50
U.S. Supreme Court 37–38, 93, 132, 134
University Hospital, Augusta 152–153, 156, 167*n*15
University of Texas at Austin 4
Urban League 87, 99–102
Utley, Garrick 68

Valente, Mickie 125
Vietnam War 7–8, 44
Volpe, John 52–53

Wallace, George 11
Walters, Barbara 91
"War on Poverty" 42, 44
Warrick, Roderick 8–9, 163
Washington, D.C.: fine arts and planning commission 50; HIV/AIDS 155; riots and aftermath 46–47, 101; Wills' apartment 10, *11*, 48, 71, 141; Wills' arrival 47; *see also entries at* Watergate
Washington Post: on Job Corps 43; Leeper on "bum squad" 59; racism 69; Watergate break-in 68, 70–72, 74, 82, 83, 84, 141; Wills' obituary 153; Wills' shoplifting arrest 120; *see also* Bernstein, Carl; Woodward, Bob
Washington Star-News 76–78, *77*
Watergate 600 54
Watergate East Apartments (Watergate East) 52
The Watergate Hero: An Eyewitness Report by Frank Wills (promotional pamphlet) 89, 110–111, 166*ch3n*1
Watergate Hotel 54
Watergate Office Building break-in: arrest of burglars 63–64; building location 12, 54; discrepancies in Wills' account 71–72, 74–75; DNC headquarters 12, 54–55; FBI investigation 67, 74–75; fifteenth anniversary 138, 139–140; fifth anniversary 110; first break-ins of DNC 57–58; indictments 75; media reports 68–74; "mystery man" 96–97; police response 18, 59–66, 170*n*1; security guards (*see* Brown, Leroy C.; Pittman, Fletcher; Wills, Frank); security log *17*; taped door latches 13–14, 17–18, 60, 70, 74–75, 162; tenth anniversary 115–117, *116, 117*; third anniversary 103; trials and sentencing of burglars 82, 109, 161; twentieth anniversary 140–142; twenty-fifth anniversary 149–150; "what ifs" 162–163; Wills and Givner's dinner 16, 75, 171*n*12; *see also* Wills, Frank, and Watergate break-in
Watergate Towne Complex 50–54, *53*, 170*n*10
whistleblowers 162
White, Ryan 156
White, Theodore 162
Wilentz, Sean 163
William Paterson College 102
Wills, Angel (daughter) *see* Brown, Angel
Wills, Catherine (aunt) 23
Wills, Cornelius (grandfather) 23, 156
Wills, Eddie (cousin) 1, 36, 45, 74, 152, 158–160
Wills, Eugene (son) 43, 118–119, 140
Wills, Francis (uncle) 23

200

Index

Wills, Frank: AIDS 154–156; *All the President's Men* (film) 104–108, *105*; annoyance with publicity 81; arrival in Washington, D.C. 47; asthma 31; awards 87, 90, 97, 98, 102–103, 132, *145*, 150, 161–162; bitterness and disappointment 4–5, 84, 97, 103, 110, 115, 142, 148–149, 150, 152, 163; brain tumor 152, 153, 154, 156; brothers 24, 167n6; Chatham Realty Company 81, 90; childhood in North Augusta 31–33, 36–37, *39*, 39–40; childhood in Savannah 20, 23–31, *29*; as cultural icon 87; death 152–158, *157*, 167n15; as Detroit auto worker 45; as Detroit security guard 12, 45–46; as Dick Gregory Health Enterprises spokesman 134–135, 137–138, 160, 179n40; education 39, *39*, 40, 41, 99–102; employment problems 81, 87–88, 90–91, 113, 114; Evans as agent for 84–89, 91–92, 96–103, 106–107, 110–111, 175n17; Evans' exploitation of 100, 101; fatherhood 41, 43, 118–119, 137–138; GED efforts 99–102; as Georgetown University security guard 103, 106, 110; Haley book project 3–4, 128–131, *130*, 138–139, 179n9; Job Corps 42–44; as loner 11, 40, 49, 98–99, 115, 137; lucky breaks 42, 43, 120, 121, 133; media appearances 87, 95–96 (*see also JET* magazine); mental health 114, 151–152; modesty 83, 84; on Nixon 93, 95–96, 103; obituaries 153–154; physical appearance 47; as pioneer whistleblower 162; "psychic forces" beliefs 114; public appearances 89, 92, 97, 111; on racism 92; relationship with his mother 140, 142–143; relationship with Hooper 136–137; relationship with Irvin 40; self-contradictions 97; shoplifting arrests 114, 117–127, 131, 132, 134, 135, 161; as unworldly 96, 98, 100; Washington, D.C. apartment 10, *11*, 48, 71, 141; West Five Notch Road home 41, 112, 142–147, *143*, *145*, *146*, *147*, 150, 158; *see also* finances of Wills

Wills, Frank, and Watergate break-in: building patrols 13–17, *17*; burglars arrested 64; dinner with Givner 15–16, 75, 171n12; discrepancies in account of break-in 71–72, 74–75; duties 12–13; FBI interview 74–75; fifteenth anniversary 138, 139–140; fifth anniversary 110; film portrayals 1; finding taped door latches 13–14, 17–18, 60, 70, 74–75; hired by GSS 12, 48–49; media reports 68–74, 77–78, 84, 92; police response 18, 60; polygraph test 78; tenth anniversary 115–117, *116*, *117*; trial of Watergate burglars 82; twentieth anniversary 140–142; twenty-fifth anniversary 149–150; "what ifs" 162–163; Wills recognized as hero 2, 74, 81–82, 163, 174n12

Wills, George (uncle) 23

Wills, Gladys (aunt) 23, 41

Wills, Hampton (uncle) 23, 31, 36, 41

Wills, Marjorie (mother): birth and childhood 23; character traits 28; death 142; donating body to science 142, 167n15; employment 26–30, 36, 167n7, 167n10; as gatekeeper for Wills 86, 139–140; jury duty 113; Mount Transfiguration Baptist Church 36, 142; radio programs 31; relationship with Angel (granddaughter) 138, 140; relationship with Frank Wills 45, 140, 142–143; return to North Augusta 31–33, 36–37; Savannah apartment 23, 24–25, 28; strict parenting 30–31, 36, 39; stroke 140; West Five Notch Road home 41, 112, 142, *143*; Wills' shoplifting arrest 119, 122

Wills, Nellie (aunt) 23

Wills, Shirley 152, 159

Wimbish, Ralph 3

Woods, Rose Mary 52, 170n10

Woodward, Bob: *All the President's Men* (film) 104; *All the President's Men* (with Bernstein) 90, 153; papers 4, 165n2; Watergate break-in reports 68, 78–79, 103–104; Wills interview 23–24; Wills obituary 153–154

Young Democrats Club 85

Ziegler, Ron 72

201